# EFFECTIVE
## DECISIONS
## AND
## EMOTIONAL
### FULFILLMENT

*the text of this book is printed
on 100% recycled paper*

# EFFECTIVE

## DECISIONS

## AND

## EMOTIONAL

## FULFILLMENT

**Rolland S. Parker**

BARNES & NOBLE BOOKS
A DIVISION OF HARPER & ROW, PUBLISHERS
New York, Cambridge, Hagerstown,
Philadelphia, San Francisco, London,
Mexico City, São Paulo, Sydney

*To my mother*
*who encouraged me with my writing*
*when I was a child*

Thus fate knocks at the door.
—Beethoven

A hardcover edition of this book is published by Nelson-Hall, Inc. It is here reprinted by arrangement.

EFFECTIVE DECISIONS AND EMOTIONAL FULFILLMENT. Copyright © 1977 by Rolland S. Parker. All rights reserved. Printed in the United States of America. No part of this book may be used or reproduced in any manner whatsoever without written permission except in the case of brief quotations embodied in critical articles and reviews. For information address Nelson-Hall, Inc., 325 W. Jackson Blvd., Chicago, Illinois 60606. Published simultaneously in Canada by Fitzhenry & Whiteside Limited, Toronto.

First BARNES & NOBLE BOOKS edition published 1980.

ISBN: 0-06-464038-8

80 81 82 83 84 10 9 8 7 6 5 4 3 2 1

# Contents

# Preface

This book develops a simple idea: The difference between a life of emotional fulfillment and one of barrenness is the quality of decisions which we make. Decisions are the very stuff of our existence. They include not only the traditional major ones, such as those about marriage, employment, and residence, but the seemingly trivial acts that fill our day. We choose the quality of our communications as we speak to our employer, doorman, children, spouse, colleagues, and friends. Each of these contacts, deceptively small and transient, builds up around us a particular emotional quality in our social world. The momentary decisions about how we will spend our time at the job create or destroy our careers. The employee who spends his optional time chatting, rather than planning something of use, has made a decision. The would-be writer who goes out to find a sex partner rather than struggling at the typewriter has also made a decision. The wife who demands attention from her husband, rather than developing her own interests and hobbies independently, has made another kind of decision. Seemingly inconsequential decisions bring us closer to our goals or detract from them.

The key to improved decision making lies in self-understanding. First, we must appreciate our individuality, special needs, and desires based upon our unique development,

experiences, and bodily constitution. Second, we have to understand how our world affects us and the feelings that people stir
up. Our ability to size up a situation, to determine if we can
function in it to our best advantage, ought to be improved.
Finally, it is vital to develop realistic goals in accord with our
values which express our potential and overcome any barrenness
in our lives.

In contrast to some authors who apply the solutions offered
by a particular, generally narrow, school of psychotherapy, I
have incorporated relevant ideas from many sources: the behavioral sciences, history, biography, management, natural science, and, with pleasure, the poetry of amateur writers I know
who have had vital experiences. In addition to the classical
psychoanalysts, the contemporary humanists, behaviorists, and
social psychologists also have something to teach us about the
nature of life. More than most writers, I stress the biological part
of human nature. Our genetic heritage places in our lives potential talents and weaknesses that define the areas in which
we can function comfortably.

I have emphasized a respect for human individuality. No
narrow definition of emotional fulfillment will serve as a goal
for all people. There is a broad range of activities and lifestyles
that enliven human spirits. At different stages of our lives various events and kinds of relationships can bring us pleasure.

Finally, I have written as simply as possible, but with enough
precision to present ideas I care about and have struggled with
for years.

Among the people to whom I would like to express my appreciation are Mr. Harold Grove, who contributed the idea of
illustrating a book about effective decisions with the lives of
individuals; Ms. Diane Harris, who offered suggestions concerning content and organization; my agent, Mrs. Bertha Klausner,
who encouraged my writing career; and my friends, who forgave
my retreating from this world in order to concentrate. I would
also like to thank my clients who shared their lives with me and
contributed to my understanding.

# The Decision Maker's Guide to Self-Evaluation

(For Maximizing Success and
Minimizing Self-Destructiveness)

This guide is based on the premise that effective decisions depend as much on the decision maker as on the external situation. Generally speaking, no one can understand all aspects of complex personal and business situations or gather all available information. Rather, we must rely on our personal effectiveness in coping with situations as they develop. This personal effectiveness includes self-awareness, special skills, and an understanding of how to maximize our strengths and minimize our weaknesses or self-destructive tendencies. The items listed are based on qualities and attitudes which research and clinical experience have shown to be important in making effective decisions.

Directions: Read each of the following statements. If you feel a statement is clearly true most of the time, place a + after it. If you feel a statement does not describe you, or that you deviate from it frequently, place a − after it.

## SELF-UNDERSTANDING

1. I try to understand my feelings when I am in social relationships and when I make decisions.
2. I try to understand what effect I have on other people and how they see me.
3. I have a clear sense of my own identity in terms of my past, how I lead my life today, and my goals for the future.
4. I have carefully evaluated my goals in terms of my capacity, including a realistic assessment of my education, personality, weaknesses, and strengths.
5. My standards of performance are realistic in terms of my real obligations.
6. I consider my real motives when I think of my goals and plans for the future.
7. My goals take into account my degree of persistence, self-discipline, and capacity for self-sacrifice.
8. I carefully avoid transferring to others the feelings and attitudes I develop in different and irrelevant situations.

## EMOTIONAL DEVELOPMENT

9. I can accept emotional warmth and support from others, (love, involvement, closeness).
10. I am usually able to express my opinions openly to others.
11. I can express my sexuality without guilt.
12. I can express my anger without guilt.
13. I can express my need to be dependent.
14. I can tolerate being alone without great emotional discomfort.
15. When somebody hurts my feelings, I can say "Ouch."
16. I can express emotional warmth without embarrassment.
17. I am able to make decisions without wondering what my family or neighbors will think of me.
18. I react to new situations and people with self-acceptance, that is, with confidence, self-assertion, and little vulnerability.
19. I can assert myself when an authority tells me to do something unreasonable.

## SKILLS

20. I have good communication skills: I speak and write clearly, concisely, and to the point.
21. I am competent in my job, or I am currently increasing my education or technical training.
22. I can fulfill my legitimate needs without unnecessary conflicts.
23. I have trained myself to listen carefully to others, and I reserve judgment until I have considered their statements.
24. In my dealings with others I make it a point to negotiate and compromise.
25. In my dealings with others I try to evaluate their temperaments and special needs.
26. I have friends of my own sex with whom I have a relationship of closeness and trust.
27. When I deal with others I have an appropriate degree of self-assertion; that is, I do not push others around nor do I permit them to violate my rights.

## PRUDENT ACTION

28. I read the best newspaper available almost every day, and supplement my knowledge of current events, natural and social sciences, and so on, from other sources.
29. I use foresight to avoid stressful and dangerous situations.
30. I maintain good health by systematic exercise.
31. I avoid tobacco.
32. I avoid alcohol.
33. I avoid excessive fatigue.
34. I slow down and avoid making decisions when tired or unable to concentrate.
35. I avoid situations in which I know I am vulnerable.
36. I drive safely and do not deceive myself by confusing recklessness with skill.
37. I keep pain-producing people from my life.
38. By behaving legally I avoid the possibility of losing my job or going to jail.

39. I accept my responsibilities and make those efforts that will help me get ahead.
40. I do not take on responsibilities that overburden me or that belong to others.
41. On my job, I fulfill my own needs primarily, rather than those of my employer.
42. I do not assume unnecessary emotional obligations.
43. I prefer to occupy my time in useful or interesting ways, and I avoid wasting time.
44. I do not incur financial risks through an excessively high standard of living.
45. I set priorities according to my goals, and I take care of the most important things first.

### AUTONOMY

46. If my spouse or friends have a reason for not being with me, I can let them go without arguing.
47. If I am alone for a period of time, I generally have something enjoyable to occupy me.
48. I have a hobby that does not require the participation of anybody else.
49. If I wish to do something, group disagreement alone will not cause me to change my mind.
50. If I discuss an issue with others, I can listen calmly yet maintain my independent opinion.
51. When facing a crisis, I first try to help myself before expecting aid from others.
52. I believe that my actions are more important in determining my destiny than "fate."

### SUCCESS ORIENTATION

53. I generally expect to be successful in tasks I have chosen.
54. When I am in a dull frame of mind, I usually believe that things will get better.
55. Fear of failure is not a consideration when I plan a project.

56. My services are valuable and I expect to be rewarded for them.
57. I typically persevere toward my goals regardless of obstacles.
58. I am more interested in producing work of good quality than in directly seeking prestige or power.

# 1

# Decisions and the Quality of Your Life

Decisions are the link between experience and action.

Your emotional well-being today is the result of countless decisions which you made yesterday.

Tomorrow, or next year, or ten years from now, the quality of your life will depend upon decisions that you made long ago, are making today, and will make in the future. Your emotional well-being also will depend upon *decisions that you didn't make,* or made carelessly, casually, foolishly, ignorantly, stupidly, short-sightedly, impulsively, unintelligently, unconsciously, or passively.

I will show you the basic sources of your decisions and how these sources affect your life. When you understand your real nature, you will be able to make decisions consistent with your special qualities as a unique human being. You will be more competent to avoid common pitfalls, which result in poor decisions, inferior quality of life, and perhaps downright disaster. Self-understanding will help you to make choices superior to those you now make in all important areas, including personal relationships, career, money, and even sex.

Our goal, together, is to help you improve your style of life and ultimately to achieve a state of emotional fulfillment through better decisions.

Some cynics might say, "It is all society's fault. That's the real reason our lives are all fouled up." A sensible reply would acknowledge that much misery is caused by powerful people with selfish interests, or those who are inefficient, corrupt, and cruel. But this is not the entire story.

Much of our destiny is under *our personal control*. The goal of this book is to help you to increase the amount of control you have over your life through improved decision making. You can create better decisions in those areas where intelligent choices can make a difference. As you exercise greater control, new areas of competence will open up and older ones will improve.

To increase our effectiveness, it is important to distinguish between the personal, social, and impersonal forces in our lives. The personal forces involve our own feelings, attitudes, values, goals, unconscious distortions, and expectations. They also include the effects which our personal forces have upon the people who are important to us. Social forces are the effects of the people around us; how these people influence our feeling and thinking, and how they react with encouragement or hostility to our efforts. Impersonal forces include the overall cost of living, availability of housing, unemployment rate, and so on. Intelligent decisions take into account our special qualities, an awareness of human relationships, and the general climate of the times. The relative importance of each will vary from time to time and situation to situation. However, it does not take too much "emotional common sense" (Parker, 1973) not to be insolent to an employer when jobs are scarce!

## DECISION MAKING AFFECTS HUMAN RELATIONSHIPS

Decision making affects human relationships. We have a choice in how we will deal with people. Many a relationship, job, invitation, and so on has been nipped in the bud by a wisecrack, an inappropriate remark, or indifference to someone's feelings. Therefore, good decision making is required even in the borderline area between personal relationships and the impersonal areas of our lives. For example, in times of a job or housing shortage, both planning and the ability to get along with interviewers or rental agents will be needed to increase the odds in your favor. Therefore, by becoming more aware of the subtleties of your own personality and then making suitable changes, and through greater understanding of people, your capacity to make useful decisions will be greatly magnified.

I emphasize setting *realistic goals*. Goals are helpful in organizing your thinking so that you can decide what are the chief issues in your life, and then choose among alternative courses of action. In this way, you increase the likelihood of achieving what you want: emotional fulfillment as a feeling human being, with a unique history and special qualities.

The question of goals is closely related to the kinds of *values* we have. Values are our subjective way of defining what is rewarding and what is distasteful in the vital areas of our lives. There are many abstract ideas we pick up along the way which influence our decisions. Values tell us the kind of person we want to be, how to react to people, and with whom to associate. We will take a look at these values and decide whether they stand the test of experience. Are your values your own, or are they the pet philosophy of your grandmother's religious advisor? Maybe they really belong to your rabbi's wife's aunt.

I would like to have you explore values in terms of their effects upon your decisions, taking into account your own special characteristics and needs, and the realities of the environment. (You can evolve a useful philosophy for yourself and determine what you can really expect to achieve from life.) Then you will be able to make decisions toward goals which are consistent with the real world. The choices you make no longer will be haphazard. Your batting average in life will be substantially increased.

These are not unrealistic promises. Your life is made up of many decisions each day. You probably don't recognize many of them. Merely by improving a number of seemingly small decisions you will have greater success in the arena of your life.

You might also decide to make some major changes. This book will help you to decide when to make such a change, and to recognize which influences you will have to consider.

What are the emotional costs of decisions which we have made or that others have made for us which we were too vulnerable or ignorant to cope with?

All of us experience areas in our lives which are barren or dead, spots where our spirit is undeveloped or crushed. Sometimes we are aware of these only vaguely; we sense only that our spiritual and mental capacities are far greater than our achievements. We look coldly into our mental mirror and cruelly tell ourselves that we have failed, that our inadequacies are avoidable. We see our personalities as weak, our wills as flawed, and our discipline as yielding before trivial satisfactions. No doubt you have spent thousands of hours pursuing trivial or false goals, associated with people who depressed your spirits and misused your money so that you were controlled by economic insecurity.

This emptiness or depression, this emotional underachievement, can be overcome with the right tools. What does it take to make a spiritual void blossom? You can develop for yourself a program, a plan of action which will create excitement in your life, improve your motivation, and give you a sense of purpose. You can really make your blood flow! However, this cannot be achieved without some discipline, without some study of yourself and others, and above all, without giving up some cherished illusions and wrongheaded values.

### IMPROVING YOUR LIFE REQUIRES SELF-UNDERSTANDING

The key toward improving your life is self-understanding. This is not all that it takes, but no sensible plan can be devised which does not take into consideration your very special characteristics as a person. The techniques which you use to cope with stress, the kinds of people whom you can relate to or must avoid, the personal and professional goals for which you strive and make sacrifices, must be based upon a realistic consideration of your basic nature.

You will learn to observe situations and yourself more accurately. Thus, you can modify your actions as you go along so that they can bring you closer to your goals. You will learn to recognize poor decisions, before it is too late, as those decisions which do not bring you satisfaction or help you to achieve your goals.

I suggest we start by looking at your life today. Are you aware how many decisions you make? If you think there are only a few you are kidding yourself. I hear you counting them— whether to go to college or increase your training, which job to take, whether to marry a certain person, whether to rent or buy a home—maybe a few more.

Wrong.

Each day you make dozens of decisions that influence the quality of your life. You make decisions from the time you *decide* to get out of bed to the time you *decide* to go to sleep. Making decisions is the essence of freedom. Part of the most important difference between being free and being a prisoner is the greater number of choices the free person has to make. Decisions are made *for* the prisoner: where he lives, what he eats, the quality of his accommodations, whom he talks to, what he reads, where he goes and where he doesn't go, what he wears, when he stands, when he sits, when he exercises, when he sleeps, when and what he eats, when he comes and when he goes.

To utilize self-understanding as a tool toward leading a happy, productive, and emotionally related way of life, let us use an analogy: a marksman shooting a rifle at a target. Let emotional fulfillment be the target we are shooting at. Two sights on the rifle must be lined up. They are *clear understanding of ourselves* and *appropriate, realistic goals*. However, these two sights are insufficient in aiming *precisely* at our target. The experienced marksman knows that weather conditions can cause his bullet to go off target. He compensates for this by "taking Kentucky windage," or changing the sights on his rifle to correspond to realistic conditions. We also must take Kentucky windage through understanding how other people and social considerations affect our plans.

Most persons have little awareness of themselves and how they differ from others. They consider their most vital characteristics either to be accidental or easily changed (if they would only make the effort). Many have the illusion that everybody shares the same values and attitudes that they do. Others feel they are totally alone and different. Actually, people share the same needs and drives, but to a startlingly different degree. We all need love, but for some it represents a greater pressure than for others. No man is an island, but some persons tolerate or even crave greater isolation than others. All people have some need for security and dependency; yet some individuals from birth seem fearless and crave excitement, while others are anxiety-prone and easily startled.

What does all this mean to you? It means that your basic personality sets limits on the kinds of situations you can enter into: it easily influences you when you select friends and a mate; it shapes your relationship with your supervisor; and it determines in part the kinds of stress you can overcome, the problems you can solve, and the ease with which you will achieve your goals. To a degree, some of your characteristics are God-given; they come with your body. They may be changed slowly, if at all. I myself was a very phlegmatic child. Under the pressure of circumstances, however, I have become intense and energetic. My temperament during each phase conditioned the kind of life I led and how others reacted to me.

Basic traits are determined both by biological factors and by the intense experiences we had as children. My goal is to help you think clearly about your basic nature and how you developed. A thorough understanding of your temperament and how your bodily characteristics (constitution) shape your activities will help you to make better plans and to set more realistic goals.

I also want you to learn to see your associates more clearly. As you form relationships, or counsel your children, or supervise your subordinates, you will be able to utilize their strengths and to help them compensate for their weaknesses.

Further, you will become sensitive to the significance of *discrepancies*. It is the discrepancy between capacity and goal which leads to humiliation and frustration. Many of my patients, who were shy and inward from an early age, had submitted to vast frustration in an effort to overcome their weaknesses. Some became salesmen; one became a marine. There are more sensible ways to handle emotional difficulties. One way is to accept yourself, with all your characteristics and limitations.

Thus, one goal in your reading this book might be to identify deep needs and basic characteristics which cannot *easily* be changed, and also those attitudes, weaknesses, and values which *must* be changed. The first set will be the framework upon which you will build your plans and efforts toward fulfillment. The latter are garbage and debris; they are to be cast out because they are self-destructive. Improving self-discipline can enhance the development of a realistic, yet optimistic, attitude.

I hear a wiseacre out there sneering: "Why make this so complicated? Stop confusing me! I don't want to be an amateur psychologist. My goal is very simple. I want to be happy. I want to be fulfilled. I want peace of mind. What's so hard about that?"

If it were easy you wouldn't be reading this book. Besides, in five minutes we could figure out a couple of ways you are kidding yourself. If we chatted together we might discover that your life is so full of self-destructive habits that you couldn't possibly be happy. Secondly, you picked up goals during your confused youth which might be out of reach of your capacities and personal qualities. Perhaps they are inappropriate in terms of your present realities and your current personality and development. They might be fantasies developed when you were an acned little kid, or were pushed around at home or on the block, or when you felt like the worst klutz in the world.

Most important, I think that happiness, fulfillment, and peace of mind are not goals. They are fortunate results of appropriate choices made when you are on the road to meaningful and realistic goals. These are goals which are appropriate to your nature and the kind of personal life you wish to lead.

It appears to me that when a person says that his or her goals are happiness or peace of mind, this statement shows a serious lack of understanding of the nature of life. It is naive to think that one can constantly maintain that combination of inner and outer worlds which will keep us steadily happy. Rather, a more meaningful goal is to try to reach fulfillment. By this, I mean the idea that one has lived life to the fullest, has experienced deeply many kinds of human events, has made a contribution to the welfare of those around us, and has developed capacities to work and love and be friends to a significant extent. *In the process* of experiencing life deeply and of developing our personality and our relationships, we will often have peace of mind and happiness and even elation and hilarity.

Honesty demands that we realize that life is built upon shifting sands. No sooner do we achieve a goal than there are new circumstances to master. Perhaps we are a bit older and stronger so that we try a more challenging goal. Maybe we have become weaker so that we cannot achieve the same level. Our emotional supports may fade away or die, the institutions on which we rely may fail or betray us, or acts of God may radically change the conditions of our life. As a result, the state of contentment is disrupted and the tasks of living are again upon us.

## PERSONAL FULFILLMENT IS A PROCESS

Thus, personal fulfillment is seen as a continuous process of development and striving. Enjoyment, happiness, peace of mind, and self-acceptance are but signposts that we are on the right road. They may give us a signal to stop for a while, to enjoy life, to relax, to refresh, to be with others. But take heed! The road is growing dark, the wolf is at the door, the storm clouds are gathering, and the grass is growing under our feet. Each cliché is there to remind you that life is always changing. Even to remain in the same place often requires considerable effort.

Do you accuse me of being a nihilist? I hear you assert that life has meaning, that unless there are definite, lifelong goals people feel valueless and purposeless. I am no nihilist. On the contrary, I have been accused of setting excessively precise goals for people. However, let's look at the kinds of goals that people set for themselves.

*History I–1*: A thirty-year-old, unmarried woman is depressed and lonely. She wants to get married and believes that when she is ready the right man will come along. In the meantime, she is engaged in ambivalent relationships with younger sisters and a brother. Ever since her father died when she was 10, she has been in the habit of being emotionally and financially supportive to them. Now they are all in their twenties, and she is unwilling to give up her role of Older Sister. By becoming in her mind the exclusively caring person, she completely ignores her own needs. Though she wants to marry, by setting up the simultaneous goal of being parent to several grown siblings she exhausts her emotional resources and sets up further stresses that do not leave her free to relate to an appropriate man. Furthermore, she has been taught a self-destructive passive attitude. She thinks that the "right man will come along." It would have been better for her if she had been told that she would have to take the initiative to meet a man.

*History I–2*: A middle-aged man solemnly assured me that since he was happiest "living day by day" I was wrong in asserting that people ought to set meaningful goals for themselves. Let us look at this man's way of life. He enjoyed being a "gadfly." It brought him pleasure to torment others because of what he considered their weaknesses or contradictions. We can infer his real goal: it is to create a place for himself in the world as a nuisance. Only as a nuisance could this unfortunate man feel that he was noticed. Obviously, he had given up the possibility of being loved. Should there be a crisis in his life, he might have to confront it alone. He has not developed a lifestyle which would encourage others to care about him.

In the next chapter we shall begin discussing how the choices and decisions you make and the goals you follow all contribute to emotional fulfillment—or perhaps to outright disaster. I shall try to demonstrate that if you *believe* you control your life, you are more likely to be able to do so than if you take a fatalistic attitude.

# 2
# Choice:
# Success or Failure

You are living in a rough and vicious and mindless world. Nevertheless, it is moderately possible to control one's life in a beneficial way. It is not necessary to be always under the sway of others, to be motivated by irrational feelings, and to make decisions based upon faulty evaluations of your situation and needs. Sometimes we make social decisions which are obviously poor by treating others in a fashion which causes us to be isolated or retaliated against. We antagonize people who are emotionally and materially important to us. These self-created situations cause stress and result in disabling neurotic symptoms.

Self-destructiveness can be avoided (Parker, 1973b). I define self-destructiveness as making mistakes which are predictably wrong, those which we would counsel our friends against. We frequently do things which our experience teaches us will result in failure or other emotional pain. You can recognize that choices can be made which maximize the likelihood of emotional fulfillment. However, to accomplish this end it is vital that we exercise some insight and discipline to avoid predictably self-destructive courses of action. Further, we can constantly engage in trivial experiences so that the resulting emotional emptiness has the same effect.

I see achievement of emotional fulfillment as *a series of*

*choices or decisions.* You may tell me that you or somebody you know is happy through living in the present, being aware of the moment, the here-and-now. This may be correct, but I don't believe it is more than accidental or temporary. Any circumstance that requires few or only minor decisions must inevitably change. One does not have to be too old to remember a war, political scandal, unexpectedly high inflation, devaluation of the dollar, or substantial increase in violence. The current energy crisis affects the pattern of living of every person. New conditions which we must cope with are unexpected, and frequently more difficult or dangerous than those they replace. In today's world, you must be able to take an unbiased look at your environment and your own capacities to deal with it.

I live in New York City. Sometimes my travel route takes me through the infamous Bowery. There one can see a good sample of the wreckage, the derelicts of human life. Invariably there are men who sprawl on the sidewalk, stop cars for a handout, or swill cheap booze alone or in small groups. Some of these unfortunates are psychotic. It is likely that many of the remainder planned their lives poorly. At particular forks in the road they did not understand their needs, and perhaps made a series of wrong choices. Then gradually, self-esteem gone, reputation gone, capital gone, the only solution was the Salvation Army handout and the flophouse. Further, they were generally not aided by the social/political/economic policies of those to whom we entrust our welfare.

Let us take a cold look at statistics to observe what really happens to people. This is meant to make you aware of the real cost of failure and to motivate you to explore your own situation and actions.

## NOT EVERYBODY SURVIVES RISKS OF THE REAL WORLD

Let us look at what happened to us in recent years. Some people's lives are so hateful they destroy themselves. In the United States during a recent year, the suicide rate was 98.8 out of every 100,000 men and 32.5 out of every 100,000 women. Curiously, it was twice as high for whites as nonwhites, although the figures for nonwhites were increasing compared to the 1956–57 period. (Those who claim the inferiority of blacks never quote these statistics.) Elderly men and postmenopausal women had the greatest casualty rates by suicide (*World Almanac*, 1973, p. 955).

When people cannot survive in the real world, they usually do not go out peacefully. Of 6,507 deaths by suicide recorded by the U.S. Public Health Service in one year, 3,054 took poison, 841 hung or strangulated themselves, and 1,911 shot themselves. The penalty for not overcoming the tasks of living is excruciating (*Associated Press Almanac*, 1973, p. 291).

There are other ways of failing the tasks of living. The National Institute of Mental Health estimated that over 1.6 million people received outpatient psychiatric services, and another .37 million were serviced by community health centers. The total number of inpatients has doubled since 1955 (*World Almanac*, 1973, p. 961).

Let's look at the rates for murder and manslaughter. It is important that you ignore for the moment your feelings about crime in the streets and related attacks by strangers. It is generally agreed that in most cases of murder the victim knew the killer. In a sense, murder is a family sport. The likelihood of getting killed in the United States in 1971 was 8.5/100,000, up from 7.8 the previous year. If it is of any interest, the rate for an accidental death due to firearms was 1.46, compared to 4.21 for homicide, and 5.33 for suicide (*Associated Press Almanac*, 1973, p. 147). The likelihood of having an accidental death was 55.8/100,000. In that same year, the cost of accidental injuries and deaths was estimated at 18.2 billion dollars (*World Almanac*, 1973, p. 953).

While the number of marriages (*World Almanac*, 1973, p. 952) was 2,192,272, the number of divorces was 689,704, an estimated failure rate of 31.5%.

Don't put the book away, we're not finished. In 1970, 196,429 or 967/100,000 of us were incarcerated in federal and state prisons (*American Almanac*, 1973, p. 160).

You can see that the likelihood of our personally experiencing an avoidable, human-caused disaster is quite high.

A cumulative series of choices can make the difference between enjoying life and disaster. Let us start an extended analysis of some of the conditions which lead people to make worthwhile or foolish choices.

The topic with which we shall begin is whether you believe it is worthwhile to make any decisions at all. We have already referred to a passive hoping-for-the-best, life-is-a-flow-so-I'd-better-move-with-the-current attitude. If this is your bag, stay with it, but be careful it doesn't get over your head.

## What Controls Your Life?

One important consideration in the quality of your decisions is the question of whether you believe that you control your own life or that the control exists outside through superior forces. This dimension of human experience has been called by students of personality the *Internal v. External Locus of Control* (Maddi, 1970, 1972; Rotter, 1971). *Having the correct attitude could save your life!* John H. Sims and Duane D. Baumann studied the "disproportionately higher frequency of tornado-caused deaths in the South" (1972). Why more or fewer people die in a tornado is a complicated matter, depending *only in part* upon the strength and frequency of the twisters, the type of construction of dwellings and other buildings, the frequency and quality of the warning system. Since none of these factors correlated highly with the number of deaths (in fact, parts of the South have less severe tornados than the Midwest), these scientists decided to look into the *human* factor.

They decided to compare the responses of residents of Illinois with those of Alabama on a test of *Internal v. External Locus of Control*. Here are some selected comparisons. The table illustrates the questions asked and the percentage of people in the two states who offered these responses.

|  | % of Respondents | |
| --- | --- | --- |
|  | *Illinois* | *Alabama* |
| As far as my own life is concerned, God . . . | | |
| Is active in it: "controls it" | 36 | 59 |
| Is a protective Presence: "watches over me" | 30 | 8 |
| I believe that luck . . . | | |
| Is of major importance | 6 | 49 |
| Is of minor importance | 27 | 17 |
| Getting ahead in the world results from . . . | | |
| Religious moral power: "God willing it" | 9 | 46 |
| Work: "hard work" | 67 | 29 |

The responses indicate that the people from Illinois felt they had more control over their lives than the people from Alabama. Now, how did they feel about the part they play in surviving a natural disaster?

| During the time when a tornado watch is out I . . . | | |
| --- | --- | --- |
| Am attentive to weather conditions: | | |
| "Watch the sky" | 9 | 2 |
| Am attentive to news media: "TV" | 24 | 0 |
| The survivors of a tornado . . . | | |
| Require assistance: "need to be helped" | 24 | 8 |
| Experience negative emotions: "feel terrible" | 3 | 21 |

Sims and Baumann suggested that Illinois-type persons, who believe that they direct their own lives, "use their heads and the technology of their society, and they take action." Alabama-type persons, believing that God (or fate) or luck controls their lives, "place less trust in man's communal knowledge and control systems; they await the fated onslaught, watchful but passive."

Nevertheless, it seems that when the risk is some time in the future, a hidden belief in one's personal immortality, together with an unwillingness to make sacrifices, can prevent decisions to change our lifestyle, even at the risk of death! One study (Nager, 1976) showed that when people of even above average socioeconomic level and education were offered information concerning their personal risk of suffering heart disease, practically none of them did anything in response. Even their physicians were passive in attempting to motivate them to change their habits. The scientists who ran the study speculated that "the rewards of a preventive medical program are way off in the distance and people just don't buy that kind of reward system." The subjects' personal physicians had no hope of motivating their patients to make changes in their lifestyles in order to avert diseases which would occur many years in the future.

Whether you believe that you control your destiny (Internal) or that outside forces control you (External) can have a significant effect upon your ability to handle a potential or actual crisis. Your belief also plays a role in many other significant events in your life.

Consider the following situations. One research study found that the belief in control over one's own destiny was more highly associated with achievement than all the traditional factors which are usually thought to play a part in school success. Prisoners who were Internals had more information than Externals on how to obtain parole! Black civil rights activists have a greater belief in their own power than those who do not take part in this movement (Maddi, 1970; Rotter, 1971). Those persons who are hospitalized for mental illness believe they are controlled by external forces (aren't they?), particularly if they have been admitted for a second time (Levenson, 1973). Actually, if you are an External you can be more easily conditioned to new situations, and under some conditions you can be more subject to majority opinion (Maddi, 1970; Rotter, 1971).

Externals prefer tasks which lessen their chances for failure. They seem to forgo opportunities to attain skills which would result in achievement. This attitude creates circumstances which reinforce their belief that external events are the chief influences in their lives. Internals seem to expect success, even in tasks where they cannot explain away their failures. In fact, they seem to continue to hope and to persevere, even where failure has reduced their expectation of success (Phares and Lamiell, 1974).

There is some research evidence that belief in internal control is more prone to change according to circumstances than is belief that control exists in "powerful others" or in "chance fate"

(Levenson, 1973). Since there seems to be little connection between belief in internal control and political activity in some studies of mostly white persons (Abramowitz, 1973), I suspect that many persons have a deep pessimism concerning their capacity to influence their government.

How do people develop attitudes which make such a profound difference in the manner in which they handle their lives? Perhaps it is a belief in the logic of events. If your early experiences led you to believe that your actions were potent and that you could influence your parents and the people and events around you, then you probably act as though your life is controlled from a place inside your cranium. But if you have been trained to believe that spiritual forces are the real determinants of your destiny, or that your feelings are worthless, then you may be passive during a crisis. At one of those forks in the road of your life, a right or wrong decision will have a profound effect.

## COMPETENCE OR HOPELESSNESS

Success is more than a matter of what you were taught by your parents. The model they created is also important. The assertive parent, one who grasps life in his hands, might set a model for capable coping with crises. On the other hand, such persons sometimes have such confidence in their own capacity to handle matters that they disparage the capacities of the growing child. The growing person is not permitted to have the experience of plunging into a situation, learning about it, and having an honorable success or failure.

Conversely, a meek, frightened parent can either set the example of letting superior forces take charge, or leave living space for the child to learn what he can do for himself in his life.

*History II–1*: An overworked immigrant widow does not satisfy her son's need for prestige and acceptance by others: A middle-aged man feels unable to make contact with the kind of men and women which will bring him warm human relationships. He recalls a typical day when he was fifteen. "Just another day. No finances, no security, no affection, no parties, no girls, not going anywhere. I feel second-rate, inferior because I don't have a feeling of coming from anywhere or having anything. I need a fancy dressed-up mother before I can be proud of her. I feel helpless or hopeless."

The extreme passive attitude is *hopelessness*. It evolves from the belief that one is helpless in controlling one's fate. There are many documented cases of people who died suddenly, for no apparent cause, because they believed that they had no control over their destiny. Of course, some of these unfortunates were in extreme circumstances: They were prisoners of war or were suffering from cancer. Others were in no danger except from their belief that they were about to die: for example, they were condemned by witchcraft, taboo, or voodoo rituals. Still others were subjected to arbitrary treatment in hospitals or old-age homes, or were discharged from their jobs at age sixty-five. Children in hospitals or homes who are well-treated physically but who are given no emotional warmth also develop feelings of depression. Often they die unpredictably (Seligman, 1974).

To develop the belief that control over you is in the outside world can be the first step towards passivity. Further experiences creating discouragement may lead to refusal to take constructive actions. Ultimately, personal disorganization, deterioration, and actual premature death can be the consequences.

Hopelessness is one of the core characteristics of people who suffer from depression. Let us look at the extreme experience of depression, people who have recently attempted suicide. It appears that they have an unrealistically negative attitude towards the future. The seriousness of their attempt was more connected with a feeling of the unhappy outcome of their efforts than with the feeling of depression. In addition, successful experiences created increased optimism but failure caused more hopelessness (Beck, Weissman, Lester & Trexler, 1974).

### EXPERIENCING SELF-ASSERTION

Experiencing control has additional effects upon our personality and thus the quality of life we create through our decisions. We can contrast the "individualist" (Maddi, 1970), with the "zombie" (Maslow, 1971, p. 73). The individualist does not feel powerless in the face of social forces and his biological urges. He believes that he can understand and influence them. He is less likely to take actions simply because they are socially desirable. The zombie lacks signals from within as to what to do. He is experientially empty. Therefore, he turns to the outside world for guidance—to other people, calendars, rules, and so forth.

Looking to outer rules for guidance is particularly dangerous, since we are trained from the beginning to accept the authority of parents, teachers, and so on. We generalize that it is important for our welfare to give in to the social demands of the people around us. It also makes us see the rules as something real, something independent, not the product of somebody else's mind (Hogan, 1973), *set up for his advantage*. We obey orders, we follow rules, never thinking whether they are in our best interest, whether they can be questioned, or whether a touch of disobedience might not be helpful. Well, not everybody does. I had a supervisor who, while putting her feet upon the radiator, would look up from her trashy novel and tell the rest of us to work harder. When this did not improve our productivity, she told us to record just what we did during the day. The first time I noted the minutes I spent in the men's room was the end of this nonsense.

The dangers of yielding unquestioningly to rules and orders may be illustrated by the actions of, and consequences to, the German nation. Even after they had lost the war, and stood accused by world opinion of war crimes and mass murder, many major and minor German officials justified their actions on the basis that they were merely following orders!

Although there can be severe consequences from refusal to make independent decisions, many people seem to be actually afraid to do so. There are a variety of ways in which we can utilize abstract beliefs to determine our actions without evaluating alternatives. These include allegiance to religion, political movements, a school of thought, a cult or other authority, or some set of writings. Sometimes we develop a subjective feeling of certainty and never try to determine whether our beliefs are valid. Perhaps we make a decision seem ridiculously easy by ascribing all virtue to one cause and all evil to the opposite side (Kaufman, 1973).

The key principle to be learned is to form the habit of making your own decisions. Develop the habit of attempting to understand your situation, then taking definite action to control it. However, this process is quite complex. To improve your batting average, you had better understand yourself. How do you really make your decisions?

# 3

# Self-Awareness
# and Priorities

Who makes your decisions? We will see that students of human nature, who have been brilliant and learned, have not been able to decide who makes your decisions. You can't even be certain that you make your own decisions! Even if you should convince me that you make your own decisions, it might be claimed that some of your decisions have been formed before you were born, before you can remember, or have been shaped by countless vague forces or by people who might not even have known your name! The complex effects upon human decisions may have caused Jung (1933, p. 179) to assert that while there exists only one science of mathematics, of zoology, and so forth there are many psychologies and philosophies.

A person who tries to understand "what makes him tick" (how he chooses among alternatives or makes decisions) by following the leader of any particular school will be sadly misled. He will certainly find that the proposed explanation for his personality, emotional disturbances, and perplexities definitely will not cover all of the complexities of his emotional life. On the other hand, if he seeks the answer through exploration of the fantastically rich literature on human behavior, he will be stunned by the contradictions and varied emphases. Nevertheless, I cannot accept Jung's explanation that psychology is a discipline "which cannot be fully experienced and therefore cannot be comprehended by a purely empirical approach . . . thus encouraging speculation." Rather, the solution to the problem of understanding ourselves lies in focusing upon the basic differences between people, the complexity of the human mind, and the diversity of human experiences, as well as in trying to overcome the incapacity of any one explorer of the psyche to take into consideration more than a few factors simultaneously.

Thus the most honest way to approach decision making, so as to increase the emotional fulfillment in your life, is to lay before you the *range of ideas* which have been presented. It is likely that *all the ideas are partly correct.* One is reminded of conflict between two men in one of the little Jewish settlements (Stetl) in Eastern Europe. A crowd gathered, and finally someone suggested the traditional remedy: to ask the Rabbi for his opinion. So everybody went to the Rabbi's study, where he solemnly asked one man to present his case. When he was finished, the Rabbi said: "You're right." At which point his opponent exclaimed, "Wait, I haven't told my side of the story." When he was finished, the Rabbi intoned: "You're right, also." At which point a third man cried: "How can they both be right?" To which the Rabbi answered, "You're right, too."

My own model in this case will be that most remarkable professor I had at New York University, Presley D. Stout. An ex-minister with the build of a wrestler, he would slowly pace back and forth in front of the room, gathering his thoughts, and presenting each "school" of psychology with such clarity and conviction that I would think: "This is what he believes." Then, he would proceed to the next point of view, present its analysis of the weaknesses of its predecessor, and state the fundamentals of its position. I would then think: "Ah, *this* is what he believes." And so forth.

You will be able to make substantial changes in your approach to life through understanding how the various facets of your personality affect your decisions. You will begin to realize that there are many different determinants of behavior, and that what influences you may vary from occasion to occasion. What I propose to do is illustrate some of these forces so that you can learn to identify them. Some of these will come under your control, and through various experiences ultimately be modified. Those which cannot be changed will be taken into account so that your personal goals will be realistic, and so that you will be spared the frustration of trying to achieve the impossible.

If we define a decision as the beginning of an action, as well as a choice between alternatives, we can conceptualize at least six important influences upon the direction of your behavior. The cumulative effect of all your decisions can easily tip the balance toward emotional fulfillment; or it can bring regression to emotional discomfort or even psychosis or suicide. As I analyze the situation, the key areas of decision making which have been determined are:

1. Natural forces of physics, chemistry, and biology
2. Inherited neural and visceral patterns
3. Unconscious attitudes
4. The Self as an active force
5. Potent environmental reinforcers (rewards and punishments)
6. Social factors

I believe that all these areas influence the way in which we run our lives. I will try to present a sympathetic explanation of each point in separate chapters. I affirm a scientific, nonmystical, and practical approach to human affairs. I believe that human life is influenced by *natural* forces, and we can achieve emotional fulfillment by understanding, accepting, and utilizing them.

As Herrick (1956), a distinguished neurologist and student of human evolution, pointed out: "Physiologists have succeeded in explaining so many vital processes in terms of the laws of inorganic mechanisms that some of them are convinced that all functions can be so explained when our knowledge is complete. . . ." (p. 46). This is the ultimate statement of scientific determinism.

It has been estimated that "98 percent of our actions are not free-willed but automatic, and that is a boon to us" (Thomsen,

1974). If these scientists are correct, then the anatomical and physiological apparatus with which we are born controls our fate. After all, the body is made of physical structures, each composed of organic (carbon compounds) and inorganic substances. These inevitably must follow the laws of physics, the objectively determined pathways of chemical processes, etc. Whether we speak of muscular events (playing at sports, making love, driving a car), or of internal or visceral ones (digestion, heart rate, brain processes), they will eventually be totally describable in terms of physical-chemical-environmental fields. The psychiatrist Carl Jung (1933) wonders whether "we must ask ourselves if the psyche is not after all a secondary manifestation . . . completely dependent upon the body . . ." (p. 178). So much for free will!

I do not know whether our decisions, goals, and way of life are totally created by our atoms. However, we will take a look at why the process of making a decision is sometimes so complex. You can also see that with so many pressures upon you it is hard to tell just why you took a particular position. It is obviously difficult to balance the various forces acting on you, integrate these with the information available to you, and then come to a correct decision. Sometimes events occur at a lightning rate and we function intuitively, without much chance to think. Nevertheless, by becoming aware of how your mind functions, you will sharpen your thinking, improve your capacity to plan ahead, strengthen weaknesses in your personality, and overcome present blind spots in your decision making ability.

## WHY IS IT HARD TO MAKE A GOOD DECISION?

Why do we frequently make decisions which bring on emotional disasters, such as suicide or the destruction of relationships, imprisonment, severe accidents, violence, and all the other terrible events of life? Why do we make decisions which subtly and cumulatively reduce the quality of our life and destroy our emotional well-being? There are many different reasons, such as emotional problems, lack of self-understanding, lack of suitable knowledge, inability to set priorities, and inflexibility. Let's examine the situation. We will start with a couple who increased their difficulties through poor decision making.

*History III–1:* Due to the husband's prolonged education, a couple have been under serious stress for a number of years. Despite economic deprivation there has been the need to care for young children. Recent pressure from the university for the husband to complete his education has caused them to defer vacations and reduce to a minimum their time together. This also prevents the husband from assuming certain domestic responsibilities. His wife becomes frustrated and angry since she is extremely dependent upon him and acknowledges herself to be demanding. The unexpected deprivation due to her husband's requirement for extra time for school causes her to experience rage and hopelessness. Above all, she feels that her efforts to be less demanding were rewarded by a kind of provocative, unnecessary attempt at independence on her husband's part. She believes that she has been patient while he made many errors of strategy which interfered with his completing his education. She has "had it." Each day is endless, without affection, without joy, because of her struggles to take care of children and household. The husband, on the other hand, sees her as inefficient, demanding, and unsupporting.

## What decisions does he make?

1. To become authoritarian, for example, by demanding a hot meal at 10 P.M., although he knows that his wife is exhausted because of a physical condition and the need to care for two small, active children;

2. To express his dissatisfaction with her and to withhold affection;

3. To telephone at the last minute that he would come home late because he wanted to engage in his hobby;

4. To find time to help his parents, who are young, healthy, and completely able to take care of their own needs, while at the same time telling his wife the household tasks are totally her own responsibility.

*What decisions does she make?*

1. To increase her demands upon him to the point of insisting that he cease his education or reduce the investment of time, even though this would be professionally, and therefore financially, disastrous;

2. To abuse her mother, upon whom she is also dependent;

3. To become involved (for the first time) in community activities when household cares require attention;

4. To keep him up late after his return with demands for attention, despite the fact that in addition to working and studying, he is traveling two hours each way.

Who really makes their decisions? Their decisions were made for them a long time ago. They were made by parents who conditioned them to relate by arguing, instead of accommodating. The wife's parents, by creating a model, taught her that people are divided into those who are dominant and those who are submissive. The other set of parents taught the husband to be ingratiating through reinforcing his antics as a cute boy by unconditional acceptance. Their characteristic styles of relating cause only friction with each other. Neither of them was taught how to understand personal needs, or to relate to others in a manner calculated to bring satisfaction.

### Lack of Self-Understanding

No decision is worth anything unless we have the personal resources to carry it out. It is simple enough if we want a piece of chocolate. Either we have enough money, or the speed to steal it and run. Nothing else is required. However, when more complex problems are involved, the demands made upon us become numerous and sometimes obscure. An effective decision is one which can be carried out, and which also brings satisfaction. Therefore, if we do not know our personality, with its assets, skills, aptitudes, and serious liabilities, we cannot make decisions which can be carried out successfully. Furthermore, unless our decisions are consistent with our values and goals and do not require an excessive investment of effort, we will not accomplish anything which we will enjoy. Consequently, we will not create a lifestyle which enhances emotional fulfillment.

People lack self-understanding for several reasons. Since personality is very complicated, it is really difficult to grow up and have a total grasp of the kind of a person we are. It is like trying to read something in a foreign language of which we have an incomplete understanding. We will understand some of the ideas well, some incompletely, some in a distorted way, and some not at all. Your goal should be to develop ability to make decisions consistent with your abilities and emotional requirements.

## LACK OF INFORMATION

Some people make terrible decisions because they do not know all of the facts which can affect them. They start a career, buy a house, enter a love affair or marriage, or have children without getting enough information to decide whether they can succeed or not.

A young man I know recently decided to apply for law school. He has the intellectual ability to succeed. However, I advised him to look ahead and determine what the market for lawyers was likely to be in the future. With changes in auto insurance laws towards "no fault," instead of the standard liability-adversary policies, lots of business for the legal profession might be lost. When I mentioned this, he said that he might not want to practice law as such. Rather, it would give him training to function in a variety of careers. At least, he had suitable alternatives if the primary objective could not be reached.

What I want to encourage you to do is to explore all the areas affecting any decision you will make. True, it is a popular philosophy today to "hang loose, trust your feelings, do what you really want to do." You should (regretfully) put this aside as nonsense. I don't know anybody who follows this philosophy who is either happy or has achieved anything worthwhile. On the contrary, they are willful, impulsive people who don't care about the effects of their actions on others (or on themselves for that matter).

Since you have the disposition to invest time in self-study, I can safely encourage you to perform research concerning the relevant facts in any important area you are entering. In this way, you will minimize the hazards and maximize the likelihood of success. I would particularly emphasize the area of human relations, since most people do not have an adequate education in this area. A fine way to ruin any plan is to lack knowledge of how people react and of the most constructive ways of influencing them. This explains my contemptuous attitude towards those who espouse the hang-loose philosophy towards expressing feelings. Certainly, it is a sign of emotional well-being to be spontaneous and emotionally expressive. But you had better learn where it works, where it doesn't work, and how to recognize the signs of people accepting or rejecting you.

### POOR PRIORITIES

One of the chief characteristics of good decision making and planning is a fine sense of priorities. What are the chief issues? When must a plan be completed? When must it be communicated to other people? When do you start operations? How will you get feedback so that you know what adjustments need to be made? Will the task be finished in time for a shakedown cruise before becoming operational?

This sounds complicated, but it is the way wars, scholarships, and contracts are won. It is also a sound way to move one's residence or change a job. Even having a baby involves deciding one's priorities if the ship of life is to be smoothly launched.

Since this is all obvious, what actually happens with most people? A combination of anxiety and lack of self-discipline interferes with setting up and implementing priorities. If you are nervous about failure, then you may delay planning or carrying out any plan at all. In your mind the risks are too great. This will be particularly true if you have a low idea of your own ability. Another important reason why decisions are not carried out in a timely way is lack of self-discipline. There are many people who never get anywhere, because they do not study, concentrate, or avoid trivia. Thus they don't concentrate on whatever is necessary to achieve worthwhile goals. Curiously, while I was writing this paragraph a woman called and told me she was not yet working, but stayed up late every night watching TV! How could she go on job interviews with that style of life?

Frequently, in mature years, after people have children, and their capacity to concentrate and learn is distracted by adult responsibilities, they decide that their existence has no meaning and their opportunities have been wasted. Such people do make a radical change, but only with the self-sacrifice they didn't invest when they were younger.

Priorities and self-discipline can also play a part in personal relationships. When you have a greater understanding of your reactions to other people, you will be able to judge whether a given relationship brings you toward your personal goals, or downgrades your emotional life. Unfortunately, many people remain in relationships which are poor for reasons of "family" or "friendship" or to avoid loneliness. As a consequence, their time is used up, their spirits are ruined, and their life is much less successful than it need be.

### LACK OF FLEXIBILITY

Inflexibility about decisions is yet another way in which the quality of your life can be spoiled. This is an outgrowth of our discussion of priorities and timeliness. I cannot think of any kind of important decision that might not be altered by unpredictable events.

*Each day you make a decision to continue or discontinue what you did the day or year or decade before.* Many people stay in a job after it is clear that the road to advancement is blocked. This is more than inertia. It is a decision not to move. This is only one example of inflexibility in decision making.

Only when we have a clear idea of our emotional capability and our aptitudes can we set up a time schedule to determine whether we are achieving what we think we can attain. A situation may appear promising for a while, but because of deception, new supervisors, changed attitudes, unpredicted political and economic events, deaths, new products, or numerous other reasons, it may no longer be what you intended for yourself. Be flexible.

## SELF-DESTRUCTIVENESS

I believe that self-destructiveness is the most frequent contributor to poor decision making. I define self-destructiveness (Parker, 1973b) as making decisions whose harmfulness upon ourselves we can predict in advance. If the same situation should arise in the life of a friend, we could offer great advice; but we don't take it for ourselves!

*History III–2*: A woman is very dependent upon her husband because of paralyzing anxieties. Despite the fact that she has low self-esteem and feels incapable of working, using public transportation, and so forth, she makes a variety of decisions which create an intolerable home life. She believes that her husband has been unfaithful (the evidence is slight) and she harasses him into confessing. She refuses him sex with the excuse that he is not attentive enough. She feels hurt that he is disinterested in her, but neglects her personal appearance and doesn't take care of their apartment. Although money is short, she runs up vast phone bills and forces her husband to eat out by not shopping or preparing meals.

This is an extreme case, but there is something of this woman in all of us. How many times have we been able to give good advice to the next person, and refused to give it to ourselves? To a large extent, we all have a fund of wisdom which would be sufficient to help us to avoid bad decisions and thus increase our chances for satisfaction and ultimate emotional fulfillment. Why then is self-destructiveness so prevalent in life?

I believe that the chief force behind self-destructiveness is *a lack of priorities*. Most people do not decide what is important for them, and then ruthlessly eliminate from their lives the trivial or the damaging. *A clear awareness of one's values is one of the greatest assets in reaching emotional fulfillment.* When you know your real rewards, you can make decisions which will enable you to reach them (see Chapter 6: "Impossible Dreams vs. Realistic Goals").

Another decision-ruining, self-destructive tendency is the willingness to settle for *momentary gratifications*. We all engage in trivial actions, temporarily pleasing, for which we curse ourselves the morning after. Cumulatively, these slightly pleasing acts can divert our energies or create undesirable situations. These ruin any opportunities that we have for a good lifestyle and a fulfilling emotional life. There is no substitute for self-discipline, not even ten years of psychoanalysis five times a week.

A third serious cause of self-destructiveness is *taking other people's opinions too seriously*. This originates with the realistic fear that children have of disobeying or displeasing their parents. It ends with becoming frozen in action until we can check out what the neighbors—real experts, they!—have to say.

*History III–3*: A young man was a student at the famous College of the City of New York during the period when its distinguished faculty was enabling the children of immigrants to get an education. He was encouraged by two of its greatest faculty members, the distinguished philosophers Morris Cohen and Harry Overstreet, to go to England to study at Oxford. Now, what was the logical thing for his parents to do? Obviously— consult the neighbors. These eminent authorities said, "No, whoever heard of such a thing. Nobody from our group ever studied at Oxford." Results: He spent most of his life in the garment industry and in years of conflict with his wife who lacked sympathy for his philosophical preoccupations and attempts to write. His attitude towards his mother? Don't ask. Her inability to make up her own mind and to grant freedom to her son was self-destructive because instead of aiding her son's development it caused him to have contempt for her weakness.

Here is an example of a couple's decision to maintain the status quo, which keeps them functioning at cross-purposes. This prevents them from enjoying life and fulfilling themselves.

*Histroy III–4*: A married woman in the forties, with children, is in conflict with her husband for a variety of reasons, including his lack of support for her efforts in gaining a college education and preparing for a career. Her husband yells at her or the children when he hears something that he doesn't like. I suggested to her that sometimes she should still maintain her position and let him yell, and tell him that she is an adult who is entitled to her own opinions. She has been so trained to be obedient that she couldn't even imagine saying this to her husband. I suggested to her that, "when you're conditioned to obey it's hard to be spontaneous . . . to realize that there are alternatives. . . . The two of you seem to be always on the defensive, as though there might be a fight at any moment."

This brought tears to her eyes. "I felt like crying when you said that we were always fighting."

I asked her, "What does fighting mean to you?"

"It is an admission of my unhappiness. I might lose the fight. People become irrational, they hurt each other over irrelevant things. I don't want to hurt him, I don't want him to hurt me."

I suggested that she was also guarding a romantic image of life, that people really can get along without fighting. Then I said, "Maybe in some ways you will have to fight more, and in some areas it isn't worth fighting about."

Her reply was, "I feel like sinking when you say we'll have to fight more. We fight, but they are not good fights. We're afraid to face what is really there." After a while she commented that her husband looks much older than he is, although he tries to maintain good health.

Therapist: "He's under a lot of stress."

Patient: "Well, so am I."

Therapist: "Well, why don't you tell him that you both are? Why don't you try to collaborate with him?"

Patient: "You make it sound like two armies and they're both on the defensive. I won't know how to handle peace and contentment in the home."

Therapist: "You will have to confront some issues you have been avoiding, and not fight over others."

Patient: "The things we argue about are all peripheral things and we don't argue about the things we're really angry about. When I had the crying jag in group (therapy) you came close. I can't accept it from you, and you pointed out how I could accept it from D. (a male group member)."

Therapist: "Maybe that's why you fight, it keeps you from being close."

Patient: "I was able to feel more intimate with my husband that night when I got home. I was able to say to him, 'Let's go to bed and enjoy each other instead of watching TV.' It was very good and I was able to reach orgasm. After this, I would have expected him to be in a better mood the next day, but he got scared. He can't handle intimacy."

Therapist: "You will be taking steps in your therapy and perhaps leaving him behind."

To obtain the quality of life we call emotional fulfillment requires both *maximizing decisions which lead to a constructive lifestyle, and recognizing and then changing circumstances which are degrading.*

Avoiding poor decision making requires that you start by evaluating your personality and above all your frame of mind. Your emotional condition is a complex product of your basic nature, the real world, and the kinds of adaptations which you have used in order to survive. As a consequence of your experiences, you feel a certain quality of self-esteem or self-hatred, emotional fulfillment or deprivation, social competence or inadequacy, and so forth.

There are certain key moods which signal to you that basic changes are required in your life. Your poor decisions have brought you emotional self-destructiveness.

*Emotional neediness*: The inability to obtain basic satisfactions casts a pall on all other parts of life. It results in making great demands upon friends, mates, and others so that we end up by being rejected or resented. The decision to demand fulfillment from others instead of creating it for ourselves (autonomy or self-sufficiency) destroys relationships.

What are our basic needs? They are those emotional responses that we require from other people in order to be satisfied and happy, which we cannot easily provide for ourselves.

1. *Love*: The feeling of being wanted and cared for

2. *Security and dependency*: The belief that in time of trouble there is someone who cares

3. *Sex*: The ability to relate and to have pleasure with one's body

4. *Recognition*: To belong somewhere, to believe that you play a definite role in society, and are valued for your contributions

5. *Companionship*: Wanting to be in the company of peers

Millions of years of evolution built these needs into the human nervous system so that our ancestors could cling together for survival against a pitiless world. Human beings who reject these needs, or who do not know how to have them satisfied by others, do not get close to people.

*Existential Sickness*: Maddi (1970) defines this as a failure in the search for meaning in life. There is so much strife, struggle, disappointment, and downright anger today, that many people wonder "What is life all about?" Not everybody asks this question. Some people achieve an understanding of the meaning of life through the religious, philosophical, and mystical experiences. After a while, the person experiencing existential sickness has a chronic inability to believe in the truth, importance, usefulness, or value of any of the things he does, or even can imagine doing.

Nevertheless, the rest of us require a reason as to why we are alive and struggling. We do not choose to be born, nor the kind of world which envelops us. We do not choose our parents, nor our teachers, mentors, nor our relatives. Why do we have to cope with such a terrible world without any choice if there is no reason and life has no meaning?

Some of the possible ways of coping with this existential sickness are being a *nihilist, crusading,* or *vegetating* (Maddi, 1970).

The *nihilist* attempts to discredit the beliefs and traditions which have meaning to others. His primary feeling is despair, and his chief pleasure is destruction.

The *crusader* seeks out dramatic causes. However, even social action movements, as dramatic and exciting as they are, can also be disruptive and dangerous to others. For an enlightening explanation of why peace is threatening to some people, and why social conditions are constantly being shattered in the name of idealism, you might turn to a symposium on *The Emotional Stress of War, Violence, and Peace,* which I edited (Parker, 1972, particularly the chapters by Parker, Sturm, Schuman, and Riscalla).

The *vegetative individual* sinks into indifference, apathy, and aimlessness because he no longer employs any effort to attain some sense of meaning. This is a type of regression.

Existential illness is a belief that there is no possibility of fulfillment in this world. It is overcome through clarifying your values, and thereby improving your motivation. Among the consequences are increased activity and involvement, as well as the reduction of emotional problems and stress.

# 4

# Emotional Problems
# and Stress

Emotional problems sabotage efficient decision making. They interfere with the ability to see either oneself or the world clearly, and they destroy congenial human relationships.

Emotional problems keep people from seeing themselves realistically. They cause us to repress our true feelings and impulses, or to be unaware of their origins and meaning. In addition, they cause us to view ourselves unrealistically. We exaggerate our true worth or minimize it. This is disastrous for good decision making since a minimum requirement is that we understand correctly what we are capable of achieving.

Emotional problems also distort our view of the world. Our philosophy and concept of what life is like develop to a large extent when we are children. Since children are vulnerable to the greater force of adults, are less competent, and think differently than adults, our life map based upon these old experiences is outdated. One effect of having a troublesome emotional life is that we tend to keep the viewpoint we developed years ago. Instead of (a) evaluating a situation in terms of real abilities and personality, and (b) matching it to an accurate assessment of the outside world, we fail in both areas. After all, even with a totally accurate picture of ourselves, we cannot make plans without seeing clearly the people and other resources of the world which can affect our progress.

In this way emotional problems interfere with information gathering, logical analysis, and/or attempts to reach one's goals. It does this through feelings and attitudes which are irrelevant to what we want to achieve. Putting it another way, we spoil the way we function in life because past experiences create moods, anxieties, prejudices, distortions, fears, expectations, or misinformation which ought not to be part of a problem we have to solve. Consequently, we are tossed and turned, or we are afraid to proceed, or we do not see the world clearly. We may not even be aware of those experiences and feelings which are functioning so destructively. As a result, our thinking and actions deviate from achievable or worthwhile goals.

Emotional problems affect decision making in two general ways: first, in our relations to people; second, in the way we approach a task. It may come as a surprise to you that decisions and personal relationships are connected. In fact, we do decide how and when to obtain the cooperation of others, what to say to them, when to establish or break relationships, whether to express warmth or anger, and so on. In this way, our decisions affect transactions and relationships with our mates, neighbors, people who work with us, servicemen, teachers, friends, lovers, and all the rest. When it comes to particular tasks, we gather more or less information, proceed impulsively or slowly, work with greater or lesser care, volunteer for or refuse assignments, all on the basis of an emotional life which is functioning constructively or self-destructively.

Emotional problems destroy congenial, cooperative relationships with people. In the old days, if you had a mystical bent, or just hated people, you could become a hermit. Now even if you could find an unoccupied place you wouldn't survive for long because of animal traps, coyote poison, or drunken hunters. No, your fate is to have to get along with people. If you cannot, you are in trouble. Every basic feeling can affect human relationships. Any distortion existing in sexuality, anger, dependency, assertiveness, etc., will have some effect upon how we like people and get along with them, and how they react to us. There are few decisions that we make which sooner or later won't require getting other people to interact with us. Thus, *any disturbance in human relationships interferes with our capacity to carry out our decisions, or even to get into a frame of mind to make decisions and to plan.*

## COMPULSIVENESS

This is the emotional problem which probably has the worst effect upon effective decision making and implementation of decisions. Some people experience the intrusion upon their minds of thoughts, images, impulses, or actual actions which are unwelcome and which they feel they ought to resist. On the surface these individuals would seem to be efficient since they are thorough, consistent, punctual, and orderly. However, they may expend much energy but produce little. In fact, many of their thoughts and actions are due to a high level of anxiety. Compulsive people believe there is a high probability that any situation will have an unfavorable outcome (Carr, 1974). In some subjective way, the intrusive thoughts, impulses, and actions seem to reduce the possibility of something dangerous happening. There are two forms of this condition that we must recognize if we are to counteract its effects upon ourselves and appraise adequately the persons with whom we must deal.

*Goal-less thinking or obsessiveness* can be characterized by working at a solution all day and not coming to any kind of a decision because unrelated thoughts intrude upon our minds or interfere with our rumination of the problem we want to solve. After we come to a conclusion we immediately decide to do the opposite. Then, we may return to the original conclusion. This is called obsessive doubting. Sometimes threatening thoughts caused by feelings of guilt or other anxieties also may make us stop doing something we feel will have undesirable consequences. In this way, we feel that we have some control over the situation, even though the connection between our thoughts and the real world may be so tenuous as to be superstitious.

*Unproductive actions or compulsions* consist of doing things which are repetitive and time-consuming but getting nowhere.

We might be filing papers, taking out the garbage, or cleaning the closet, at a time when something significant awaits our attention. We do not recognize this as stalling because we attempt to justify the necessity of performing trivial actions. We might find that we have actually accomplished something and then spoiled it, perhaps time after time (undoing). We end up exactly where we started, but emotionally exhausted, frustrated, and self-hating. Perhaps we work on relatively minor aspects of a problem and never get to the major aspects at all. The decision to do this is bad judgment, and we do not conceal our lack of productivity from those who care. Another way to avoid confronting our decision to work unproductively is to utilize excessive care or preciseness. Deciding to improve on an already good product is a great way of not delivering the goods. Keeping a house excessively clean is an equally marvelous way of preventing our family from enjoying it.

What do goal-less thinking and unproductive activity have in common? They conceal our true feelings from ourselves or the world. At least for some time. Many of these activities and thoughts screen from ourselves our angry and destructive or hostile wishes. Nevertheless, our true feelings may show indirectly. For example, the care with which a teacher corrects a paper may keep him from being aware of his dislike for a particular student or of a generally critical attitude. Excessive attention to details serves to keep a situation from being completed. It is hoped that no one can then judge the completed task and say that its author is incompetent. Fear and anger are concealed. In general, goal-less thinking and unproductive actions *conceal the unconscious decision to harm somebody*.

## DEPRESSION AND HOPELESSNESS

Depression is a very complicated mood with a variety of causes. It is the feeling of being melancholy or "blue." From the point of view of effective decision making, depression is accompanied by a variety of changes in one's personality which interfere with competence in dealing with matters great and small.

Therefore, it is important that you learn to recognize the signs of depression in yourself, and in those upon whom you rely, in order to prevent interference with the accomplishment of your goals.

Depressed people lose interest in life (Klein, 1974), are pessimistic (Beck, Weissman, Lester & Trexler, 1974), experience loss of appetite, ability to sleep, and interest in sex, and are easily fatigued (Beck, 1973). They frequently feel guilty and valueless.

Depression can be accompanied by other strong feelings and bodily complaints which serve to disguise its presence. Anxiety ("nervousness") can be prominent (Prusoff & Klerman, 1974; Downing & Rickels, 1974), as well as hostility (Klein, 1974).

There are a number of causes for depressive reactions, which have been divided into *reactive* or *exogenous* (stemming from life stress) and *endogenous* (internal, perhaps caused by physiological changes). According to *The American Handbook of Psychiatry* (Mendels, 1974), "There is considerable evidence that genetic factors (heredity) play an important role in the etiology of affective illness."

*Reactive depression.* This type of depression has its origins in certain childhood events, which leave us vulnerable to the loss of relationships, and to certain symbolic events, which make us feel valueless and cause life to lose its meaning. Examples might be the death or the disinterest of our parents when we were young. However, depression is also caused by the inability to express our anger when we are attacked (Parker, 1972, "The patient who cannot express pain"; *Emotional Common Sense*, 1973, Chapter VIII: "Coping with Emotional Pain"; Chapter XII: "Handling Depression").

Because of the particular peculiar constellation of feelings and attitudes which we have when we are depressed, it becomes difficult to work our way out of this state. The depressed person frequently permits his own life to come to a halt by giving up his plans. It also becomes difficult for others to make decisions which include depressed people since they are preoccupied with their misery. They may feel unworthy of any efforts which are shown for them. Depressed people often have a quality of reproach which puts a burden of guilt upon their families and other associates. Thus, in the presence of depression, the vital issues affecting many people become sidetracked in order to provide support for one person. One often sees that there are unconscious feelings of hostility behind the depression. We are dealing with somebody who is full of resentment.

Depressive people do not relate effectively or appropriately to present conditions because (perhaps under the impact of stress) they are reliving old feelings about themselves and the significant people who were formerly important to them. These older beliefs may have included ideas of worthlessness and pessimism, and the events of the real world are screened and molded to conform to the content of these older "schemas" or complexes of feelings and attitudes. Because of the pessimistic ideas which are created, the severely depressed person experiences a feeling of incapacity to cope with his present problems; and he feels hopeless about obtaining satisfaction in his future (Beck, 1972).

We have already seen how a pessimistic attitude can lead to inaction in a crisis, with fatal results. However, it is noteworthy that depressed people sometimes can be mobilized to action in emergencies upon the threat of hospitalization, or through fear of being regarded as peculiar (Beck, 1973, pp 23–24). Hopelessness may be recognized by an attitude such as this: "There is no use in trying to get something because I probably won't get it; my future looks dark to me; all I can see ahead of me is unpleasantness" (Beck, Weissman, Lester & Trexler, 1974).

Since reactive depressions have their roots in the past, they cripple our effectiveness and make us vulnerable and overly sensitive to rejection. In the last chapter I will point out techniques of developing autonomy so that we can feed ourselves emotionally when there is no support from others.

How can we learn to avoid hopelessness? It is critical that we live in the present. During periods of stress we must make every effort to obtain information about the danger facing us. We must obtain feedback concerning which of our activities are successful in reducing stress; and we must avoid those which are unsuccessful. We must be alert to unlearn habits which worked at one time but which do not solve the problems facing us right now. It is also extremely necessary to maintain a high degree of physical fitness because of the deleterious effects of stress upon the brain and the rest of the body.

Some forms of depression are relatively amenable to psychotherapy. Other forms are aided by medication (Klein, 1974). It is important that a depressed person seek consultation with a competent psychotherapist, who will offer support, insight, and opportunity to express anger. In my experience, depression does not automatically require prescription of psychiatric medication. Nevertheless, a competent psychotherapist will have contact with psychiatrists on those occasions when medical consultation is indicated.

We can get a picture of depression from the feelings expressed by three members of a therapy group. Although none of them was crippled by depression, all were severely affected.

L: I feel dead. Like a burden. Just going through the day. A dull pain. I'm bored by everything. Going to work, to the gym, to a party. The people I meet are the same types. It's a lack of hope. I feel very blasé.

Therapist: Talk to the feeling.

L: I wish you would either go away or hurt *more*. If you hurt more I could understand it. Maybe I would be able to work it out.

G: I lack enthusiasm for anything in particular except checking on the price of tuna fish. There is no joy in life and there is nothing that gives me joy.

M: I see myself in L. Get off my back. All of me has to be alive or dead.

*Endogenous depression.* There is some evidence that obscure defects in biochemical functioning, perhaps on an hereditary basis (Dunner, 1975; Winokur, 1975), can play an important role in depression. Where depression does not seem to be a direct result of an emotionally charged situation, it is sometimes called endogenous in contrast to reactive. Of course, an endogenous depression may be the last step in a series of other kinds of emotional stress. This type of reaction seems to involve a reduced amount of those chemicals (neurotransmitters) which transmit impulses within the brain (Van Praag, Korf & Schutt, 1973; Fawcett, 1975). One such substance which seems to be depleted in some depressions—and following severe emotional stress (see below)—is called *norepinephrine* (NE). Depletion of NE may be so profound that a seeming state of helplessness in solving problems exists ("learned helplessness"). Apparently, whether or not particular biochemical mechanisms are involved, severe or prolonged stress can result in that combination of defective coping and weakness which we know as one form of depression.

### PASSIVITY AND INDECISIVENESS

Passivity and indecisiveness are also involved in depression, although they have separate identities as well. Depressed people have lost motivation. They may begin by losing initiative in complicated tasks requiring much expenditure of energy; and they may end by being unable to take care of themselves, even in eating, personal cleanliness, or taking medication. In addition, they have difficulty in making decisions, or choosing between alternatives (Beck, 1973, pp. 23, 25–26). This is certainly related to their pessimistic attitude about the future and their belief that it is hopeless to try to improve the situation and thereby eliminate emotional pain from their lives.

However, there are also other psychological reasons for a passive attitude when the time comes to make decisions.

What is behind passivity? Look closely enough and you will find that it is really motivated by particular attitudes about life. Sometimes there is a wish to sabotage somebody else's expectations. If you do nothing, then mother's wish that you show the world what a genius you are will be frustrated. Besides, if you secretly doubt that you have any brains at all, if you are inactive there will be no evidence that anybody can produce to prove that you are defective.

It might be that you were led to believe that somebody else

would carry the ball for you. Being spoiled as a child doesn't train one to take initiative and accept responsibility. A great deal of discouragement also contributes to a passive attitude because the person says to himself, "Why bother? It will be all wrong anyway. I will just end up by being hurt for the millionth time."

A passive/lazy attitude is troublesome to overcome, and we must learn to recognize it in others. We certainly know about it in ourselves because we have been told about it by others repeatedly! Few people have so little energy or ambition by nature that they can't handle the ordinary assignments which come their way.

## CONFLICT

There are a number of ways in which the ability to make choices can be disturbed by a combination of desire and anxiety (Dollard & Miller, 1950, Chapter 22). Conflict occurs when we have difficulty in making up our minds because we have to choose between alternative solutions. The issue is beclouded by different amounts of reward and/or anxiety associated with each choice so that our path is not clear.

Frequently, we have no anxiety about a person or an action when we are at a distance. However, as we come closer to having a relationship, or doing what we want to do, then some old fears come closer to being realized and we become more and more anxious. Often we don't anticipate our nervousness when confronted with the actual situation. The closer we come to the outcome we desire, the more nervous we get; the further we retreat, the more reassured we feel. In this way we fluctuate back and forth. The closer we get to our goal, both anticipated pleasure and anxiety become simultaneously greater. Much energy and time are used up trying to make up our mind: do it or don't do it. The ultimate outcome will be decided by whether the joy or the anxiety is greater as we come closer to our goal. The very anxious person will remain quite far from situations which ordinarily create pleasure for others, such as an active social life, career advancement, and so on. When we can't choose between two seemingly pleasant alternatives, it may be that there are hidden antipathies towards both.

Since most anxieties are based upon out-of-date conditions, to be caught in a conflict frequently indicates an emotional problem which can be resolved through psychotherapeutic consultation. To ignore it does not mean that it will go away. People frequently avoid situations, and feel better, only to have the same unpleasant feelings crop up again. If there is a constant pattern of avoidance, the result is a significant crippling of one's emotional life because too many important activities are hampered.

## STRESS AND DECISION MAKING

*Stress* can be defined as a reaction which we experience when we cannot cope with a situation. The result is emotional or physical discomfort in the face of danger. Stress is a signal to you that, without radical changes, your emotional life and perhaps your health will get worse and not better.

Stress is often the result of somebody's faulty decision making. There may be a tyrannical employer or spouse who has decided to sacrifice you to meet some personal need. Stress can also be a result of your own faulty decision making. Requiring two jobs to meet the bills of an extravagance is one example. To fall ill, or to have poor stamina, because of a combination of poor diet and insufficient rest is another.

When you are under stress you must find the time to analyze its causes. Then, be firm in your resolve to make those changes in your world or life which will eliminate it. Stress leads in the opposite direction from emotional fulfillment. Inappropriate goals, in the light of reality or one's personal characteristics, can lead to serious stress.

## EMOTIONAL DISCOMFORT: A SIGN OF STRESS

There are important advantages to identifying the various signs of emotional discomfort, or reaction to stress:

1. You can learn to associate cause and effect. As you sense that you are under stress, you will be able to identify the cause and eliminate or avoid it before it becomes too harmful.

2. You can recognize your own sensitivities and weak spots.

3. As a parent, teacher, supervisor, or counselor, you can fulfill your responsibilities by being able to guide or inform others that there is a serious problem.

4. You can guard yourself from such harm as bad temper and defects of judgment if you recognize that somebody in a position of authority over you is experiencing stress.

Signs of stress include the following:

1. Somatic symptoms; for example, high blood pressure, pulse rate, cholesterol
2. Anxiety and fear
3. Guilt
4. Tension
5. Anger or rage
6. Tension-caused irritability
7. Feelings of emotional deprivation
8. Feelings of rejection, humiliation, hurt
9. Job dissatisfaction, inability to self-actualize
10. Low self-esteem
11. Unpleasant fantasies
12. Sleep disturbance
13. Apathy
14. Depression
15. Feelings of helplessness and hopelessness

I have found it useful in my clinical practice to consider the stress which has brought on an emotional problem, and the particular vulnerability of the individual which created the weakness. When one also considers the world which one has created around oneself, then stress analysis points up the need to take particular decisions to (1) reduce stress, (2) strengthen our resources, (3) change our way of dealing with our world, and (4) perhaps to make a significant change in the world around us.

## SOURCES OF STRESS

*External sources*: Sometimes "the world is too much with us." We shall see later that the human mind and body developed under vastly different circumstances from those of an urban environment, with the particular economic and material conditions of modern society (Chapter 7). The requirements of a combination of job, travel, education, maintaining a household, taking care of children, and so on may be too complex or exhausting for a particular person. One's constitution, training, education, and other resources may be inadequate to meet environmental demands. It is impossible for one person to prepare himself for all possible conditions, and the force of circumstances or a lack of prudence can confront us with an excessive environmental overload. In addition, if we find ourselves in an alien world, that is, one with which we are not trained to cope, this form of external stress can easily make us break down in one way or another.

*Social sources*: We have been conditioned by generations of natural selection and years of personal dependency to require, and be sensitive to, the quality of the relationships we have with the people around us. Interpersonal relationships can be stressful in a wide variety of ways. It is important that we recognize them, and then proceed to improve their quality. It is important that we remove from our lives those who insist on being degrading influences. Hostility and degradation have obvious stressful qualities. People also often cave in when they are separated from those they love. Furthermore, the social requirements made upon us (our "role") can create severe problems. Sometimes these demands are vague, for example, when we do not know how to act in a new situation such as a job, or when we are in somebody's home with whom we are unfamiliar. At other times different roles can be in conflict, for example, the middle management executive who must be subservient to the vice-president of his department and who believes he must in turn be a terror to those whom he supervises. An important, but infrequently recognized source of stress is an incompatibility between a person's lifestyle and temperament. The world we have created and our way of dealing with it may make unrealistic demands upon the basic qualities of our personality.

There are many sources of vulnerability to social stress. They include excessive dependency upon others; lack of support from important people when things go wrong; fear of, or actual punishment for errors; and conflict or lack of clarity in our values and goals. If we do not understand ourselves, then we cannot determine the kind of social life which will lead to emotional fulfillment on the one hand, and freedom from social stress on the other.

*Personal sources*: At times our own body betrays us because it is unable to deal with the world in its expected way. I refer to illness, brain damage, and fatigue. Under these circumstances, we think that we can cope with demands, but indeed may be literally unable to do so, and yet completely unaware of our disability. *The most frequent cause of personal stress in my opinion is fatigue.* This leads to more unforeseen problems and complications than any other stress factor.

Personal vulnerability may also be due to ignorance, imprudent expenditure of energy in high living, inability to deal with external, social, or internal stress, or genetic vulnerability. Hereditary weaknesses can make us susceptible to any form of stress if we have been placed in some situation for which we are constitutionally poorly endowed. Ignorance, fatigue, or poor habits also lead to personal vulnerability. This, in turn, can make us unable to handle other situations for which we are ordinarily competent, turning them from mere details of our world to stress factors reducing our ability to handle decisions and other aspects of daily living.

*Internal world*: We are often our own worst enemies where stress from our emotional life is concerned. Sometimes we are troubled by our thoughts and feelings even when there is no stress affecting us in the world around us. Early experiences have created diverse attitudes toward certain kinds of people and situations, and sometimes a tendency toward angry or melancholy moods. In addition, if our emotions confuse our thinking, or if we have not trained ourselves to deal with problems in a disciplined, rational way, the solutions we create may be worse than the problems they are designed to cope with.

Of course, the disturbed inner world of the people around us may also be a source of profound external stress if we are their targets. We shall discuss this topic further in Chapters 9 and 10 ("The Unconscious," "Feelings and Your Decisions").

Internal conflicts are some of the most serious saboteurs of good decision making. When you have conflicts within your own personality you may end up by making no decisions, or decisions which are impulsive, trivial, infantile, stupid, contradictory, hateful, cowardly, or just plain wrong. The trouble with internal conflicts is not only that are you fighting with yourself, but also that you may not even know you are in a fight! You may have repressed some of the reasons behind the struggle.

Internal conflicts are generally the result of our having been subjected to several sets of values while we were growing up, perhaps at different stages of our lives. We may not even be aware of the pull of one set of feelings.

### EXAMPLE OF CONFLICT AS A FORM OF STRESS

*History IV–1*: A woman in her thirties was unable to decide whether to take an apartment by herself. She had been living for many years with a man who had originally shared her lodgings out of necessity. After a while a closer relationship had built up, but it had eventually cooled off. During part of this time, the man had been unable to work, and his dependence upon her was clear. Now, his presence in the apartment was a source of inconvenience and embarrassment, interfering with her ability to establish a relationship with a new man. Nevertheless, she felt that a decision to take an apartment by herself was a terrible thing to do. She felt guilty.

What were the sources of her conflict? As a young child during the Second World War she had been separated from her parents in order to survive. Unconsciously, she identified with this man and felt that she would be performing a shameful act by "abandoning" him, as she had been "abandoned" as a child. This feeling was in conflict with her mature wish to be independent and to be able to form a new sexual relationship. She was able to move when her therapy group convinced her that she was contributing to the infantilization of this man by yielding to his guilt-provoked tactics!

When you find yourself in a situation where you cannot make a decision despite the urgency of doing so, then you must explore the various values which are pulling you in different directions. If you find that the force behind one of the choices is derived from events which no longer apply, then the correct decision will become clear.

Stress, then, can come from almost any direction. It can build up gradually, or can knock us down suddenly. I would like to present a poem written by my friend Jane Morrin, who was suddenly stricken with the terrible pains of a perforated colon of unknown origin. After repeated surgery and several life-threatening complications, respiration, fever, cardiac arrest), she expressed her feelings about this stress as follows:

### ARCHITECTS OF SAND
### Jane Morrin

Living as we do at the verge of the sea,
We all become sometime architects of sand,
Makers of sand castles, simple or grand
According to taste or ambition . . . or pride.
    But defense is essential at the edge of the deep;
Shoring up walls, getting shapes redefined,
We constantly battle the incoming tide.

Playfully, wavelets come curling up the strand,
Tumbling froth down slopes of sculptured sand,
Vanishing darkly with a damp, hissing sound.
Now skyscrapers topple, great castles are drowned.
Behind each wave trembles another, then more.
(Water's needed for building, but repairs are a chore.)
    We dig in, determined, or move up the shore.

Soon, heaving scuds of water take on menacing looks
As surf comes up higher. We abandon the heap,
Yielding to that ultimate adversary, the indifferent deep,
Feeling that perhaps luck, fate—maybe even divine will
Had a say in what happened in that trivial play,
   We brush that away feeling silly, but recall bitter times:
   Adversity "winning" in spite of foresight and skill.

But what if the winds grow in sound deep with mourning?
What if opposing winds fling spume high like a warning?
Buffeting waters are birds spreading to pounce,
While far out, waves contort into mad, frothing mounts. . . .
What if, slowly looming up, a wall like black blood,
A ferocious black tide roaring out of the flood,
Assaulting soft builders, slammed into the mud?

Bad enough to see plans often smashed, washed away—
An old bitter cliché most men live every day.
How much worse then when the planner is crushed by disaster
   Say a fall or a fever—what of his plans then . . . or after?
Once a wave shoved me deep into the sea. . . .
Now I am washed back up on shore, entangled
in sea wrack; smelling of iodine and salt and decay.

Should I, when I'm able, pick myself up from this ruined place
And start building sand castles again? I am filled with grief.
I, whose guts were scraped in passing the terrifying reef,
Who could not breathe while burned in a limitless ocean of pain,
While tumbled to the edges of hell—what can I gain
Building castles of sand at the playful edges of laughing
      beach days?

Some day perhaps I will build castles again . . . some day . . .
     Now I cannot.
Instead, I have a hunger for meaning, an urge, a need to search—
To brush sand and salt out of my eyes with battered fingers
And comb this place for something . . . perhaps a pearl
Flung back up on shore with me, for understanding. . . .

Jane has made a marvelous recovery, and she is resuming a life full of constructive influence on those around her.

## BODILY REACTION TO STRESS

The physiological reactions of animals offer some insight into what occurs in our bodies when we are subjected to continuous or severe stress. In this way we can learn to defend ourselves against overwhelming conditions. Our capacity to withstand stress must be taken into account, in addition to our courage, our training, and so forth. We can improve our decision-making abilities by becoming aware that at certain times we can undertake new projects, while at others we might be excessively vulnerable to failure and pessimism.

Animal studies indicate that following intense stress there is a reduction of norepinephrine in the brain. Repeated exposure to the same kind of stress encourages *habituation,* or return to normal levels (Weiss, Glazer, & Pohorecky, 1974; Glazer, Weiss, Pohorecky, & Miller, 1975; Weiss, Glazer, Pohorecky, Brick, & Miller, 1975). One consequence of the reduced neurotransmitter level is hampered capacity to learn relatively difficult ways of dealing with new stressful situations immediately after high stress. Learning ability improves with time, paralleling an increase in brain NE (Weiss & Glazer, 1975).

It is significant that if you test ability to learn before habituation takes place, then a relatively long-term deficit in ability to learn *in this particular situation* occurs. This would not occur if testing is delayed until recovery from the initial stress had taken place (Weiss & Glazer, 1975). Apparently, inability to perform correctly *the first time* results in the learning of extraneous acts. These mistakes are conditioned, regardless of their irrelevance, because the stress (e.g., electric shock) is ultimately removed anyway. These incorrect responses interfere with subsequent learning of correct evasive tactics. We shall see that hormones affect this situation considerably.

One way that the body copes with stress is through secretion of hormones from the cortex (covering) of the adrenal gland. This occurs through control by the adrenocorticoptrophic hormone (ACTH) secreted by the anterior pituitary gland, which is affected by the adrenal cortical level and other bodily functioning through the brain and blood vessels. A two-way interaction (feedback) develops whereby the level of one hormone has some influence upon the level of the other (as well as other effects). There is evidence that ACTH *prevents* unlearning (extinction) of old responses, whereas glucocorticoids (adrenal cortical hormones) *suppress irrelevant actions,* which leads to effective new learning. These hormones have even further influence upon changing behavior because they affect processing of external information. Adrenal cortical hormones seem to influence the functioning of the hippocampus, a brain (temporal lobe) center which processes new information during memory formation (all of the above from Levine, 1972).

Feedback is important in determining whether there will be adverse effects from stress. For one thing, the knowledge that we are actively doing something while in a dangerous situation seems to reduce stress, in contrast to being helpless in the same situation (Miller, 1973). This was observed in studies of combat pilots, who were more active compared to their copilots. It has also been observed in studies of animals. Information—for example, a signal that a shock was about to occur—appeared to reduce the likelihood of getting ulcers (Weiss, 1971a). If a conflict situation was set up (for example, by shocking the animals when they tried to escape), more ulceration developed in active animals than in helpless animals receiving the same treatment (Weiss, 1971b). When the animals were permitted to escape from ulcer-provoking situations, and when they received feedback that they had responded appropriately, ulceration was greatly reduced (Weiss, 1971c).

There are also sex differences in physiological reactions to stress. In comparable stressful situations, males secrete more adrenalin (from the interior of the adrenal gland) than females do. Females tend to remain relaxed while under the same stress that sends the adrenalin of males squirting into their bloodstreams. Whether this is an actual sex difference, or is due to socially conditioned differences in reactions, is not yet known (Frankenhaeuser, 1975).

# 5

# Toward a Definition of Fulfillment

Emotional fulfillment is a hazy idea, difficult to define, and problematic to achieve. The only way to study it sensibly is to recognize these difficulties, and then to approach a definition with full awareness of the differences among people. For example, a recent article in the *New York Times* reported that a motorized caravan of 5,000 vehicles containing Libyans was marching into Egypt, demanding unification, and stating their willingness to die for this ideal. Few would empathize with this deeply held wish, yet many adults were ready to make sacrifices and take risks in order to achieve this, to me, obscure goal.

This example teaches us that a useful definition of emotional fulfillment must take into account the considerable variability among people, and it must avoid such a degree of vagueness that would categorize everybody!

## What Is Normal?

The first question is: What is *normalcy*? Kinsey, for example, approached this definition by asking what people actually do sexually. In a sense, if we exclude the criminals and others suffering from well-defined emotional problems, one might conclude that an exceedingly wide variety of sexual behavior is normal, and therefore potentially a part of an emotionally fulfilling experience. For our purposes, I shall define *normal* differently, even negatively. To me, normal emotional development is unhampered and lacking emotional distress. A normal person has developed without feelings of inadequacy and can express his feelings warmly and openly. The underlying patterns of development have unfolded without crippling effects (Saul and Pulver, 1965). The normal person does not have to exert excessive energy to control his feelings or impulses because of unreal fears. Rather, a normal person can express himself or herself without self-destructiveness (Parker, 1973).

## How Does Tension Affect Emotional Life?

Another question affecting emotional fulfillment is the nature of emotional reactions. Is it the nature of emotional life to relieve tension, to obtain pleasure, and to avoid pain? This is largely the approach of Sigmund Freud (1924). The ebb and flow of tension, of which the sexual experience is the best example, is clearly related to the feelings of pleasure and displeasure. If this view is correct, our emotional life is dominated by the desire to remove tension, or at least to keep it from reaching intolerable levels.

A very different approach to the nature of emotional life is offered by Maslow (1962, 1971). He suggests that people who are in the process of developing (self-actualizing) experience "fully, vividly, selflessly, with full concentration and total absorption" (1971, p. 45). Such people are more likely to build up and maintain tension for long periods of time. But it is a tension which is *constructively utilized* toward important, realistic goals. The rewards are those moments of fulfillment and happiness so well described as "peak experiences."

How can we resolve these two points of view? It is important to distinguish between basic needs (see Chapter 3), which must be gratified before we can develop wholesome attitudes toward life, and the wish to develop our personality beyond the immediate necessity of coping with life's problems.

People differ considerably in the extent to which each need must be fulfilled at any stage of their lives. If any one of these needs is frustrated during development, the result is an *emotionally hungry attitude*. The person who has been deprived of sex or affection during long periods finds it difficult to be satisfied by most relationships. After such a person has received some emotional satisfaction, he can then devote his efforts to personal development. However, there are degrees of striving. I wish that my readers could have shared with me a recent group therapy session.

*History V–1*: After a long period of passivity a young woman took an active interest in the group and was much more reactive in sharing her feelings. Then, quite unexpectedly, she announced that she was leaving.

She had actually made considerable progress after coming into therapy. She had unexpectedly separated from her husband because of his deception. A long history of emotional deprivation caused her to become exceedingly nervous if she had to spend an evening alone. At that time, the alternative to "going bananas" was to sleep from 8 p.m. until she had to go to work the next morning. Now, as she described it, she had a new romantic interest, and if this went well, she did not anticipate any important problems. When her boyfriend went away on long business trips, she had no difficulty in remaining alone. However, the group told her that this was a good opportunity for her to continue exploring the remainder of her emotional reactions while her life was enjoyable and calm. Particularly, they felt that she was closed off to information given her that was potentially troublesome. Furthermore, they believed that she was "settling for less" by leaving at this time.

To some extent, this young woman illustrates the person who is satisfied with the status quo, who feels that it is not necessary to reach her potential for development once her most troublesome needs and tensions have been satisfied.

## USING ADVERSITY CREATIVELY

This is not a universal experience. There are some individuals who utilize even overwhelming stress to enhance their productivity. In 1802, Beethoven, for example, came to grips with the fact that his increasing deafness would interfere with his career as composer, conductor, and virtuoso pianist.

"Born with a lively temperament, inclined even for the amusements of society, I early was forced to isolate myself, to lead a solitary life. If now and again I tried for once to give the go-by to all this, O how rudely was I repulsed by the redoubled mournful experience of my defective hearing; but not yet could I bring myself to say to people 'Speak louder, shout, for I am deaf.' O how should I then bring myself to admit the weakness of *a sense* which I once possessed in the greatest perfection, a perfection such as few assuredly of my profession have yet possessed it in.... Recreation in human society, the more delicate passages of conversation, confidential outpourings, none of these are for me; all alone, almost only so much as the sheerest necessity demands can I bring myself to venture into society; I must live like an exile; if I venture into company a burning dread falls on me, the dreadful risk of letting my condition be perceived" (*The Heilegenstadt Testament*, in Schauffler, 1924, p. 91).

What was the result of this crisis? Self-pity? Not for Ludwig. Out of this depression, this total doubt that he could fulfill himself, came the *Eroica* symphony. From the inner turbulence came a work, longer and more complex than any written before, breaking the formal constraints of the classical symphony, one which was certainly never exceeded subsequently by any other composer for poignancy, originality, and subtle expression of human emotion. It is a symphony whose originality, form, and intensity changed the entire course of Western music. This creation, this attempt to cope with despair, remains a challenge which separates to this day the great conductor from the merely talented.

One can find other examples where the combination of intense deprivation and extreme external anxiety mobilized a totality of creativity.

The following is a description of cultural life in the German Theresienstadt concentration camp, a way station for extermination:

"A rich supply of talent worked creatively in the very jaws of death. Scholars discussed metaphysical problems; physicians and nurses tended the sick and dying; craftsmen repaired watches, shoes and clothing; gardeners tilled over plots of land and beautified them. Musical and dramatic activities engaged and even consumed highly gifted artists. There were master performances of Smetana's *Bartered Bride* and Verdi's *Requiem*; a delightful opera especially written for children, *Brundebar,* was presented. Actors played *Liliom,* read *Faust,* and recited Villon's poetry. The great plays of the European repertoire were presented to audiences. In the *Zwangsgemeinschaft*—the compulsory community of Theresienstadt, feverish intellectual and artistic effort wrestled with dread of the pink slips—the signal for transport call-ups [to the crematoria of Auschwitz]" (Levin, 1973, p. 484).

We can learn from these two examples that the urge to function at the deepest and most complex emotional levels, to continue to develop psychologically, can continue even under conditions of the utmost stress which threaten all that one has built up. Looking at the problem of emotional fulfillment from another angle, the process of functioning in ways which have proven vital in the past, which mobilize all of one's spiritual, emotional, and intellectual resources, can actually maintain one's sanity and will to resist under the worst circumstances. This is another example of tension serving important emotional functions, being not merely an unpleasant feeling to be eliminated at all costs. The price to be paid was worth it: continued life with dignity. The Nazis made clever and systematic attempts to degrade the inmates of concentration camps. Those who survived were frequently people who were able to remember their life callings and in other ways to see themselves as not totally submerged by the bestiality. The odds of survival were insignificant, but those who valued their selves sometimes made it by using their wits.

## PREVENTING STRESS

Another issue which must be encountered in the quest for emotional fulfillment has to do with the relationship of a person to his society. People who claim that it is all society's fault give me a pain in the neck. I am not an apologist for the catalogue of injustices which occur around us, but what I have noticed is that many individuals who blame the world for their troubles tend to be passive. They have not been trained nor have they trained themselves to find out what is important for them emotionally. They do not struggle to make over a piece of their soul so that it is beautiful.

A person who shows significant deterioration under stress rarely will function later at a higher level than before. This has a specific implication for the course of your life. As an individual, by learning some kind of self-discipline and developing your resources, you are in a sense preparing yourself to come back from disaster. This is as good a reason as any for parents to encourage their children to do well in school, to have hobbies, or in any way to integrate and strengthen their intellectual, emotional, and physical powers. It is the well-put-together child or adult that comes back from the brink. We have already seen Jane Morrin's poem as an example of an artistic, deeply experiencing person who was able to gather her thoughts and express her feelings about a devastating experience through poetry.

Another friend of mine reacted to multiple operations for cancer with a book of beautiful poetry (*A Paper Nautilus*, Ruthanne Wolochin, copyright 1977, by permission).

### WHAT TIME I HAVE

I do not know how much time I have—
    It may be none at all.
I long to make each day so real—
    To put to full use all of my faculties
    To alert all of my senses
    To titillate my intellect
I yearn to feel—to touch—to love
    I YEARN TO LIVE!

We can see then that the process of striving toward emotional fulfillment has multiple rewards: peak experiences; developing ourselves to the fullest; a sense of independence from the more painful events of the world; and even strength in the face of disaster.

What are the areas in which you might look to develop yourself? There are at least four which lead toward emotional fulfillment: (1) love, (2) friendship, (3) employment, (4) avocation.

Very few people achieve their utmost potential in all four of these aspects of life, and certainly not simultaneously. I presume, however, that you experience some dissatisfaction in some of these areas, and that you have the motivation to start to improve your life.

Because of the need to respect individual differences, only a brief description of emotional fulfillment in the various areas will be offered.

1. *Love*: the capacity to exchange intense experiences with another person, without the need for crippling emotional distance, without transferring angers and expectations from childhood, and with sufficient commitment to overcome the inevitable posthoneymoon blues.

2. *Friendship*: experiencing other people as emotionally important to you, being able to exchange support, and warmth, and viewing these contacts as important in sustaining one's sense of value in other situations.

3. *Employment*: the experience of a job as utilizing one's talents, offering a place where one has made a contribution to the world, and adding to one's sense of identification and security.

4. *Avocation*: an activity performed for the love of it, which enriches one's private world and serves as a source of pleasure, and which can be enjoyed without the necessity of making emotional demands upon others. (Thus, more than other means of emotional fulfillment, an avocation serves the function of autonomy.)

## CHARACTERISTICS OF THE EMOTIONALLY FULFILLED PERSON

You might consider yourself in each of these facets of emotional fulfillment and thus determine in which areas efforts will be needed to bring you closer to the ideal.

1. *Capacity for Deep Experience*: The fulfilled person is not emotionally blocked. He is stirred by the events of the world and the people around him. A relationship, a concert, a beautiful thing he himself has created, the suffering of an individual or group, the success of a close one, even the achievement of an astronaut—these have meaning in his guts.

2. *The Sense of Striving*: There is a goal out there, realistic, worthwhile, and sensible, that mobilizes one's life energies and makes it worthwhile to sacrifice, to anticipate, to share, and to dream. You have the experience of developing your personal projects and working them out with zest.

3. *Self-Awareness*: This is an interplay between knowledge of the real reasons why we take action and make decisions on the one hand, and our sensitivity to the feelings that others stir up in us on the other. Thus, there is a continuous network between our outer and inner worlds, and we should be able to listen in at any point.

4. *Acceptance of Others*: The emotionally fulfilled person is reasonably willing to see that other people have faults, that they cannot be perfect merely to supply his own needs. Also, the fulfilled person is not destructive. He avoids transferring anger or needling others, and he can express praise warmly.

5. *Self-Acceptance*: After striving for your goals, and trying to relate in a warm way to others, you come to the point of believing, "I have a valuable place in this world." By this I do not mean the fantasy of relaxing totally and taking an early retirement in Tahiti, but a realistic estimate of one's worth, one not based upon childhood values and overcompensations for inadequacy. The self-accepting person is not defensive; the neurotic, abrasive efforts of others are ignored or rejected as unacceptable.

6. *Relating to Others*: To be emotionally fulfilled means to live in a social world, and to believe that one's feelings and efforts and achievements, and those of other people, are meaningful. While autonomy is vital in order to avoid making severe, unpalatable demands upon other people, the emotionally fulfilled person still wants to feel that what he does and the kind

of person he is are important to others and have a beneficial effect.

7. *Autonomy*: The mature, fulfilled person believes that part of his life may be usefully, if temporarily, spent without sharing it with others. He respects his own individuality and does not believe that satisfaction must come only from the approval of others, the constant companionship of another person, or the support of a supervisor. The autonomous person tries to get some of his emotional needs fulfilled by other people, but when he senses that his demands are excessive, or that nobody is available, he creates his own satisfactions.

8. *Personal Development*: The fulfilled person is aware of his capacities and has struggled to express them. These include his emotional, physical, and intellectual potential. This idea is similar to self-actualization (Maslow, 1962) . To be fulfilled, after coping with life and contemplating one's experiences, one must determine what he can do best; then he must make sacrifices and take risks in order to develop and express that which is best within him.

The goal of becoming an emotionally fulfilled person is worth striving for.

# 6

# Impossible Dreams vs.
# Realistic Goals

*History VI–1*: A middle-aged woman was deeply depressed because she had to leave her home in the country to take a job in the city. Although there were realistic economic reasons for making this step, she was resentful about the difficulties of living and working in the city. However, when one considered her experience closely, the depth of her feeling seemed excessive and somewhat hard to understand since she still had access to her property at her convenience. It developed that she had set for herself a dream, an "impossible dream," which was violated by the reality of returning to the city for employment. Her goal had been to become one of the "beautiful young people" whom she had met and enjoyed in the community. To return to the city meant that she was emotionally entering another category, that of the divorced woman who must cope with the economic and spiritual problems of the city, and could not be one of the carefree, spontaneous younger generation in a lovely country setting.

## THE DESTRUCTIVENESS OF 'IMPOSSIBLE DREAMS'

I was outraged by the popular song "Dream the Impossible Dream," for a number of reasons. My own false goals and ideals had caused me a considerable amount of pain and wasted effort. Also, as a practicing psychotherapist I could observe the futility of setting unattainable standards. Childhood and adolescent fantasies are poor soil from which to harvest a lifestyle and mature planning.

When I saw the film "Man of La Mancha," I observed that it was a typical example of how the mass media create disastrously false values. In brief, Cervantes is portrayed as being arrested by the Holy Office (Inquisition) for participating in a play which is offensive to them. In a confused sequence, he is being sent to a dungeon, his property is seized by the other prisoners, and he consents to being tried for some unclear crime. The viciousness of his fellow prisoners is terrifying. He convinces them to play various characters in Don Quixote, including a servant girl whom he idolizes as his Dulcinea. She is mocked by some ruffian muleteers, who are defeated en masse by Don Quixote. As an act of forgiveness, she volunteers to bind their wounds, and puts herself in their hands, only to be abducted and mass raped. Don Quixote and Sancho come upon her after she is freed, and she abuses the Don for making her into a target through his distortions. Nevertheless, she later seeks him out without knowing that he has given up his madness. In other sequences, also not in the original book, she pleads with him to recognize her and they eventually reaffirm "The Impossible Dream."

It is true that the film with great artistry shows in a number of scenes the brutality which people perpetrate upon others. There is an insane sadism, a primitive and poorly directed vengefulness that we may experience when we are mistreated and exploited. Here, instead of being taught the lesson of cautiousness, that plenty of people are downright rotten and ought to be avoided or guarded against if possible, we are told to be idealistic and ignore reality. When the (predictable) disaster occurs, we are told to maintain our inappropriate ideals concerning the importance of fighting for abstractions.

The real Cervantes (1547–1616) actually blended both prudence and a desire for vengeance. He had had the experience of having his creation (*Don Quixote*) stolen from him by another author, and his outrage inspired him to complete Part II of the massive novel. As his talented translator Starkie noted, (p. 30), "He would show the difference between the work of an artist and that of a literary hack." Cervantes had emotional common sense. In his own words: "I am not likely to persecute any priest, above all if he happens to be a familiar of the Holy Office into the bargain" (p. 546). Even the character of the author is misused for the commercial purposes of the writers of the modern version.

What Cervantes really told the world was a message opposite to that in "La Mancha": "These foolish tales . . . that up to now have been my bane may with Heaven's help turn to my advantage at my death. Dear friends, I feel that I am rapidly sinking; therefore, let us put aside all jesting. . . . At such a moment a man must not deceive his soul. . . . My sole aim has been to arouse men's scorn for the false and absurd stories of knight-errantry, whose prestige has been shaken by this tale of my true Don Quixote, and which will without any doubt, soon crumble in ruin" (pp. 1046, 1050).

We all have impossible dreams. Our decision to be guided by them can be the difference between genuine success and emotional fulfillment on the one hand, and being full of doubts, emotionally worn out, and tormented by regrets on the other. The real issue is the definition of what is impossible. Because I have expressed my reservations about people following excessively difficult goals, I have been reproached for being negative, or expecting too little of others.

## INAPPROPRIATE GOALS

What is an impossible dream? Which standards and goals are suitable, and which are inappropriate?

Consider the following:

*History VI–2*: An exceptionally anxious man in his thirties decided to go back to graduate school in order to develop a career in an area that interested him. This involved accepting some financial support from his parents, who made it clear that it was a burden to them, and that they felt by now he should have been self-supporting. He did well in graduate studies, and handled his assignments competently and promptly. This required him to overcome really massive amounts of anxiety and self-doubt since he really saw himself as incompetent. On several occasions he wondered whether he should continue in his chosen area because he compared himself to certain "creative" teachers. He believed that since he "lacks imagination" he was in the wrong area and doomed to failure.

His doubts can be traced back to early childhood. Among his earliest childhood recollections were those of his being toilet trained. "We had a maid. My mother worked, and the maid sat me down on the potty. I remember in kindergarten soiling my pants. I was taken home. I was embarrassed." His earliest recollection of his father involved being chased by him from the cracker barrel he was sitting on in his father's store. His earliest memory of his mother was of her leaving him in the hospital for a tonsillectomy. From these recollections we can infer that he developed a picture of himself as basically inadequate: he couldn't even control his bowels. Furthermore, there was no sense of security with his parents. His father wouldn't accept him as being part of the store. His mother left him when he was frightened and sick. His first memory of other children was going with the kids next door to their country place. He was aware of a religious difference, but felt warm because he was included within a nice family, an experience he hadn't had before. Within his own family his place was not secure; he had no status.

Today, after his infrequent visits to his parents, he comes back feeling depressed and sometimes suicidal. He has become aware that his father is much more destructive than he realized. His father would be satisfied if his son would open up some kind of a store, anything, so long as he was earning a living.

Let us look again at the question of being "creative" and the function that it plays in his life. He is extremely sensitive to the fact that he has to accept financial help from his parents late in life, and that they offered it ungraciously. Probably, to him, merely earning a living at some profession would not be enough to feel adequate. To still the "voice" of his parents he must do something exceptional. He must be as good as the most successful people in this field. He expects this of himself while he is still a student. This is self-destructive, because he cannot be certain that he will function at the peak of his field. His excessively high standards could keep him from seeking employment; make him accept less responsible offers than he could handle; make him devalue his actual success; spoil his initiative; keep him from demanding adequate remuneration; and prevent him from enjoying his work.

How does he actually cope with his anxiety? He says to himself, "I have no alternatives." He realizes that to yield to his doubts is to take the road to disaster. So he plunges ahead to complete his studies and obtain employment.

Let us look at another man's goals.

*History VI–3*: This man's goal is to enter into the relationship of father with as many people as possible. He is himself a husband and the father of several attractive children who seem to be on the way to having successful lives of their own. He is attentive to them. He pals around with a son, devotes spare time to editing the school reports of a daughter, and so on. One would even think that he had enough burden as parent to want to reverse roles and achieve the status of child for himself. Oh, no! He seeks the father relationship with the dozens of men in the company which he heads. This is a service organization whose employees are chosen for their level of accomplishment so that they can help other organizations do their own jobs better. One wouldn't think that as a group these men needed fathering.

What is the result? He feels constantly overworked because he has too many material and emotional burdens. He has not succeeded in surrounding himself with competent associates who can take a larger share of the load; probably he unconsciously does not wish to work with highly responsible individuals who are task oriented and thus do not seek paternal guidance. The emotional strain of having a successful, expanding company is large because he sees his responsibility to them as "having them all eat at my table." Think of feeling personally responsible for the welfare of two dozen men and their families.

How did The Father of Them All develop this goal, this impossible dream?

"My first memories are of November, 1932. I was four years old. I remember the apartment we lived in in great detail. There was a window box in the kitchen that looked out. We kept our garbage can in that built-in area. There was a presidential campaign going on at the time. Roosevelt was running against Hoover. There was a campaign song that said 'Hoover in the garbage can.' I got very confused when I looked into our garbage can and did not find Hoover (whoever that was) there. I had already discovered that adults did not always tell the truth.

"My mother and father both worked at a small family business. Most of the time a maid was my parental identification, if I had any. Sometimes they could not afford a maid and I was on my own. I remember my father as a man who was always too busy or too tired to spend time with me. I was thirty years old before I realized that he liked me, and even then I still wasn't sure. Mother was kind but she too was extremely busy and burdened. I knew that she loved me but she did not have my love as her only task.

"Things got worse as I got older because the Depression got worse, or at least it did for my parents.

"When I went off to school I found that the teachers were no more responsive to my needs for love and attention than were my parents. They did not like the fact that I needed to look at the airplanes flying to relieve the boredom of the classrooms.

"When I was about eight we moved into a basement apartment in a small multifamily building. There were two rooms. A kitchen–living room and a bedroom. The bathroom was in the boiler room area. At night the grill on the coal furnace formed weird shadows of the fire within. The area became a terror to me and my little bladder surrendered to my mattress rather than face the fears created by the boiler's shadows. This did not endear me to my already overworked parents.

"By the time that I was ten or eleven I found that I was a successful street fighter. I thoroughly enjoyed the role of bully and I have never lost that joy. I do not like any authority but my own.

"I change my environments to serve my needs. I am the poppa. I sit at the head of the table and I decide when the meal shall be served. I take the biggest and best morsels, if I choose.

"I sometimes say in jest, 'I wish that I had a father like my children have' but in reality I am intellectually aware of the fact that if I did have a father like my children's father I would not be the person that I am today and that I would not like that at all because I like myself a great deal."

He could remember his apartment in great detail. He learned the value of being inquisitive. By looking into the garbage can he learned what he thought was an important lesson, that adults did not always tell the truth. While this is true, he assumed that he understood what the song meant, which he did not. He still has some difficulty in empathizing with others when they have a different feeling about their experiences than he has. He assumes that others have the same sense of self-confidence, and is puzzled by their anxiety or sense of being rejected. Two further themes are developed. First, he felt rejected, and did not have one person from whom to seek support or with whom to identify. He felt rejected and began to develop the image of a father who would be interested in him, and who would be materially successful so that the family would not undergo the deprivations and stress of a Depression. In school he did not find the affection he craved. Remembering this is a way of saying that he went to school to find something different from what was offered: affection instead of learning. This was an important theme in his life. To this day he cannot completely satisfy himself with affection within his family, possibly because he fears disappointment.

The next theme that was presented was his anxiety. As a fearful boy he experienced the humiliation of wetting his bed rather than facing the terrors of the night. This further jeopardized his parents' affection. Subsequently he became able to overcome his anxieties through bullying. It is satisfying to him to assert his ego over others, and thus reverse the fearful, inadequate role that he played as a child. In his profession he combines the qualities of bully and skeptic. It is his task to find out why something goes wrong and he enjoys putting his client through a series of "why" questions until the source of an inadequacy is revealed. Furthermore, by taking the position of leadership in his company (a position with which he feels uncomfortable and which he realizes he does not fulfill as well as somebody else might), he plays the strong, successful father. This way he ensures that no one will be in a position to push him around or play on his weaknesses. Nevertheless, since he does not select his associates with complete success, he finds himself "playing" far less that he chooses because of the excessive chores he must handle. There are times when this situation breaks through his defenses and he actually becomes panicky; he realizes that the people he deals with are in deadly earnest, that the stakes are large, and that life is not a game.

To present a total picture, one would have to state that this man is successful in many areas of life, but his emotional discomforts stem from the futility of assuming that he can always be the master of a situation. He confuses dominance with altruism by assuming that grown men will always respond as grateful children.

The concepts of Alfred Adler (1929, 1931; Ansbacher and Ansbacher, 1956) are most useful in helping us to understand how people develop goals which divert them from reality. The child early in life experiences feelings of inadequacy and frustrated dependency. He feels as though he is not equipped to solve the problems of life. Inferiority feelings are not by themselves abnormal. "They are the cause of all improvements in the position of mankind" (Ansbacher and Ansbacher, 1956, p. 117). From these feelings the person develops some goal, perhaps a goal of superiority or of perfection. The particular goal will depend upon the meaning that he attributes to life.

Although Adler's position is forthright, people are not so simple. The real origins of their goals become repressed. We organize our life around some situation in the future which we

think will make us happy, without being aware of our real motives. The man who tried to compensate for his childhood
humiliation of wetting his bed does not say to the world, "I
don't want to pee in my pants." Rather, it became transformed
to: "I feel like a father to many people." After all, fathers don't
pee in their pants.

### FREUD'S "EGO IDEAL"

Another important contribution to the understanding of excessively demanding goals was made by Sigmund Freud (1914,
1923, 1933). He spoke of the *ego ideal* by which we judge ourselves. This is an ideal image of how we ought to be. It develops
in order to please our parents, to ensure that they will continue
their support and affection. We assume some of their good qualities so that they will continue to love us. Initially our parents
seem overpowering to us because of their capacity to control our
lives through doling out love. The ego ideal develops at a time
when we feel relatively incompetent to control our world. Therefore, to compensate for this weakness, the ego ideal has to be
especially beautiful, potent, powerful, famous, lovable, and so on.

Two images develop within us which are complementary and
which later hamper good decision making. First, we fantasize
*how we should be* in order to be happy and successful, and to
show up those who were derogatory to us. This is the ego ideal.
Secondly, we invent *an image of other people* who will give us
what we want emotionally. These images, or the motives behind
them, are often unconscious. However, they significantly affect
our goals. As adults we then try to act out our lives as we
imagined the characters and scenario in earlier life. We look for
people to play the characters we have invented, and we try to
manipulate them into playing emotionally significant roles. To
treat life as the scenario of a play can be tragically self-destructive
since others will not accommodate themselves to our unconscious wishes. An exception is when two people enter into some
unconscious arrangement in which they are each fulfilling the
unconscious needs of years ago. They keep each other in the

immature position of experiencing petrified juvenile fantasies instead of developing and maturing. Sexual relationships frequently develop and are maintained this way.

For these reasons an "impossible dream" is frequently the neurotic expression of early discontents. It ignores both the real world and the mature capacities you have developed to make a good life for yourself.

*Satisfactory decision making requires recognizing and exterminating false goals.* There are a number of steps you can take so that your decisions are based upon goals which are suitable to your current life.

1. *Distinguish between your current needs and the unfulfilled deprivations of the past.* It is absolutely essential that you realize that what the world did not give you as a child cannot be made up. Therefore, your goals should be developed on the basis of your mature, up-to-date estimate of what you want out of life. If you think that you cannot overcome or recognize these old feelings by yourself, then you should seek a warm, supporting therapist.

2. *Develop self-esteem.* Participating in activities that you find worthwhile is a suitable way of breaking the cycle of frustration caused by impossible goals. It is also vital that you eliminate from your life anybody who makes it a practice of being degrading to you. Don't argue the point, just do it. You will feel much better.

3. *Obtain a realistic assessment of your personal and professional assets.* Self-understanding is indispensable whether you are overestimating or underestimating what you can get out of life. Repeated failures in the social or economic spheres give you a message that you are doing something wrong. It may be a matter of learning new skills or improving your competence. On the other hand, you may be trying to move in social circles or function in positions in which you cannot succeed because you don't have what it takes. I know one woman who was advised to divorce her husband and marry a millionaire. She really enjoyed this advice. The trouble is that after she separated from her husband she discovered that she didn't know any millionaires! I

suspect, also, that she could not compete successfully with the women who do marry into money. Another man wanted to be a professional writer. He was confronted with the fact that the way he spent his time was unsuitable to being productive in this area.

4. *See people as they are.* One of the most common causes of the failure of personal goals is expecting something from people who cannot or will not perform for you. Do not expect a man to be a self-reliant aide when unconsciously you have selected him to play the role of grateful son. If you wish to marry, the expression of indifference by your intended ought not to be misinterpreted as a little game concealing the opposite intentions. Constantly match your goals, your feelings, and the activities of the other person. When there is a discrepancy, you may be experiencing some misperception of the other person's actions or personality. Your unconscious needs can be affecting your information gathering, and thus your decisions.

5. *Accept people for what they are.* Good decision making in the service of your goals generally involves cooperation from others, unless you are actually in a position to enforce demands. If you want the esteem of other people, then you must surround yourself with those who like you. Don't waste time convincing the antagonistic person that you are valuable, unless he is essential and stands in the way of achieving your goals. Frequently, we get locked in combat with people as matters of prestige, rather than because the other person is indispensable. The individual who doesn't want to work for you shouldn't be counted upon. I remember handing in a master's thesis to my advisor and receiving it back with vague marks in the margin. It became apparent to me that the professor was disinterested. I went to my department head and asked to be assigned to another advisor.

6. *Understand your values.* These determine what it is which is worth struggling for, and thus what results are ultimately rewarding. This topic is sufficiently important to warrant an entire chapter (Chapter 11).

In the next chapters we shall help you achieve self-understanding. In this way, you will be able to make prudent decisions which are consistent with your real needs and your basic nature.

# 7

# The Evolution of Human Nature

The surest approach to correct decision making is a realistic evaluation of human nature. The models usually offered are in my opinion frequently unrealistic. Consequently, our expectations of ourselves, and those which others create for us, cause frustration, dissatisfaction, and ultimate failure. For example, the most influential model of human personality has been that of Sigmund Freud. Although he was originally a brilliant neurologist, and though he spearheaded a realistic appraisal of many aspects of human life (notably the unconscious), his thinking had severe limitations even in his own day. As the prominent evolutionary zoologist George Gaylord Simpson states, his "biology was outmoded in his day and is now almost completely rejected." Freud's thought emphasized inheritance of acquired characteristics, as well as the concept that we repeat the characteristics of our forebears (recapitulation). Also, the various concepts of human life created by theologians, philosophers, mystics, and others do not take into account important qualities which make human beings "a peculiar, specialized kind of creature with great abilities and surprising limitations" (Washburn & Harding, 1975).

Human nature has not evolved very far from primitive times. In fact, although there are substantial apparent differences between man and ape, biochemical studies show that hardly any differences exist in protein formation between man and chimpanzee (King & Wilson, 1975). While the expression of the genetic qualities differs between man and our primate relatives, the physiological underpinnings of life have diverged less than we might think.

Many of our current characteristic reactions exist only because they were useful for the survival of our ancestors. Reactions that enabled us to survive as a species might be harmful to particular individuals today (Bakan, 1968, pp. 20–21). When we consider what is really happening to our species, we observe disastrous overpopulation and violence, emotional and physiological signs of stress, dissatisfaction, alienation, emotional conflict, war, criminality, mental illness and mental retardation, and so on. All these conditions are evidence of maladaptation to a civilization which our species created. These conditions are totally different from those which shaped us as a species. Our physical and mental adaptation is to a simpler way of life. An insufficient number of generations has occurred to select genetic qualities which are appropriate to civilization. Furthermore, the furious rate of change ("future shock," Toffler, 1970), plus enforced mass dislocations, wars, and so forth, places too great a burden upon our genetic apparatus. We may conclude that our bodies and minds were designed for a "caveman" level of existence, and today's world is a poor environment for our emotional survival and fulfillment.

## SOME CONCEPTS OF EVOLUTION

The idealistic reader may wonder how decision making is related to mankind's evolution from dirty, uncouth, hairy creatures. Human nature has been shaped by the principles of heredity, natural selection, and adaptation.

Darwin's concept of natural selection taught that particular characteristics or combinations of characteristics give a species a greater advantage in surviving and propagating more of its kind. In this way those traits which enhance the likelihood of successful mating tend to be passed along to a new generation (inherited), while those which interfere are likely to be bred out of existence (Simpson, 1972). Until the development of civilization, human evolution was affected by this principle just as the evolution of any other species.

All living forms evolve and adapt as separate species. In addition, individuals also adapt to the world around them. Adaptation may include changes in bodily structure, in the functioning of organs, and in behavior. Successful changes enable either the species or the individual to survive or flourish. Most characteristics of a species can be understood as having made a contribution to its ability to function properly, to withstand its enemies, and so forth. Of course there are exceptions: the bulk of the dinosaur, the diminished wings of the dodo, and the strange qualities of the human mind. More of this later.

One of the most important factors in shaping our development as a species, i.e., the way we think and function and the structure of our bodies, was the interaction between radically changing weather, geological, and biological conditions, on the one hand, and the changing psychological and physical characteristics of our remote ancestors, on the other. As the external world changed, we adapted to it by developing new mental and physical qualities. Some changes involved modest variations in our genes (large changes are generally lethal). Other changes were merely the recombining of qualities already present into a more advantageous form. These new features in our ancestors permitted them to survive more effectively under difficult circumstances, or enabled them to explore new worlds which were superior to the old one.

The new features were changes either in forms of behavior or in the brain and the rest of the body.

More effective means of behavior enable a group or an individual to compete with or destroy other living creatures or to cooperate with members of the same species. These behavioral qualities can be more important for survival than differences in anatomical structure. Our ancestors not only out-fought other species (and the related human-like races), but they out-thought them as well.

Another adaptive change involved alterations in bodily structure—for example, the brain, hands, skeleton, teeth, and reproductive organs.

We have first to consider a curious fact. Since the human species exceeds in size 99 percent of the world's creatures, we have to eat more than most other species. What your ancestors needed to survive was some combination of brain, glands, muscles, and skeleton to enable them to kill a saber-toothed tiger with a massive blow of an axe. While this made your ancestor happy, it is an illegal way to deal with the landlord, gas station owner, or your employer! Thus, formerly effective ways to eat and protect oneself still play an important, though negative, role in human nature.

## HUMAN ORIGINS

Since many of our characteristic ways of expressing violence resemble those of the rat, it is significant that the primates seem to have evolved from rodents perhaps 70 million years ago (Paleocene era, A. E. Wood, 1972). (Be careful when you call somebody a rat because you are degrading a distant cousin!)

Perhaps the first distinctively primate feature to develop was locomotor behavior, i.e., climbing and suspension by the forelimbs (Fleagle, Simons & Conroy, 1975), as our forebears moved through trees and bushes. Then, the capacity to converge the eyes (and related development of the brain) permitted our remote ancestor to estimate his victim's distance without having to move his head (Carmill, 1974).

An important character in our epic is a prehuman (hominid) ancestor called Ramapithecus (15-20 million years ago). This creature probably descended from ancestors that lived in trees and had a largely vegetarian diet. While Ramapithecus was but three feet tall, he had a pretty good brain volume of about half a quart (500 cc). His teeth and jaws were adapted to crushing and grinding. They seemed to be adapted for picking up, digging up, grinding, and digesting large quantities of low-energy grass seeds, roots, and other similar tidbits available in the savannas and plains of East Africa (Harris, 1972). Perhaps their first tools were sticks for getting at roots which could not be dug up manually.

At this point, climate drastically affected our evolution. The forest areas in which Ramapithecus lived became dryer. Hominids were selected who were more adapted for land living than tree living. This was a real opportunity since it is inconvenient to use an axe while swinging by one's arms through the trees. It is controversial whether Ramapithecus, and those hominids that followed, were vegetarians (Harris, 1972; Pilbeam & Gould, 1974) or whether they ate up to 50 percent meat during the dry season (Campbell, 1972).

The next prominent member of our ancestral tree was Australopithecus, who weighed in at 50-90 pounds, although his brain was comparable to that of a 600-pound gorilla (Gould, 1974). Remains found in Africa indicate that Australopithecus lived from 5.25 to 1 million years ago, perhaps coexisting with hominids even closer to the main line of human evolution (*Science News,* 1975, 108, p. 292). He was also a ground feeder, but with a difference. Instead of the stooped-over, knuckle-walking gait of Ramapithecus, he developed slender digits and walked more upright (Washburn & Harding, 1975). Consequently, arms became free to make tools or weapons. Sticks and rocks became usable objects (Mayr, 1970; Buettner-Janush, 1966). Since some African cultural elements have an antiquity of about 2 million years (Brace, 1970), perhaps Australopithecus is the originator of a line of culture which extends into today's world. He seems to deserve the designation of human, however primitive he might have been.

It is significant that around this point in our evolution, the increase in size and ruggedness (and probably viciousness) of our ancestors created the differences in size and strength between males and females (*sexual dimorphism*), because the male had to defend his family on the ground from competing individuals and groups. Selective pressure also created evolution of a brain which enabled these creatures to make and to use weapons effectively. It does appear that this greater destructive potential eventually was used to eliminate competing races of mankind. Even the stick-wielding baboon does not needlessly assault his peers in other troops!

## Brain Development

Our hominid ancestors were walking on two feet before the evolution of the disproportionately large brain characteristic of later human evolution (McHenry, 1975). The essentially human organization of the brain (as opposed to relative size) was formed about 3 million years ago. Perhaps beginning with Australopithecus, or a subsequent form (*Homo habilis*), human evolution changed in the direction of larger bodies and proportionately larger brains. The relative proportion has remained the same over several million years. The initial relatively large visual area of the occipital cortex (supporting particular kinds of hunting habits requiring intensive use of the eyes) became smaller while the parietal and temporal areas (involved with touch and hearing) became more highly developed and remain so to this day.

## Interaction of Brain and Environment

At about the time of increased brain expansion, "evidence occurs for tool manufacture, meat eating, use of a home base, and probably food sharing, indicating a new adaptive strategy which becomes typical of later hominids" (McHenry, 1975).

As Australopithecus learned to hunt big game, selective pressures led to the evolution of a much bigger brain (Mayr, 1970). The origin of the human brain may have been paralleled by the initiation of human social behavior, perhaps predating even the systematic use of stone tools and the large-scale practice of hunting. It has been said that "part of the nourishment the brain requires is social as well as dietary" (Holloway, 1974). Parts of the brain develop in a feedback relationship with other aspects of human evolution, namely manual skills and language. Selective pressures for skillful performance shaped the evolution of the cerebral cortex and the cerebellum, as well as hands and vocal apparatus (Washburn & Harding, 1975).

Hunting also entered into social evolution; hunting is a social enterprise requiring planning, cooperation, and division of labor. Memory was developed to retain knowledge of the movements and other characteristics of herds of animals, seasonal changes, the best way to make and use weapons, and so on. Knowledge and memory increased the capacity to plan for future needs (Campbell, 1966). Since hominid posture was now erect, and they used their hands instead of a prominent face (muzzle) to obtain and cut food, the shape of the head could evolve toward the use of speech for communication. Increased sensations (neural input) from lips, tongue, eyes, hands, and so on encouraged brain evolution in the direction of increased memory and foresight, as well as the capacity to utilize these new functions. Symbolic thinking and language created the capacity to digest and communicate information (Dobzhansky, 1973). Eventually, the brain became genetically programmed to learn language with even relatively small amounts of training (Asenberg, 1972).

## THE BRAIN AND MATURATION

Development of a brain proportionately larger than most other species had a profound effect upon human anatomy and rate of maturation. The female pelvis changed in size, shape, and orientation so that babies could come into the world with substantially larger heads and brains. According to Gould (1976), the human brain continues to develop at the characteristically high fetal rate long after brain growth has ceased in comparable primates. In fact, the human level of development which compares to birth in other primates is *six months after actual birth*. Human birth has become so difficult, due to the constricting effects of pelvis size, that the limit of human brain development may have been reached. The consequence is that human infants are born relatively early, before their brain and heads become too large; and therefore they are quite immature and dependent. Nevertheless, one advantage of a period of immaturity is that there is a longer exposure to family life, during which skills and culture can be transmitted.

### NEUROLOGICAL FACTORS

Neurological research of lower primates and human beings is beginning to shed light on why our mental life is so complicated. The qualities which are beginning to become clear must have evolved during our species' evolutionary struggle for survival.

For a long time, the question of differences between the way men and women think has been a topic for gagsters, partygoers, and all other philosophers. Now it appears that, in young male and female monkeys at least, parts of the brain that control aspects of learning may develop at different rates. These parts have close connections with regions that influence emotions and other internal functions. Differences between the sexes in the rate of development of brain regions would affect the organization of behavior in such a way that the results would outlast the formative years. These might be as important as anatomical differences in influencing how males and females think and act (Goldman et al., 1974).

Additional complications are added by the fascinating fact that, while lower primates seem to use corresponding parts of both sides of the brain for particular mental functions, in mankind each side of the brain has a specialized use. We shall see later that this could lead to the formation of conscious and unconscious attitudes as separate qualities of our intellectual/emotional life. In human beings, the left side of the brain seems to specialize in speech, skilled movements, arithmetic, and analytical thinking, while the right side emphasizes spatial relationships, music, musical functions (nonverbal auditory patterns), and perception of a whole unit rather than analysis of parts (Milner, 1971; Galin, 1974; Bever, 1975).

Human beings appear to be the only animals whose left and

right cerebral hemispheres perform different functions (Early, 1975; Bever, 1975). This would ordinarily seem to be disadvantageous, so there must be some evolutionary advantage that has caused this trait to be selected for posterity (Bever, 1975).

## WEATHER AND RECENT EVOLUTION

An additional pressure affecting human evolution is weather change. Modern man has lived during an extended Ice Age (D. G. Klein, 1974). Since our species originated in the tropics, survival in colder climates made demands upon our "ingenuity to devise protective facilities such as clothing and tents" (Campbell, 1972). The brighter ones coped successfully with environmental conditions that could have killed them overnight or caused starvation. With the ability to maintain some security despite varying weather conditions came significant changes in sexual life. The sexual drive came under increasing control of the cerebral cortex (outer brain layer) and less under hormonal and seasonal factors. Thus, we can lay to rest the stereotype of the caveman seizing his mate and dragging her into a fur-lined cave. Muscles were not all. Those males with leadership, ability, and initiative were desired as mates. That's why we evolved a bulging cerebrum instead of enormous biceps. The Miss of 100,000 B.C. probably picked her mate by his I.Q. rather than his muscles. Brain was in. Brawn was out.

## INCREASED POPULATION

Nevertheless, there was a sudden halt in the growth of brain size some 100,000 to 200,000 years ago; and there is no evidence that the brain has improved since that time (Mayr, 1970, p. 386). Part of this lack of brain development can be attributed to the limiting factor of female pelvis size. Another part is due to successful (agricultural) technology. With social groups becoming relatively large and with improved food gathering, mankind went into a kind of surplus economy. Particular individuals provided leadership, and division of labor permitted efficient use of skills. There was sufficient food to go around for the first time in evolutionary history. Even the less effective individual had a place in the group or could be permitted to survive. Probably intergroup cooperation in hunting and foodsharing also contributed to the increase in total population (R. G. Klein, 1974). If adaptive success is measured by numbers, mankind was fewer in number than monkeys until long after the development of agriculture (Washburn & Harding, 1975). Ultimately, humans spread into more areas of the globe than any other mammalian species (Mayr, 1970, pp. 394–395).

## SOCIAL ORGANIZATION

Although study of living nonhuman primates can reveal some possibilities of our ancestral hominid community life, they are too varied for any generality to hold. Many combinations of single individuals, single males, and groups of various compositions exist. Groups of similar or related species can live together without elimination of one of the competitors. Social organization evolved because of the advantages in caring for the young, in maintaining vigilance, and in controlling aggression among individuals (Bernstein, 1974).

Where there is plenty of room and little population pressure, the natural size of the group might be merely a few families. The evidence for this comes from archaeological studies of Paleolithic and Mesolithic times (perhaps 8000 B.C. and 7500 B.C.) (Schild, 1976) and of contemporary Bushmen of Africa (Yellen & Harpending, 1972).

As larger communities became prominent in human existence, relating to other people became a condition for survival. The young were dependent upon their elders for a lengthy period during which they became educated in the techniques of survival. As the psychoanalyst Heinz Hartmann (1958) said, "the task of man to adapt to man is present from the very beginning of life." Those of our ancestors who were not "person oriented" (Miner & Dachler, 1973) had a poor chance of surviving or mating. Social orientation was selected as a genetic quality. Unless you could adapt to a human environment your line would die out.

## VIOLENCE

The earliest members of the species Homo, perhaps 3.75 million years ago, seemed to have been meat eaters. This can be determined by the prominence of sharp canine teeth, in contrast to the predominantly flat surfaces for grinding characteristic of their contemporaries and ancestors (*Science News,* November 8, 1975, p. 292). About the time that cranial capacity increased, smaller cheek teeth developed, indicating that "members of the Homo lineage had a decreased dependence on roots and tubers for food and increased dependence on meat." Thus, early Homo may have had food habits similar to contemporary hunter-gatherers, who eat meat regularly, in contrast to nonhuman primates who rarely eat meat. Furthermore, the increased use of tools could have processed plant foods in such a way that there was a decreased need for large cheek teeth for crushing and grinding (Kolata, 1975).

The change of diet toward meat and away from plant products signifies vastly changed need and habits. Instead of gathering stationary, passive food, Homo had to locate animals, pursue and kill them. These same aggressive traits could also be utilized against human competitors and enemies.

While mutual dependency and aid were successful in pursuing game, these traits did not suffice to cope with the problem of violence. Even the evolution of a dominant male who selected his mate, was relied upon for strength in mutual defense, and cooperated in the search for food, did not undo the genetic capacity to use violence against other humans or similar species.

## WEAPONS AND EVOLUTION

Social structure created an opportunity for skilled craftsmen to teach others (perhaps the young) how to make weapons. Thus, capacity to communicate, to be social, to learn, to utilize skilled movements, to be aggressive and cunning, all became hereditary qualities selected for survival (Jolly, 1972, p. 356).

Fossil mankind in Africa had small skulls. In this area, there is little flint from which stone tools could have been made. Fossil mankind in Europe, however, has essentially a modern brain size. It is inferred that the presence of materials suitable for making particular weapons interacted with genetic evolution to aid in the development of larger brains. Stone tools and weapons are considered to be the earliest evidence of "sufficient neurological material for culture" (Buettner-Janusch, 1966, p. 349). The brightest weapon makers prospered and begat their kind. The most effective weapons—points, spear throwers, bows, and arrows—were probably invented in the last 100,000 to 50,000 years of the 15 million years of hominid existence (Harris, 1972). These weapons were the ultimate cultural contribution of prehistoric man!

### ORIGIN OF AGGRESSION

In my opinion aggression (action) and anger (feelings) are far more important in shaping personality and human nature than sexuality. In this section the evolutionary origins of human destructiveness will be illustrated. The writer has written an extensive discussion of the irrational quality of anger in human life, with its interpersonal and other social effects (Parker, 1972b).

Lorenz (1963, Chapter X) describes rat aggression in a manner that makes it appear as a forebear of human social organization. We have already said that humans are descended from rodent-like creatures. Lorenz's description reminds us of our own primitive origins.

> In their behavior towards members of their own community, the animals ... are models of social virtue; but they change into horrible brutes as soon as they encounter members of any other society of their own species. ... The tolerance, the tenderness which characterizes the relation of mammal mothers to their children, extends in the case of the rats not only to the fathers but to all grandparents, uncles, aunts, cousins and so

on. [Furthermore, rats learn to avoid man-laid poison by] . . . operating basically with the same methods as those of man, by traditional transmission of experience and its dissemination within the closed community. Rats attack members of other groups, informing their in-group of the stranger's presence through mood transmission. . . . The constant warfare between large neighboring families of rats must exert a huge selection pressure in the direction of an ever increasing ability to fight, and . . . a rat clan which cannot keep up in this respect must soon fall victim to extermination.

It has been observed, however, that this type of aggression is more characteristic of rats in closed quarters (e.g., laboratories), which parallel the density and lack of easily obtained supplies of mankind's environment in cities. In areas with easily available food and mates, and shifting locales (food warehouses in India), the situation is different. Social organization is weaker, strangers are tolerated, or can more easily escape (Frantz, 1976).

Lorenz notes, further (p. 239), that "there is evidence that the first inventors of pebble tools, the African Australopithecines, promptly used their new weapon not only to kill game but fellow members of their own species as well." Further, when modern man (Cro-Magnon) appeared on the scene 35,000 years ago, he became "dominant" (Mayr, 1970, p. 394). This is a polite way of saying that our ancestors may have murdered everybody who was different. Genocide has a long history in our species.

Human beings evolved from a primate line in which aggression and dominance certainly played an important role. Aggression is considered "a biological mechanism shaped by natural selection into an adaptive force which helps to establish and maintain primate societies" (Bernstein & Gordon, 1974). The following discussion is based upon Lorenz (1963), Jolly (1972), Hamburg (1972), Bernstein (1974), Bernstein & Gordon (1974), and Bernstein, Gordon, & Rose (1974).

## SPECIFIC FUNCTIONS OF AGGRESSION

Aggression serves several specific functions. They include the following:

1. *Increasing the effectiveness of defense,* namely by taking the attack to the predator (source of threat).

2. *Obtaining access to resources,* for example, to food and water.

3. *Defending the young.* Loss of offspring was serious when our species was few in number and subject to death through weather, disease, and being eaten by animals such as saber-toothed tigers. No doubt fear and utilization of kidnapping mobilized aggressive instincts.

4. *Maintaining territoriality.* Violence spreads individuals throughout an area, thus ensuring that food resources of a particular location will not be exhausted.

5. *Stabilizing a group through dominance.* The presence of a hierarchy stabilizes a society, since fights are avoided when each individual knows the other's strength. Conflict in primate groups is typically between individuals of closely related dominance ranks, rather than between those high in the hierarchy and juveniles and females (Bernstein & Gordon, 1974). It is motivated to preserve established positions and prevents upward mobility, until the dominant figure is overthrown, perhaps by fatal assault. When stabilization does not occur through submissiveness, then aggression can persist at high levels (Bernstein, Gordon, & Rose, 1974).

6. *Providing leadership.* Some individuals serve a group both through vigilance against outside disruption (from predators or competitors) and also through control and limitation of intragroup aggression. In this way social structure and order is preserved (Bernstein, 1974).

7. *Selecting mates.* Aggressive males generally have their choice of mates, thus ensuring passing on of their genes at the expense of less aggressive group members. Furthermore, it has been observed that aggression is used by males to punish straying females, thus "maintaining social proximity . . . a social bond" (Bernstein & Gordon, 1974).

It can be seen that aggression has played a significant role in primate behavior. What is the significance for mankind? Lorenz (1963, p. 239) makes an interesting point concerning a basic difference between the hostility of mankind and that of nonhumans. Other species seem to develop inhibitions which control aggression toward members of the same species (p. 240; also Hamburg, 1972; Bernstein & Gordon, 1974). However, the submissive gestures and appeasing attitudes which work in other species were suddenly rendered ineffective by "the invention of artificial weapons (which) upset the equilibrium of killing potential and social inhibitions" (p. 241).

A second substantial difference between human aggression and that of other species, is the variety of irrational targets we have, and the inappropriate reasons we utilize to express it. The capacity to think in abstract and symbolic ways, together with the formation of images and fantasies associated with deep feelings from very early in life, contributes to aggression being expressed with unlimited variety and intensity. Inevitably, aggression and fear shape our personality, human relationships, and decisions. We are frequently unconscious of the role that it plays.

You may ask whether competition is inherent between organisms surviving in the same space—that is, competing for identical, limited resources. There is evidence that it does not have to work this way in nature. Closely related species of fish (Kaust, 1974; Sale, 1976), species whose brains I did not admire until reading these articles, succeed in getting along nicely with each other. They utilize various structural adaptations and changes in behavior to make varied, alternate use of a particular reef or lake. Mankind, on the other hand, developed the habit of decimating all competing species, even when our numbers were few and the world was wide open. Outrageous justifications for harming the out-group are still with us through exaggeration of their differences and power to harm us (Hamburg, 1972). However, the complexity of human aggression must be recognized, and the labeling of aggression as such is partly social definition, as well as a scientific process (Topoff, 1975).

## RAPID TECHNOLOGICAL EVOLUTION

While animals merely adapt to the world that they are born into, mankind has created a tempo of change so rapid that our physical-emotional resources cannot keep up with it. In some sense, part of our brains and bodies are designed for the Stone Age, while our creativeness has brought us to the Age of Atomics and Moon trips and Overpopulation. The pace of technological development began to quicken around 40,000 years ago. The New Stone Age "was the start of the destruction of man's natural environment, and as the rate of population increase grew, the rate of destruction increased" (Campbell, 1972, p. 53). The use of fire to convert forests to grasslands started 35,000 years ago. The ability to cook permitted mankind to penetrate into cold climates where vegetable food is unavailable much of the year, and also permitted the use of otherwise toxic foods (Leopold & Ardrey, 1972). Fishing seems to have begun 32,000 years ago. About 12,400 years ago mankind began to exploit migratory animals. For the first time this permitted a sedentary way of life and led to the development of home bases which could be occupied for longer periods (the origin of cities). Mobile hunting bands were no longer required, since the paths of deer and birds could be predicted. More complex social groups then developed; we now call them hunter-gatherers (Campbell, 1972, pp. 51–52). At the end of the Ice Ages (10,000 years ago), mankind changed from gathering foods to growing them (Brace, 1970; Zokary & Hopf, 1973). Since peas, lentils, wheat, and barley are nutritious and easy to store, their availability encouraged the introduction of metallurgy around 7,000 or 8,000 years ago (Wertime, 1973).

These differences in living conditions placed emphasis upon radically different and changing physical and emotional capacities for survival. The small group which followed game evolved characteristics useful for hunters. Subsequently, mankind evolved both personal characteristics and a society useful for agriculture or for seasonal migration with herds of domesticated or wild animals. Even the relationship to the weather changed, since it could cause crop failure and thus famine (Bohannan, 1971).

Thus, a great diversity of cultures existed in our primitive ancestry: hunters, cattle raisers, and farmers. Each of these types survived only if they were sensitive to the characteristics of their game, herds, or crops (Darlington, 1970). The human traits selected for survival enabled them to be in touch with the animal and vegetable worlds.

The most recent significant change in our external world has been the result of technology and mass urbanization. Both qualitatively and quantitatively the rate of change has been enormous, with grave strain upon the capacity of human life to adapt to the world it has itself created. It has been pointed out that both the New Stone Age and the Industrial Revolution were accompanied by great population increases. "In both of these cases, there was less adaptation in terms of evolutionary changes in the human species itself (although there may have been some of that) than adaptation in terms of man's own effort in molding his environment" (Beck, 1973).

Let us review the changes which have taken place in mankind's evolution and adaptation. These have included changes from tree living in a forest to ground living on the plains; from vegetarianism to an increasingly large meat diet; from hunting small game to hunting large game; from capacity to use tools to ability to make them; from polygamy to monogamy; from hunting and farming to urbanization and industrialization (Mayr, 1970). In today's industrialized, complex, largely urban world the issues which formerly determined survival make the adaptation of our ancestors quite irrelevant. When one considers the characteristics of human settlements (Doxiadis, 1970) —nature, man, society, buildings, and networks—the last three are quite recent by biological standards. Not much time has elapsed for our brain and emotional apparatus to catch up with the world we have created for ourselves. Unfortunately, our uniquely human mental ability to form symbols, which binds up the present with the future and the past, has made our lives worse. It permits us to take feelings from one situation, labels from another, and targets from a third situation—and connect them. All kinds of inappropriate feelings and expressions of anger result (Parker, 1972b). Neurosis, war, interpersonal antagonisms, and unreal expectations are part of the real heritage from our ancestors. The burden of our past can be understood in the words of Alvin Toffler (*Future Shock*, 1970):

If the last 50,000 years of man's existence were divided into lifetimes of approximately 62 years each, there have been about 800 such lifetimes ... fully 650 were spent in caves ... only during the last 70 ... has it been possible to communicate effectively from one lifetime to another ... only during the last 6 ... did masses of men ever see a printed word. Only during the last 4 has it been possible to measure time with any precision ... only in the last 2 has anyone anywhere used an electric motor. Within a single lifetime, agriculture, the original basis of civilization, has lost its dominance in nation after nation ... (p. 14).

## EVOLUTIONARY LAG

Our evolutionary heritage plays a vital role in the quality of our decision making. It is the true basis of human nature. Our brain, body, and behavior are designed for a very different world. Human capacity to cope with changing circumstances is poor (Parker, 1967; Parker, 1973b). Don't be misled by those who call the brain a marvelous organ. It is more correct to say that we cope with current situations using the brains of our cavemen ancestors. A basically human brain organization was in existence 3 million years ago.

According to Campbell (1972), from an evolutionary point of view our troubles started long ago: "The Neolithic (about 6,000 years before present period) was the start of the destruction of man's natural environment, and as the rate of population grew, the rate of destruction increased" (p. 53). Mankind is no longer organized into social units of perhaps twenty-five to fifty people adapted to a particular region. Instead, cities or entire countries comprised of millions of people are totally dependent upon others. Los Angeles, for example, receives 90 percent of its water from other than its own watershed and thus "robs otherwise fertile valleys." The United Kingdom imports approximately half of its food from other regions of the world (p. 56). The "city" itself is an evolving organism. Today's industrial-technological complex offers stimuli which were unknown to the inhabitants of the nineteenth century's mercantile-trading community (Ittelson, et al., 1974, p. 275).

What are the effects of such enormous environmental changes? Lorenz (1950, II, p. 184) asserts that "man represents . . . an animal torn from his natural environmental niche. . . . A whole range of previously adaptive endogenous behavior patterns have become not only nonfunctional but extremely destructive. . . . When an organism is placed in novel surroundings, behavior patterns occur which are neutral or even detrimental for the survival of the species. . . . A specific behavior pattern, based upon endogenous stimulus-production and adapted for a quite specific, species-preserving function, is robbed of its normal releasing situation. . . ." Similarly, changes in the environment which preclude patterns of behavior characteristic to that setting do not prevent this behavior from being conserved and then enacted at a new time or place (Ittelson, et al., 1974, p. 95).

For those of you who are skeptical concerning the proposition that our emotional/intellectual capacities do not deviate much from those of our cavemen ancestors, consider the assertion by the biologist C. L. Brace (1968): "It is probable that if a properly clothed and shaved Neanderthal were to appear in a crowd of modern urban shoppers or commuters, he would strike the viewer as somewhat unusual in appearance—short, stocky, large of face—but nothing more than that. Certainly few would suspect that he was their 'caveman ancestor.'"

The slow pace of psychological/behavioral change is suggested by the evidence that emotional expression is similar in all cultures. Ekman (1975) speculates that "all human beings share the same neural programming, which links facial muscles with particular emotions." This is confirmed by the tiny biochemical distances between various ethnically diverse human races whose genetic distance "is less than or equal to that between morphologically and behaviorally identical populations of other species" (King & Wilson, 1975).

We should recognize that characteristics which may aid the

survival of a species can be dangerous or negative in the life of an individual. To illustrate, while childbirth is marvelously complex, during it the mother is extremely vulnerable to external dangers and medical hazards (Bakan, 1968, pp. 20–21). Perhaps other qualities useful for survival of the human population create a burden upon the individual in the unnatural environment which mankind has created.

## EVOLUTIONARY HERITAGE OF HUMAN NATURE

What actually is the evolutionary basis for human nature?

1. *Slow maturation*: A long period of development and exposure to family and cultural learning is characteristic of our species, though not absolutely unique. However, because the thinking of children differs from that of adults, and because memory influences current activity, childish ways of thinking and emotionally charged early experiences influence later decisions and attitudes toward life.

2. *Use of symbols, language, and fantasy*: We seek explanations of phenomena which are not immediate, which are abstract, and which may be distant in time or place or not immediately comprehensible to the senses. Complex phenomena such as natural events are reduced to familiar, human-oriented concepts (anthropomorphism), regardless of how inappropriate the explanation, when they are incomprehensible. The logical programs of our brain may be inherent, or developed under different circumstances from the situations we are confronting. Consequently, the symbols and feeling which we utilize to label people and events may not have a basis in reality. This is the explanation for transference of attitudes from earlier situations to present ones, for prejudices, and for many self-destructive actions.

3. *Selective responsivity*: We respond only to particular qualities in the world around us; and the kinds of reactions that are possible are limited both by our bodily structure and by our inherent neurological programming (Young, 1961, pp. 609–612). Thus the range of decisions becomes artificially restricted by the

limitations of the nervous system and by the experiences of the decision maker.

4. *Mobility*: The history of our species has certainly been to explore new worlds, to run away from danger, and to expand its range when crowding made resources difficult to obtain. Today, we tend to have a life which is restricted, not only by overcrowding, but also by the ideological conviction that movement is evidence of cowardice or poor character. Therefore, most individuals make decisions away from mobility, remaining in unpleasant circumstances because of an abstract, perhaps self-destructive, evaluation of their real situation.

5. *Conflict between social needs and aggression*: We are born totally dependent and helpless, and soon we become conditioned to feel uncomfortable without close emotional contact and support. Individuals who did not have this need in primitive times probably became isolated and died or were otherwise prevented from passing along their genes. Simultaneously, the capacity for violence is programmed into our nervous system. Destructiveness is a typical way in which primates react to threats and obtain their needs in the face of competition. Thus, the balance between closeness and violence is precarious; and expression of our feelings is not based upon the situation alone but is also influenced by symbols, previous experiences, and so forth.

6. *Poorly integrated neurological functioning*: This idea will come as a shock to those of you who have been brainwashed to believe that the brain is a marvelous instrument. Actually, it is a combination of structures, some of which have evolved little from far more primitive forebears, and some of which are unique to our species. Therefore, particular functions may be controlled simultaneously by brain structures from different evolutionary ages. In human beings, specific bodily activities may be controlled by different sides of the brain, in contrast to other species in which control involves both sides of the brain simultaneously. This problem of integration of brain function is made more difficult by the fact that previous experiences from irrelevant circumstances are not erased, but are present to influence current decisions.

In the next chapter, I shall continue to discuss the bodily characteristics which affect your decisions. Specifically, I shall examine how these characteristics shape reactions and decisions. Emotional temperament and physical constitution have usually been ignored by writers on human affairs, so many of the ideas presented may be new to you.

# 8

# Individuality and Decision Making

It is not possible to make adequate decisions (and guide your life towards emotional fulfillment) without taking into consideration your unique qualities—your individuality. This is not meant to be an abstract, spiritualistic statement which is basically vague and therefore meaningless. On the contrary, by taking into account the specific qualities of your mind and body, known to psychologists as your temperament and constitution, you will be able to evaluate your potential and construct a suitable world around you.

People differ from each other to a varying degree in particular qualities. When you consider the building blocks of life, the proteins, there are greater genetic differences in the contribution of our parents than there are average differences between members of the same group or even between average members of such seemingly diverse groups as Caucasians and Orientals. The genes, which control enzyme formation, seem to be similar over different ethnic groups when it comes to basic functions such as the blood types. However, the differences which seem so obvious are literally superficial. Many of the differences among "races," and by extension between individuals, seem to involve the "interface between the body and the environment, particularly the climatic dimension of the environment . . . the body surface" (Cavalli-Sforza, 1974). The conclusion is inescapable: much human uniqueness evolved *from the necessity of coping with non-social characteristic qualities of our world*: sunshine, temperature, precipitation, etc.!

It is estimated that language evolved forty thousand years ago (Washburn & Harding, 1975) and that the ancestors of modern man were a relatively homogeneous group of hunters and gatherers until around thirty-five thousand years ago (Cavalli-Sforza, 1974). People of this type still survive among the Bushmen of the Kalahari Desert in Botswana and Southwest Africa. Curiously, although they live in very close quarters (of their own creation), they avoid pathological overcrowding by splitting their bands or moving from one camp to another (Draper, 1973). Truly, mobility is a basic quality of human nature (Davis, 1974). However, it may be wedded to the exploitation and conquest of others.

When we consider the world-wide expansion from the Near East started by our ancestors some thirty-five thousand years ago, it is useful to know that there are points of comparison between the way children learn language and the acquisition of sign language by a chimpanzee (Gardner & Gardner, 1975). Thirty-five thousand years is not very long from an evolutionary viewpoint, and the prehuman origins of our thinking and feeling patterns are by no means lost. Hunting prey and gathering berries are a far cry, adaptively, from going to the moon or being born into a slum. We have a genetic program which makes us most adaptable to the primitive world of our ancestors. The course of civilization, constructed by the human brain as a more suitable environment, has begun to reduce instead of enhance our capacity to survive. Fortunately, there is a degree of flexibility in our potential for development because of the effect of our environment upon the specific qualities of the genes. This is known as the genotype-environmental interaction (Vale, 1974). However, it is likely that there are limits for each individual. Beyond these, certain kinds of environments will prevent them from developing to their potential or will cause various signs of stress because they cannot function successfully.

As mankind evolved from the hunter-gatherer to the relatively sedentary agricultural life, and finally to civilization, the adaptation was in terms of changing his world around him, that is, his ecology (Beck, 1973). Now, these presumably beneficial conditions have plunged out of control because of unexpected complications. Poor decisions on the part of selfish or shortsighted people have created carcinogenic insecticides, ozone-reducing aerosol sprays which reduce the protection from ultraviolet light in our atmosphere, birth control pills with an increasingly known number of serious side effects, and all the rest. Governmental indifference has magnified our problems.

By 1915 Freud (1915a) had already pointed out that our drives ("instincts") are the borderland between the physical part of our life and the mental. As a consequence, he explained, our desires are the "mental representatives of the stimuli emanating from within the organism and penetrating to the mind." Our emotional life was understood to be a reflection of the organization of our brain and body. Jung (1933, p. 186) went even further: "Man's unconscious likewise contains all the patterns of life and behavior inherited from his ancestors, so that every human child prior to consciousness is possessed of a potential system of adapted psychic functioning . . . an immense fund of accumulated inheritance-factors left by one generation of man after another."

The newborn baby copes with the world with largely biological equipment. However, the interaction between biological and psychological functioning occurs from the beginning. The sucking urge serves to create a deep bond between infant and mother —when it is permitted to occur. Since the child is programmed to expect contact with his mother, the first stress of adaptation occurs when he is smacked on the behind, a procedure some obstetricians are now changing for loving contact with both mother and physician (Leboyer, 1975). Since the child is programmed to expect contact with his mother, being whisked off to a nursery can be another early form of stress (Tinbergen, interviewed by Hall, 1974). Here the first differences in our experience begin. We learn to expect fulfillment or frustration, become optimistic or pessimistic, and so on (Abraham, 1916, 1924).

Later on other intellectual and symbolic capacities develop.

These relatively elementary, physiologically based responses remain of vital importance throughout our lives. They are a kind of scaffolding on which we hang the meanings of events. Therefore, they shape many of our decisions and our effectiveness in carrying them out. Today, some distinguished psychologists state that "many forms of behavior that are critical for individual survival and population adaptation are under genetic control" (Lindzey, Loehlin, Manosevitz, & Thiessen, 1971, p. 69).

I assume that behavior present at birth, and which tends to be stable for long periods of life, is our ancestral heritage for survival.

## WE ARE INDIVIDUALS AT BIRTH

It is important to see that we all come into the world as different people. These differences, and the reactions of our parents and others to them, are some of the chief influences upon the development of our feelings and self-image. For example, it has been shown that *from the first day of life,* infants differ in their rate of sucking (Kron, Stein, Goddard, & Phoenix, 1967). They differ in their reactions to being interrupted when sucking. Some babies are so perverse that they reject the nipple: they respond to it by crying! At the beginning of life, infants differ in their ability to learn to recognize when food is available. These differences have important effects upon early relationships. The child who does not learn the connection between sucking and food may become irritable and have inadequate nutrition (Kron, Kron & Phoenix, unpublished). These differences in adaptability might be related to intellectual ability later on. On the other hand, "vigorous adaptation to breast or bottle feeding may set the stage for good nutrition and a healthy mother-infant relationship" (Kron, Stein & Goddard, 1966). If the mother is sensitive to the particular cycles of her child and adjusts her care to them, the child learns that his internal sensations have importance. He learns to recognize hunger, how to let the world know he is hungry, and whether his parents do something about it. If this pattern is not smooth the normal hunger satisfaction cycle is interfered with and there may be feeding disturbances later in life (Kron, Kron & Phoenix, unpublished). You can see that individual temperamental/constitutional differences from the beginning have implications for our social life and capacity to obtain satisfaction.

A team of child psychiatrists (Thomas, Chess & Birch, 1969, pp. 20–24) discovered that children have at least nine separate temperamental traits even from the earliest days of infancy: 1) *activity level;* 2) *rhythmicity,* or relative predictability; 3) *approach or withdrawal* in new situations; 4) *adaptability;* 5) *intensity* of energy; 6) *threshold of responsiveness* or sensitivity; 7) *quality of mood* as pleasant or unpleasant; 8) *distractability* or goal orientedness; and 9) *attention span* in the face of opposition. Their origin is in the child's constitution. These are some of the qualities with which we adapt to our special worlds at the beginning of life.

## DEVELOPMENTALLY STABLE CHARACTERISTICS

There are some components of behavior which are stable. If they change, they do so slowly. Those qualities of our body which affect behavior are called constitutional. Those qualities which directly influence our social life are known as temperament.

## CONSTITUTION

Constitution is the biological factor in behavior. It is usually underestimated by many psychotherapists and theorists of behavioral science. Biological structure and manner of functioning differ considerably from person to person. They are determined by hereditary qualities and their interaction with the environment from the womb period and later. For example, a person's musculature, and thus his attitude towards many situations, will be determined by his genes, maternal health, nutrition, and exercise. A person's constitution influences the energy he has available, his stamina, stress and disease resistance, rate of aging, propensity to anxiety, mood disorders, psychosomatic illness, and so forth.

We do not speak directly about the inheritance of behavior because our life history (prebirth and thereafter) conditions the way our genes influence our body and mind. Most aspects of behavior, whether baseball skill or intelligence, are affected by one or several genes (operating simultaneously) as affected by our environment (Vale, 1973). Their effects might be upon the central nervous system, or upon the other parts of the body such as glands and muscles (Thiessen, 1971; Wilcock, 1971). A particular genetic heritage might be expressed very differently, depending upon what happens to us. Some scholars take the opposite point of view. They believe that the cultural aspect of life is more important than genes as the determinant of how we adapt (Dobzhansky, 1973). At the present time, we cannot categorize our actions as being *exclusively* environmental or hereditary.

Some evidence for hereditary influences on our behavior comes from studies of ethnic differences in constitutional factors:

*Susceptibility to alcohol*: It is claimed that genetic factors are more important than environmental ones in the tendency to become alcoholic (Schuckit, 1972). Animal studies suggest that differences in the amount of alcohol preference relate to hereditary differences in the amount of particular enzymes which break down alcohol (Lindzey et al., 1971). Ethnic differences exist in susceptibility to alcohol. Asiatics show intoxication and flushing after drinking amounts of alcohol which have no effects on Westerners. This was related to differences in the response of their autonomic nervous systems (Wolff, 1972). Alcoholism is also less frequent in Asiatics, as compared to Westerners.

*Physiological reactivity*: The part of the nervous system which controls and balances the life-sustaining functions (autonomic) seems to work at different rates in different ethnic groups. Any differences in digestion, blood flow, respiration, and sweating would affect a person's effectiveness and style in handling many different situations. Studies of Caucasians, Negroes, and Bedouins revealed differences between them in pulse rate and resistance of the skin to the passage of an electric current (galvanic skin response) (Lieblich, Kugelmass, & Ben-Shakhar, 1973; Fisher & Kotses, 1973).

*Physiological reaction to stress*: An interesting parallel has been found between ethnic attitudes towards pain and bodily reactions. The reaction of four groups to increasing electric shocks was studied: "old" Americans, Jews, Italians, and Irish (Sternbach & Tursky, 1965; Tursky & Sternbach, 1969). The authors believe that prior attitude determines physiological responses, but they don't exclude the possibility of actual ethnic differences. Important differences between individuals of the same group did occur. Here is how the attitudes towards pain seemed to influence the various stress responses: "Old Americans have a phlegmatic, matter-of-fact, doctor-helping orientation; Jews express a concern for the implications of pain, and they distrust palliatives; Italians express a desire for pain relief; and the Irish inhibit expression of suffering and concern for the implications of pain." I don't know which comes first, attitude or bodily reaction, but they do seem to go together.

Any variation in autonomic reactions will bring about a different response to a particular event according to the momentary status of our body. Therefore the way somebody copes with a given situation can be unpredictable (Lacey & Lacey, 1958).

There are differences in the reactions of different parts of the autonomic nervous system between neurotics and nonneurotics. Some malfunctioning of the system may predispose neurotics to intense autonomic reactions, so that bodily effects often continue for an exceptionally long time (Rubin, 1965). In this way, anxiety is conditioned to extraneous circumstances, and its cause becomes obscure and its treatment difficult.

There are also many chemical effects which take place in the uterus before our birth, which also shape our temperament. These include sexual attitudes and aggressiveness (Ehrhardt, 1973; Yalom, Green, & Fisk, 1973). Thus, there are many different constitutional factors which influence our behavior profoundly but indirectly. Some of these we call temperament.

## Temperament

One characteristic which is frequently ignored in discussions of how people make decisions is the quality of temperament. A realistic view must include the distinctive emotional characteristics which play a role in effectiveness.

Temperament might be defined as those aspects of personality and emotional life which are most stable. It includes energy level, the quality and stability of moods, and typical reactions to new situations and people. Temperamental qualities can remain constant for a lifetime, or they can vary considerably over the years. I myself was a phlegmatic child, and now my capacity to work and remain active is the envy of lots of folks.

It appears to me that the task of adapting to the world is a lot harder than even some distinguished writers think. For example, a famous psychoanalyst suggested that our behavior is tailored so that it would have survival value in any "average expectable environment" (Hartmann, 1958, p. 46). I think that people are a lot less adaptable than that. Even from the beginning we differ from each other and some of us do not fit well into the world.

Certain characteristics of mood and ways of reacting to problems have been observed in human beings for thousands of years. These basic temperaments influence the quality of our decision making and generally are slow to change. Thus temperament becomes an important consideration both in making decisions and in carrying them out.

## Varieties of Temperament

Perhaps you will see yourself in one of the following types of temperament. I borrowed numbers 1 through 5 from Millon (1969), who borrowed 3 and 4 from Cattell and Scheier (1961).

1. *Anhedonia* describes the unfortunate person who is unable to have fun or experience affection, joy, and delight. Perhaps there is an anatomical defect in a brain pleasure mechanism (Olds & Milner, 1954) or a biochemical insufficiency of certain substances in the blood or nervous system.

2. *Melancholia* is an active disposition to pain and displeasure, with thinking colored by depression. The melancholic is pessimistic and despairing.

3. *Threctia* describes the person who experiences such anxiety and threat that he avoids taking chances that might lead to physical injury and stress. Thus he is timid and hesitant.

4. *Parmia* characterizes a person who is bold, venturesome, fearless, and daring and incapable of experiencing deep anxiety.

5. *Choler* is a disposition to anger and irritability. This type of person is waspish, crabby, and quick to take offense.

6. *Cheerfulness* is the dominant quality of the person who faces the most desperate situation with good humor and kind words for all.

Most people have features from more than one of these temperamental types.

## PROBLEM SOLVING

Just as there are typical ways of experiencing life, so there are characteristic modes of solving problems. It is useful to recognize your style, and then to seek situations in which it can be expressed most effectively. It may also be necessary to learn how to cope with new types of problems if the real world does not permit you to utilize old kinds of solutions. In this case, you must develop alternate means of solving problems.

## INDUSTRIAL ASSESSMENT BASED UPON TEMPERAMENT

Here is an example of how a major industrial corporation approaches the question of assessment. It represents the projection into adulthood of many of the temperamental and constitutional qualities which are present from birth, together with developed skills and also the particular style of social relationships as they may affect business effectiveness.

The ITT Assessment Report comprises three major sections:
(Used with permission of Robert Dugan, Ph.D.)

## I.  Work Approach
This section attempts to present a picture of the man's typical work style and covers characteristics like:

| | |
|---|---|
| *Energy Level* | Activity, work pace, will to work |
| *Emotional Stability* | Relaxed/tense |
| | Placid/worrying |
| | Response to stress, pressure |
| *Conscientiousness* | Persevering/quitting |
| | Follow-through |
| *Independence* | Self-reliance, self-starting qualities, ability to accept responsibility |
| | Conventional/imaginative, risk-taking |
| *Flexibility* | Adaptability to changing priorities, coping with simultaneous assignments |
| *Reliability* | Steady and predictable/ impulsive |
| *Attentiveness to Detail* | Generalist/detailed |

## II.  Intellectual Effectiveness
This section consists largely of the statement and interpretation of results on the cognitive tests and covers therefore:

| | |
|---|---|
| *General Intelligence* | Abstract/concrete reasoning, for example |
| *Verbal Facility* | Vocabulary, use of words, ability to sell his ideas, articulateness and fluency |
| *Numerical Reasoning Skills* | Ability to use numerical concepts in a business setting |
| *Critical Thinking Ability* | Analytical, logical ability to deal with more abstract issues |
| *Imaginativeness* | Creativity, productive thinking ability |

|  | *Percentile* |
|---|---|
| Superior | 85–99 |
| Above Average | 66–84 |
| Average | 35–65 |
| Below Average | 15–34 |
| Low | 0–14 |

### III. Relationships with Others

| | |
|---|---|
| *Manner* | Reserved/outgoing |
| | Assertive/submissive |
| | Way of presenting himself |
| *With Superiors* | Readiness to accept direction |
| | Stubborn/cooperative |
| *With Subordinates* | Management style |
| | Demanding/permissive |
| | Democratic/authoritarian |
| *With Colleagues* | Team spirit, cooperativeness |
| | Insight into self and others |

The report ends with a listing of the man's principal strengths and weaknesses, followed by a brief summary of the main overall findings, viewed in the light of the demands of the position in question. Where the individual has been assessed for a particular position for which a specification exists, the final sentence of the summary should read, "On the basis of this assessment and not considering his professional qualifications, Mr. X appears to possess the necessary personal qualifications for the position in question."

You have seen how people differ considerably in the emotional apparatus which they bring into life. Emotion is a tool you use to cope with various situations. One's temperament and constitution can offer a strong body and will power to cope with adversity; or they can sabotage us, create anxiety, psychosomatic problems, or weakness when it is most inconvenient or even dangerous. Thus, our capacity to take effective actions consistent with our decisions will be aided or hampered by biological-

temperamental-contitutional aspects of our being. Our temperament also will influence our moods; and it will affect our motivation toward reaching a goal and our capacity to enjoy it when
we get there.

Some of our behavior was programmed before birth. Therefore, some decisions were partly made for you before you were
born! The effectiveness of your nervous system, the perfection of
your development, and your sexual and other role-related behavior and social criteria could be dependent upon many factors:
your mother's nutrition, the medication, toxins, and artificial
elements in her food, and the amount of stress she experienced.
All these play a part in your physiological and anatomical pat-
terning and development including the way your nervous system
functions. Yes, your capacity to make competent decisions started
to develop before you were born.

In subsequent chapters we shall emphasize the familiar psychological factors which influence your decisions and their effects.
However, you must always remember that it is the special characteristics of your constitution and temperament which enhance
or sabotage these decisions. Self-knowledge must be comprehensive in order to be effective.

# 9

# The Unconscious:
# Our Outdated Map of Life

Let us now look into our private or unconscious life, which unexpectedly intrudes into the way we think, decide, and then carry out our decisions. The unconscious causes us, and the people we have to deal with, to be irrational, even when we think that we are coolest and most logical. It shapes our decision making in areas which are really critical, including our philosophy of life, the way we react toward other people, the image we have of ourselves and of our value, and the particular role that we play in society. We shall see that the real difficulty that all of us have in making good decisions may be related to a newly discovered way in which our brain is organized (Chapter 5).

What is the unconscious? There are many different ways in which our brain functions which affect our daily lives without our being aware of it.

## OUTDATED INFORMATION

In the first place, the brain usually does not erase or properly label out-of-date or useless information. It stores it and may make all of our feelings and memories available to us when we least expect them. Therefore, much of our personality arises from the vivid experiences we had as children. Even though we and our world may have changed considerably, we react as though we were still the small, vulnerable child desperately trying to figure out a way to survive emotionally. From this point of view *unconscious experiences are timeless*. As we form impressions of what the world is like, we may not alter them with new experiences. We retain the same images of important people, write a script for how everybody should react, and then become frustrated and angry because people don't conform to it. We become "embedded" in that old childish situation (Schachtel, 1959). Both old and new attitudes become mixed up in our feelings and reactions.

The picture which we have of the world is frequently out-of-date. Our guide as to how the world is organized was called by the distinguished psychologist E. C. Tolman (1948) a "cognitive map." Because our cognitive map is frequently out-of-date, we often have the illusion that we perceive people and problems more accurately than we do. As a consequence, we do not realize how defective our information is, and we make disastrous decisions. We guide our actions like a navigator using a map to steer a massive vessel through rough seas, and when the map was always incomplete and now is years out of date!

## THE UNCONSCIOUS AND POOR DECISIONS

How does unconscious, outdated information lead to ineffective decision making?

1. Our attitudes are shaped by events which occurred at different times of our lives. We do not have a consistent point of view which can be tested at any moment to see whether it leads to constructive or self-destructive actions.

2. Many of our beliefs were formed years ago. Since we may not even remember who taught us, or even that we were led to believe a certain way, we react without knowing what is influencing our decisions and feelings.

3. Since any kind of experience can be stored, many of our feelings, values, and ideas are contradictory.

4. Some ideas are connected with disturbing feelings because they initially occurred together (Bruner, 1966, p. 132).

5. There are significant gaps in our memory as to how things really occurred, both yesterday and years ago.

6. Even if we think that we remember what happened at a particular time, our recollection may be distorted or changed into the opposite, several separate events may be combined in our mind, or the whole thing may never have really happened.

7. Even if we really do remember what happened, it is probably irrelevant to today's decision.

## CHILDREN'S THINKING IS DIFFERENT

Another reason why these distortions take place is that *children think and feel differently than adults do.* As a result, their experiences are different, and as adults, we have difficulty in communicating with and understanding our earlier memories and experiences (Parker, 1972b, pp. 23–26). The child's experiences are very vague at first. Only later does pleasure and pain become associated with particular actions or people. Eventually, the growing child develops images of the people around him, and these have the qualities of being good or bad according to whether they bring pleasure, relieve distress, or create pain.

Initially, the child's mental life (Freud, 1911) is determined by his feelings (the pleasure/pain principle) and not by logic (the reality principle). It is a great step forward—long after a beginning has been made on a philosophy of life—that the child begins to think more accurately and definitely because he has learned the use of words. Up to this point, the child's categories of thought are very different from those which adults use. These primitive ways of looking at things can bring havoc when they are used in adult life because they mix together feelings and images and actions and concepts. In the child's mind, actions, feelings, and the qualities of the objects that stir them up are all mixed together. Our concepts about the significant events of our early life are shaped by what we did at the time, not merely by any objective qualities of the people or objects around us (Flavell, 1963, Chapter II: "Basic Properties of Cognitive Functioning,"; also, Piaget, 1968, p. 2).

The unconscious in all of us is based upon the child's

different way of experiencing life. Therefore many of our actions become unrelated to real people and situations. An adult way of thinking is potentially objective; that is, our reasons and categories can be shared with others and influenced by other people's comments, rather than kept totally private.

## UNCONSCIOUS FEELINGS

Another reason we are out of touch with our early experiences is that they may be loaded with *anxiety*. We tend to avoid thoughts, impulses, and feelings which make us nervous or which we believe will lead to punishment. We repress them in order not to feel anxious, but the painful expectations are still there to mislead us. There are many distortions of our personality which we develop to keep us from remembering painful experiences, or to prevent us from being aware that our impulses are inhibited because we expect to be punished for yielding to them.

*History IX–1*: Here is an example of a woman who repressed her feelings towards her sister. She was aware of hostility towards her parents for having four children. She was the oldest and felt that she never had enough. Under hypnosis she regressed back to different ages. At fifteen, she experienced tears. At ten, she remembered her sister taking her toys. Finally, at age five, she expressed her resentment that her sister was always screaming and preventing her from sleeping. When she woke up, she said that she had not previously remembered these experiences. We can assume that she was terribly angry with her sister, but felt guilty about her aggression and was afraid of expressing her resentment to her parents for having another child and depriving her of their attention.

Here is another example of *unconscious enmity*:

*History IX–2*: A woman came into therapy as a result of stress arising in connection with her marriage. Her mother had died when she was an infant due to obstetric mismanagement. While she had been made to feel guilty about her mother's death, her real feelings of self-torture and emotional deprivation were hidden from her. They were not expressed until she was in the security of a psychotherapeutic relationship. She related this experience: "I was lying down in bed, I got a call from a woman (whom she felt made her unhappy by exploiting her). All of a sudden, ice was running in my veins. I said to myself, what is this? It's fear. My God! I feel guilty. The fear is the guilt. I was doing something wrong. I'm trying to get to the bottom of these feelings. I feel guilty. Every time I did something wrong I always got the blame. Or, I put myself in a position to be blamed. Like when somebody said, 'Who did this?' My face would give me away."

Here we see how the experience of feeling guilty for her mother's death unexpectedly intrudes itself on her awareness.

Anxiety can interfere with our being able to recollect clearly what actually happened, even though the real events are potentially available and undistorted to our memory (Holmes, 1974). One of the characteristics of anxiety is that we may feel nervous and uncomfortable, even though we don't know why. When some event takes place which reminds us of some problem we had to solve, when the consequence of failure was punishment or humiliation, we become distracted by our unpleasant feelings. In this way we do not think about the task at hand, or even about the situation which originally makes us anxious. We are just aware of our anxiety. It is this anxiety which causes many people to fail on examinations, or become tongue-tied when called in by their supervisors. Anxiety is an important factor in why many decisions are deferred past the time when they must be made or when some constructive action could be taken.

## CEREBRAL ASYMMETRY AND EMOTION

An exciting breakthrough in our understanding of how the unconscious develops and influences our lives is the finding that the right and left sides of our brain (cerebral hemispheres) have different functions.

The right hemisphere seems to specialize in spatial relations, perceiving things as a whole. An example would be appreciation of a musical selection, in contrast to breaking it down into themes, harmony, and so forth. The right cerebral hemisphere uses nonverbal means of recording our experiences, probably images of a visual, tactile, muscular, and auditory nature. It solves problems by seeing common elements (Galin, 1974; Bever, 1975).

The left cerebral hemisphere specializes in language, arithmetic, and analysis of a situation into its parts. It uses forms of logic and analysis for which words are the best tools. Verbal functions, such as writing a letter, or reflecting on a verbal question, are associated with left hemisphere functioning.

The use of electrical patterns (EEG) to estimate brain functions is well known. Now it has been discovered that the direction of eye movements is a measure of hemisphere activity. The eyes tend to move toward the side opposite that of the active cerebral hemisphere (Schwartz, Davidson, & Maer, 1975). People who tend to daydream a great deal (inner attentiveness) shift their eyes to the left, while those lower in inner attentiveness more often shift their eyes to the right (Singer, 1975). The emotional, image-laden quality of daydreaming seems to be involved. When right-handed people (with left hemisphere dominance) were asked emotional questions, they tended to move their eyes to the left, while questions demanding both verbal and nonemotional consideration resulted in eye movements to the right.

Another confirmation of the association of emotionality with the right side and rational thinking with the left side is the fact that when people have left hemisphere damage, they show a "catastrophic" emotional reaction. This means that contemplation of their disorder leaves them very anxious. On the other hand, when people suffer right-side damage, they are relatively indifferent. The balance of emotional to non-emotional functions is increased by left-side damage. With right-side damage, emotional reactions to hampered bodily control seem to be reduced.

## DISSOCIATION OF FEELINGS AND RATIONALITY

The two halves of our brain have been recording different aspects of our experiences throughout life. Perhaps the reason that some people are emotional and others are analytical has to do with the fact that they have been rewarded for different kinds of behavior. As a result, they prefer one form of expression to the other. Nevertheless, the alternate brain half and its way of thinking and responding to life is still there, and must be integrated with the preferred mode of response.

Consider the effect, that is, the kinds of information processed, when a mother says to her child, "I love you," while her facial expression is full of distaste. The left hemisphere of the child's brain hears the *words,* which are affectionate, while the right hemisphere records the *pattern* of the mother's face, body, and voice (body language, which is hostile).

It is hypothesized that the nonverbal half of the brain (or its alternate, the verbal half) can be "disconnected" by inhibiting impulses from traveling from one side to another (across the *corpus callosum*). This prevents integration of the verbal and nonverbal portions of our experiences. However, "the actual process in the right (nonverbal) hemisphere, cut off in this way from the left hemisphere consciousness that is directing overt behavior, may nevertheless continue a life of its own. The memory of the situation, the emotional concomitants, and the frustrated plan of action may persist, affecting subsequent perception and forming the basis for expectations and evaluations of future input" (Galin, 1974). Capacity to inhibit emotionality may be the reason why human beings have remarkable emotional control compared to other primates (Washburn & Harding, 1975).

The separation of important centers involved in emotionality and rationality helps us to understand some of the contradictions in dreams and fantasies, as well as why other problems occur when we create decisions that integrate emotional and other important aspects of our inner life.

## UNCONSCIOUS IMAGES

A useful concept in understanding some peculiarities of our motives and social relationships is the *unconscious image.* An image represents our belief about how people *are* out in the real world. It is a kind of memory which combines feelings and perceptions about ourselves and people who are important to us. Since images tell us what to expect, they also guide our decision making. When we first start to form images as children, we do not see people with their true complexity. Rather, we divide them into parts and create separate images of each part. For example, what we like about mother becomes Good Mother, and what causes us grief is Bad Mother. We create similar images for father and other important people. Unfortunately, we receive only limited, exaggerated ideas from these images. They are experienced as "two vaguely limited but entirely distinct people" (Sullivan, 1940, p. 79). Furthermore, we "incorporate" or "introject" our family's moral attitudes and instructions (Eidelberg, 1968, p. 929) into our values. Then we think that these codes of behavior are our own, though they really are the distorted memories of how people told us to behave.

Images in the form of *imaginary companions* also satisfy needs which are not being met. These are fantasies in which others play an important role in fulfilling our emotional deficits. These images ultimately help us to decide on our mates, or to choose unsuitable candidates.

*History IX–3*: A middle-aged man had the repeated experience of choosing women who would not marry him. He complained about his disappointment when he discovered that one woman whom he liked was actively seeking a reconciliation with her husband. "I think that she will choose me when she discovers that I am such a swell guy." I asked him to remember his fantasies when he was sixteen years old. "My entire fantasies about all women were of my being extra good, a savior; the girl was down, depressed, hurt. I was saving or protecting her. I would be more accepted if they were down. What didn't I do? There was something wrong with me. How could I make this girl like me? I wouldn't accept persons the way they were. They had to be the way I wanted them to be. I would only see the good parts of them, so if something went wrong, it must be me."

He was amazed in the middle of this to realize how he relived this adolescent dream of helping a damsel in distress and thus winning her to his side. This fantasy was designed to overcome his feelings of inferiority. He would choose women who were too preoccupied with other events to care for him. Their active unavailability created the hope that through his activities he would prove what a nice guy he was. This unconscious need caused him to court unsuitable women.

Unconscious images also keep us from making decisions when they are in conflict with each other. We experience them as though we are being accused or defended, persecuted or supported. They may eventually keep us from taking an action. We can become so uncomfortable that to get rid of them we project them onto other people and believe that the innocent people are the perpetrators of our internal torment.

*History IX–4*: A young married woman was paralyzed from carrying out her daily domestic duties because of what she called "counter thoughts." Every time she decided to do something, she would tell herself "don't do it." Both of her parents were critical of her and made her feel incompetent. As a result, when she wanted to take some initiative, an unconscious image of her parents prevented her from doing so by creating the opposite instruction. As a result, she could make no decisions.

Images can also have an important effect upon the way in which we express hostility (or brutality) to others. Dicks (1972) tells how bullying Nazis tormented defenseless inmates of concentration camps. Unconsciously, they projected their own guilt to the victims. They acted like their own critical, bullying fathers. They accused these victims of being enemies of the Third Reich. When they themselves were captured, they reverted to their own juvenile self-images of being passive victims, and pleaded that they were only "little men" following orders (M. Klein, 1929, 1945; Dicks, 1972; Parker, 1972; Sullivan, 1940; Eidelberg, 1968).

## DREAMS

Another familiar aspect of the unconscious, one which indirectly tells us which decisions we will make in the future, is dreams. Freud called them "The Royal Road to the Unconscious." From our point of view, we can also understand dreams as "The Royal *Roadmap* of the Unconscious." Dreams, more than most other aspects of the unconscious, have some of the chief characteristics of unconscious processes.

The psychology of dreams is complex, and many different processes take place in a dream (Dallett, 1973). Our dreams may reveal a problem that we are facing, and one means that we are contemplating to solve it. Dreams are also a way of incorporating daily events into experiences of the past. They also serve to balance our inner life, when our approach to the world has become one-sided. Perhaps dreams were believed by Freud to be wish-fulfilling because they can provide us with experiences which we have neglected in daily living. In addition, dreams and the unconscious reveal some of the ways in which our nervous system has been organized by natural selection and heredity over numerous generations (Jung, 1933, p. 186).

Images, as they appear in dreams, can sometimes reveal that we see ourselves as similar to other people (identification). Through this indirect route, we can become aware of our real motives.

Piotrowski (1971) has pointed out that the means of communicating with oneself in a dream differs from that of the waking person communicating with others through spoken language. Imagery has both advantages and limitations. Its greatest advantage "is the capacity to express ideas in comprehensible fragments (symbols) ; to juxtapose contradictory thoughts in the same image without causing intellectual confusion; to be far more direct, uncensored and specific than rational language which can easily be used to avoid frankness and distract the listener. . . .The dreamer truly bares his soul."

*History IX–5*: A dream revealing a woman's identification with her son displays distortions characteristic of images: "I dreamt that my son was about five years old and he was standing on a bed, and there was something wrong with his leg, and to cure him I had to cut into his ankle and I did. I sawed through his ankle but didn't take off the foot completely, just half way off. He didn't cry. He accepted it. What could I have done, how could I do it? I kept convincing him that this would make him better. But I felt that I had done something criminal. I wanted to do something for him, but it was all wrong. I woke up with terrible feelings of guilt."

This woman's son had berated her for "castrating" him, that is, for making it difficult for him to behave like an assertive male. Furthermore, her own mother had to have both legs amputated due to diabetes. She herself had been overeating, which she feels is a kind of suicide. Her identification with her son is due to her feeling that he was "so damn bright...brilliant logical mind. I would have been this if I had been of the opposite sex. Instead I feel the emotionality associated with the menstrual cycle." Furthermore, her son had abused her for making him carry something when his knee had hurt some months before. Through the memories of her mother's amputation, and her identification with her son and his problem with his knee, she is giving herself a warning: Do not eat too much or you will be mutilated like your mother and like your son (with whom you identify) in the dream. Since she is less productive than she wants to be, the dream is also a reproach for damaging that part of herself which she values, her intellectual ability. The dream also included her feeling about what she is doing to her appearance. Thus, in this dream, her decision to be more careful concerning her diet was carried by an image which represented her self-destructiveness, her mother's experience, and her anxiety about her son all condensed into one.

Here is another dream in which a decision to take action is revealed.

*History IX–6*: A young divorcee dreamed that her exhusband (with whom she has had continued conflict) had remarried. "I met him at a train station. I was wearing a wedding band. I bought a token and when I was going to put it in he was leaning against the machine where you go through the turnstile. I entered the turnstile. I saw him there. 'Oh shit.' When he saw me, I said 'It's time we talked.' Then he put his hand to his hair and I saw the suede jacket with a fur collar. His hair was down to his shoulders, cut in a shag. He had a mustache. He was wearing a turtleneck under the coat. That is the kind of physical appearance I am attracted to, the hip dresser. I woke up feeling alone and depressed."

Her association was that the dream represented unfinished business. Because of her husband's evasive qualities, she never got to say goodbye. "I don't want it to be finished." Termination of the marriage would mean that she can be disregarded. She does not see herself as a person. She has an inferiority complex. Nothing ever comes out right, including her hobbies. Since marriage is social status to her, divorce is a blow to her ego. She used to look down upon her unmarried friends. To make herself feel better, she got a haircut and went to the gym.

Dreams are many sided, and there is no objective way of determining their "true meaning." Freud said that to interpret a dream one must know the dreamer first. The dream usually represents *a preoccupation by the dreamer*. In the example above, it was the wish to undo the sudden termination of their relationship which her ex-husband had maneuvered by guile. Secondly, *the dream shows how we regard the figure acting in the dream*. She still feels that her ex-husband is desirable, and he is well-dressed. Finally, *the dream shows our attitude toward ourselves,* since every person in a dream relates to part of our personality. It is encouraging that the only other person in this dream is attractive, even though her identification is shielded by the fact that the figure is a male.

## NIGHTMARES

Nightmares reveal information about our fears, and thus the kinds of inhibitions we experience in social situations. Nightmares are experienced particularly by adults when they are anxious or ill, or when drugs have interfered with normal sleep (Hersen, 1972).

*History IX–7*: A young woman woke up in a sweat.

*Nightmare*: "Horrifying. Everything seemed to be descending on me. I woke up and sat up in bed. I was being threatened somehow. Three men were trying to get me to do something, or were reproaching me or saying I shouldn't be so stupid. They threatened to tell my parents. The first man, S, was the same one I had gone with when I first came to New York. I was more deeply involved than I realized. He and I had the same feelings for each other, but I didn't know because he didn't let his feelings show through. He took off for the West. I liked H, and didn't know he was married. I saw him on weekends. Apparently he had leave from his wife to do this during the last two months of her pregnancy. The third man J, was just somebody who works in the office and knows the other two. He has been obnoxious in the past. They were reproaching me for not marrying S. They were threatening to go to my parents with everything. They would say that I had had sex with J. My parents would be horrified."

*Associations*: "To have sex with a married man means I was slightly stupid. There were so many signs. I wasn't doing anything right. His wife did things differently. I became so agitated I couldn't sleep. I was taking various nonprescription drugs to sleep." To her, being stupid means not following her parents' wishes that she go to college, meet a nice young man, get married, and have children. "It's normal. But, I couldn't go to a college." I commented to her that instead of seeing herself as a happy immoralist, she saw herself as a disobedient daughter. "My mother sent me an article about single girls in the dangerous city. All three men are European. Now I have set goals to meet Americans. In general, you get to know where you stand with Americans. I would be surer of myself and of the man's situation. I will become more alert for signs of marital status. H was an escape from the pressure of S calling up. He didn't stop calling. He wanted to marry me, but he had not shown outward feelings of this nature." (The two men did not express true feelings. She herself withdraws to avoid being hurt.)

*Meaning*: She revolts against a part of her personality which is insincere and which prefers concealing her social activities. She also wants to be more alert to the hidden motives in other people's behavior.

A nightmare is different from most dreams. There are different stages of sleep; and nightmares generally occur when we are most deeply asleep, that is, regressed, with extremely reduced controls and defenses. Under these circumstances, we may experience deep feelings of anxiety that are generally hidden. Nightmares, and the related night terror of childhood (*pavor nocturnus*, Bakwin & Bakwin, 1960) are often characterized by intense physiological reactions such as screaming, confusion, highly increased heart rate and amplitude, and rate of respiration (Fisher et al., 1970). Adult nightmares may be of lifelong duration and related to traumatic experiences of childhood. Some experiences that can lead to childhood terrors during sleep are asphyxia (for example, from adenoidal growths) and sexual anxiety over masturbation (Sullivan, 1929, pp. 95–96). People are never the same after a frightening incident or panic. The carried-forward fear can seriously affect our lives for some time. Often the figures experienced in nightmares are symbolic representations of the parental images which we created (Mack, 1970, p. 225) or images of those we perceive as hating and destroying us (M. Klein, 1940, 1945).

## TRANSFERENCE

The unconscious is also revealed in *transference*, which is a kind of prejudgment or decision about how to behave toward others. This is based upon how we see others, what we expect from them, and what conditioned reactions we have to particular situations. Transference was one of Freud's (1912) greatest discoveries. The feelings which are deeply experienced with one person become transferred to another person. We form an impression of how someone, for example a parent or important sibling, will react. Deep feelings are experienced which do not alter much with time. Thus, as life circumstances change, even though we grow up and the parent becomes different in personality or even dies, we retain the same unconscious attitudes. It is as if there is a great deal of unfinished business.

Here are some of the ways in which transference shows itself:

1. *We believe that others owe us affection.* All authorities are perceived as potentially giving or frustrating. We become angry when we don't get what we want (but may have no right to expect).

2. *We continue to feel small and oppressed.* In this case authority figures such as teachers and supervisors are expected to be humiliating, and we react with inappropriate hostility and resentment.

3. *We want to undo the feeling of rejection.* We pursue people who are rejecting. If we can convince them to love us, then we have the illusion that the earlier feeling of rejection will disappear.

4. *We don't want to give up infantile gratifications.* It would be truly wonderful if the world would continue to gratify us as small children, if all authorities were potentially giving. We become frustrated when we don't get what we want (but may have no right to expect), and we continue our self-destructive manipulations to get it (Parker, 1967).

5. *We refuse to admit that the world is changing.* We have the illusion that the kinds of satisfactions we received in the past are good for us. Frequently, if we look at what we claim to want, which was marvelous or useful in the past and which we are still demanding, we discover that it was obnoxious then, and poisonous now.

*History IX–8: Decisions based upon transference*: A young woman felt that she was uninteresting, unattractive, and not worth much. She came to my office and said that she was considering leaving treatment. She thought that I was disinterested. When I expressed my concern for her (not for the first time), and somehow succeeded in reaching her emotionally, she was able to achieve a breakthrough and tell me how badly she really felt about herself. Since the chief source of resistance had been her belief that I was disinterested in her, I asked her about her relationship with her father. He had an exceptionally long work day, and for several hours after he returned home he wouldn't talk to anybody. By then, it would be quite late. Particularly after she reached puberty, "there would be long periods of silence. I would become very uncomfortable. He didn't know what to say to me and I didn't make the effort to tell him what I was thinking about. As a matter of fact, I rarely think of you between sessions. I tried to avoid conversations involving feelings. It probably made it difficult for my father to talk to me. I grew up in a family situation where you didn't talk about your feelings. However, when I was in bed I could hear my parents quarreling, but I didn't know what it was about. I saw you both (father and therapist) as *authority figures* that were not easy to approach. If I talked to you at a feeling level I wouldn't know what reaction I would get. Rather than chance a rebuff it would be easier not to talk about things that were important."

## AMBIGUOUS SITUATIONS AND THE UNCONSCIOUS

Another means of learning about our unconscious is through our reaction to ambiguous, vague situations. When inkblots are presented to us for our meaning, we express ourselves in ways which show our internal pressures and beliefs about the world. As with dreams, we often take important themes in our own lives, and attribute them to figures which are different from us. A young man, dissatisfied with his passivity, might see a sleeping woman. A mature woman, uncomfortable about her own resentment, might project a fighting male. Furthermore, our unconscious perception of the world is frequently expressed. The emotionally deprived person may see a scene of snow; the hostile individual, a battle or explosion (Parker & Piotrowski, 1968). An acceptable way of portraying our underlying feelings or feelings we fear others will not accept, is to create poetry and art (Parker, 1969).

## MINIMIZING UNCONSCIOUS EFFECTS UPON DECISIONS

We can summarize the effects that the unconscious has upon decision making by saying that it mixes up feelings and meanings from the past with our reaction to the current situation. Understanding this, it becomes possible to undo some of the harmful effects that unconscious attitudes have upon our decisions.

First, it is necessary to understand our real interests. Let us consider racial prejudice as an example. It is well established that prejudice permits people to displace anger from real situations (in which they could get hurt if they expressed their feelings) to an abstract collection of outsiders (Parker, 1972). Probably, like many people, you do not devote sufficient ingenuity to finding out what is really bothering you. Try to become more alert to the effect that the people and situations in your life have upon your feelings.

Secondly, watch the effect that you have upon others. You may observe that people are avoiding you, misunderstanding you, raising their voices, becoming angry, and so forth. The unconscious part of your mind may be giving off messages in addition to what you think you are doing and saying. You may be double-talking! Part of your personality may be talking about the stock market or sports, and the other part may be saying: "I am emotionally hungry! Gimme!" Or, "I want to playact being a sexy person." Perhaps, "I am terribly angry, and it won't take much to provoke a blow or an abusive outburst." Even your best friends may not tell you about these messages unless you ask them. If self-exploration doesn't give you the answer, ask somebody. If this doesn't help, seek psychotherapeutic assistance.

Finally, determine whether there are any repetitive, unfortunate trends in your experience. Are you constantly losing jobs? Do you frequently seek a love relationship with an unsuitable person? Is there a constant battle with your mate over essentially trivial matters? It may be that you are reenacting an early traumatic or frustrating experience in the futile hope of undoing it. You cannot relive the past. You *can* make the most of the present.

In the next chapter, we will look at the effect that your feelings have upon your decisions and way of life. Your knowledge about the unconscious will add meaning to this material.

# 10
# Feelings and Your Decisions

In this chapter I will stress the role of feelings in influencing decisions. By clarifying your understanding of your own moods, you will be able to label your feelings and decide whether they guide you towards or away from your goals.

What are feelings? Feelings are intimately associated with the physiological functioning of our bodies, from which we can conclude that they are related to *survival and adaptation*. Awareness of bodily changes was useful to our ancestors. With the development of *consciousness,* and with increased ability to learn and to sense the passage of time, the role of feelings became extremely complicated. The frustrating task of making order out of mankind's emotional life even motivated one author to write a chapter entitled "Twenty Theories of Emotion" (Strongman, 1973). Nevertheless, there is evidence (Ekman, 1975) that all human beings share the same neural programming for expressing feelings, insofar as they utilize and recognize the same facial muscles throughout different cultures to react to similar events.

It is even difficult to define feelings. They seem to refer to some self-awareness which is pleasant or unpleasant and which has meaning. The statement "I feel anxious" indicates that there is some displeasure, and that something bad may happen.

Why do we have feelings? William James pointed out a long time ago (James, 1892, p. 162) that feelings tell us about our relations with objects that concern us. "Feelings are more than an inward state of mind; they are associated with movements." Today we call this effect nonverbal behavior. Darwin (1872, Chapter XIV) put it quite clearly when he indicated that most expressions of emotion are inherited. Those few which are voluntary have such objectives as escaping from danger, relieving distress, or gratifying desires. Emotional expression is a means of communication. The unlearned screaming of the child becomes conditioned: it is first practiced and then brought under control when the child learns that screaming brings relief.

What happens when we have feelings? The mechanism of emotional experience and expression is quite complicated. The emotions often represent a disturbance in normal physiological functioning (homeostasis or the steady state) since the body reacts as though survival is at stake or stress has to be coped with. Ordinarily, we need approximately level quantities of oxygen, nutrition, and water in order to maintain a constant bodily temperature, provide energy and so forth. Under certain conditions our energy requirements are changed, as for example in the famous "fight or flight" reaction (William James, 1907, p. 375). In order to supply our muscles with sufficient energy, the heart pounds, blood pressure goes up, the diameter of arteries and capillaries becomes greater in the muscles (permitting blood flow) and less in the gut (temporarily stopping digestion). This change in the pattern of physiological functioning is part of what we call feelings.

Sometimes we react as though we are in a constant fight when none exists. A chronic, inflexible physiological and emotional reactivity is called *psychosomatic*. It is as though we are in a constant state of tension which we do not eliminate through taking action. A typical symptom is hypertension (Lachman, 1972, p. 81). The physiology of feelings is extraordinarily complex. Therefore, not everything we experience is a realistic result of prior and current events.

## FUNCTIONS OF FEELINGS

*Feelings Give Information.* A feeling can be information increasing self-awareness. Probably feelings have evolved from the fear, anger, hunger, sexual desire, and satiation which our cavemen ancestors required for survival. Using the same bodily sensations, we have to size up what is happening to us in the context of modern society. We give labels to the changes inside our body and associate them with particular meanings. Generally speaking, psychophysiologists have not been able to relate specific bodily patterns to particular emotions. This is unimportant for our purpose so long as you understand that a feeling is associated with a meaning we attribute to events. We take action on the basis of these meanings, for example, "I am depressed so I know I have lost something important," or "I am humiliated, so somebody is trying to degrade me." However, we have already seen (Chapter 8) that it is easy for our brain to assign misleading or hidden meanings to our feelings; so it is useful to check them out.

Perhaps you decide against trying out for a particular job, calling up for a date, contacting a new friend, starting a new project, and so on, because you feel anxious. Sometimes we make self-destructive decisions because our feelings tell us that danger or rejection lies ahead, when this is not the case. On the other hand, sensitivity to our feelings can tell us that there will be stormy weather. We learn to see the signs of anger, rejection, or perhaps acceptance and love in those around us. You must decide whether your track record is a good one. Have your feelings given you information or misinformation?

*History X–1*: Decisions based upon inappropriate feelings: A young man came in and announced that he had been laid off from his job at the direction of the union. His habit of taking excessive absences (even though unpaid) had caused him to have his vacation time eliminated. He made a violent objection and they had responded punitively.

During this session, we had been scheduled to work with

hypnosis on the problem of his inability to get close to a woman. On the one hand, he had pursued a girl who in many ways made it clear that his demands were excessive and that she didn't want a permanent relationship. On the other, when a woman came close to him, for example, putting her arms around him, he would react with anxiety. On one occasion he literally threw a girl out of bed. I started to relax him, and he indicated that he was becoming panicky. He wanted to talk about an experience he had the previous day. His dentist had used nitrous oxide; and suddenly he became white, saw a kaleidoscope of colors, and felt that he had no room to breathe. His heart had pounded rapidly. I asked him to associate to the idea of being restrained. He said that as a teenager, "I wanted to get away, if my grandmother [to whom he felt close] wasn't there I would have taken off.... I just felt as if something was grabbing me right here in this chair. . . . I called my grandmother yesterday and found out that she had a stroke. . . . This chick I was with came behind me and put her arms around me; it felt like tugging. I broke away almost violently. [This is reminiscent of his abrupt threats to leave his therapy group when something happens that he doesn't like.] I see a double image, a spinal tap when I was in military service and as a child . . . thousands of hands. I want to get up in the worst way but I can't. I want to scream and sleep but I can't. I saw myself as an adult, then a child; thousands of hands hold me down. Fear. Frightened. I can see my mother. I don't know if she's there or not. I have a 106-degree fever. My doctor and ice cream. Cold, it's wintertime. Snow, just cold, being carried home, wrapped up in thousands of blankets. More blankets than I was big. An infant, my mother just walking with me, and endless walk, in the direction of home. Like a treadmill, just staying in the same place. I think I was sleeping. I'm blank. I see me upstairs in my crib just piled under thousands of blankets. I had spinal taps as an adult. I was slapped, belted because I was jumping all over the place. (I suggested that he felt restrained by the anesthetic masks and tubing at the dentist yesterday.) I almost felt relieved. I used to have terrible temperatures. People thought I should have been dead. I probably had a spinal tap. My headache has increased." (I suggested that as a child he had a spinal tap to aid in study of his repeated high temperatures.)

When he asked my opinion I replied "I hope that you can accept a woman's putting her arms around you as a friendly gesture."

This patient's case illustrates the principle of how early experiences can have a pervading effect upon the rest of our lives. Apparently, as a young child he had had fevers of unknown origin, and his physician may have given him a lumbar puncture. We can surmise that he was frightened, that he had to be restrained by several people ("thousands of hands holding me down"), and that subsequent experiences of being held are reacted to as though they were the experience of being a tiny child overwhelmed by many people while he was sick. In this man's case, it is likely that it affected him in at least three areas:

1. *Intimate experiences*: He avoids becoming close to women, and unexpectedly, following sex, he pushes them away. He is not so disturbed that he lets it interfere with the sex act itself!

2. *Employment*: He has an unsteady attendance record on his job, offering unacceptable excuses for absence.

3. *Groups*: When he does not like what is happening in a session, he reacts abruptly, as though overcoming restraints by saying: "I'm quitting."

We can see that this man could not trust his feelings. The unconscious basis for many of our decisions lies in feelings which are uncomfortable, unhappy, and which absolutely, totally mislead us. This is one of the greatest hazards of the cult of the here-and-now which has recently sprung up. Sometimes, without the opportunity to explore in depth why we have feelings which cause us to make wrong decisions, we cannot function appropriately in the present.

*Feelings have social effects*. When we show our feelings directly or indirectly we communicate to those who are in our lives. The aggressive supervisor creates one kind of motivation, and the friendly supervisor another. A father's face will encourage his children to ask for assistance with their homework or send them on their way frustrated and feeling inadequate. A man's angry or frightened look will reduce the likelihood of a woman accepting his invitation to dance. Conversely, a seemingly detached or unfriendly appearance by the same lady will discourage male interest.

Emotions and behavior occur together, as in the lover or the fighter. The person talking to himself is experiencing unconscious images which have become vivid. The person smashing her hand through a pane of glass (see History X–3) or through a wall, has decided to express her frustration against an object, rather than towards the person directly. Emotional behavior goes on even when we hold back showing our feelings. The person who gnashes his teeth at night, or works his jaw muscles, or feels tense, is in conflict between doing something and doing nothing.

The following vignette shows how emotional meaning, subjective feeling, and physiological reaction on the part of a mother were communicated to her daughter.

*History X–2*: "When I am relaxed, my daughter is relaxed. There are fewer toilet accidents. But when my husband and I have a fight, time just crawls so slowly. When I'm lonely, waiting for my husband to come, I am unhappy and frightened. Waiting becomes physical. I feel everything about my whole body. Everything slows down. My fingers tingle, every minute takes so long. I can't feel each point in my arm. It's almost painful, the feelings."

*Feelings Affect Action.* Feelings are an important part of our motivation. They supply much of the energy which keeps us working consistently toward some goal in the future. Anger, love, anxiety, and all the rest can help to sustain our actions even when there is no immediate consequence. Feelings also serve to terminate action and tell us when to quit. Depression, anxiety, fear, resentment, and fatigue are all signals that we expect something bad to happen or that our body is exhausted. Sometimes we stop progress toward our goals because of constant warring images or feelings inside our own personality. Feelings can also keep us going toward an impossible dream or discourage us and make us cease progress.

*History X–3*: This young, attractive, intelligent, married woman couldn't make decisions. To those who knew her, she seemed to be enjoying a great life: prosperity, a cheerful husband, children, no apparent problems. Actually, her mother's manipulations of her feelings and her husband's refusal to accept them affected her mood to the point where she alternated between indecisiveness, apparent calm, and attacks of hysterical anger in which she put her hands through glass and threatened suicide. Deeper inquiry revealed that she felt her life was meaningless, and she did not know *which decisions* would lead her to greater fulfillment.

She commented that their therapy group was being hard on her husband for being emotionally shallow, giddy, and ignoring other people's feelings. Upon inquiry, she admitted that her own emotions were involved. "He was affecting me more than I was telling you. At one time I had to put my hand through a window. He wasn't merely affecting me mildly. In order to deal with him I had to become numb also, in order not to go to the extreme of letting him bother me. (Then her feelings would build up.) It's complicated with my own personality and the temper that I've always had. It's admitting to myself that my husband had a part instead of just saying it's my doing. I used to think that my father was henpecked. He had two jobs and would give his paychecks to my mother. But he would do exactly what he wanted. My mother would say, 'Come home early, we have to go out.' He would come home when he wanted. Rather than get what I want, I'm happier giving him (her husband) what he wants. If I am strong enough and nagging enough it will get done, but I don't know which gives me more pleasure, getting angry or pleasing him by ignoring it. I could bother him until he does it but it makes him happy to see me lax. Even with my parents I used to do what they wanted in order not to make them unhappy. After I nagged my mother so that I got her OK to do something, and she said, 'Go,' I wouldn't go so as not to make her unhappy.

I'm never sure of myself when somebody else expresses an opinion strongly. My parents used to point out all things that could go wrong so that I wouldn't experience disappointment."

She was told that a "klutz" like her ought not to try out for the cheerleading squad; that somebody else would win the beauty contest; and so on. If she did make a decision, she was told that she could have done better. Her ability to react decisively, normally, without hesitation, was sapped by early frustrations. Once, when she was five, her mother would not accept her anger about something and she became so frustrated that she pulled her scarf around her neck. One grandmother would engage in an elaborate game to get her to admit she liked her more than the other grandmother. Although her mother was efficient around the house, she had no outside interests. Therefore, even a model of making decisions involving nondomestic affairs was lacking. Her husband was dedicated to the ideal that only a light-hearted attitude is a suitable one for life, so that she could not get through to him with serious feelings. When she talked about something important, he responded with jokes and carefree humor. A variety of group therapeutic approaches and experiences enabled him eventually to become somewhat more able to relate appropriately to his wife.

How does this woman react to even the basic decisions of caring for a home? First, we observe that she lives in a private house whereas she was raised in an apartment. Then, we see that only part of her home is furnished, after many years of living there. Finally, we conclude that those parts of her home which do not correspond to anything her parents have had experience with are complete, for example, the swimming pool. Those parts about which her parents can make comments on price and quality are incomplete. Only in decisions which are free from feelings about her parents does she come to a conclusion.

We can observe in this instance how the complexity of this woman's emotional life affected not only her mood, but also her ability to function. When she said that in some ways she was getting to be more self-assertive, I asked her how her husband is taking the "new you." She replied, "I don't know, but I like me much better."

*Feelings Control Our Attention.* Our feelings cause us to select people, events, and other details of the world upon which to focus our attention. They also distract us from other important events which may vitally affect us (Holmes, 1974). These facts are important in shaping our decisions. We look for something out there which will suit our purposes or meet our needs. We may also ignore events which make us anxious. The unmarried person, through feelings of loneliness, sexual desire, or wish to marry, will first decide to go to a social affair. Then the feelings which he habitually carries with him will intermingle with those new ones which are stirred up by the people he sees there, the nature of the event, and the social hall. These feelings will combine with images from the far and recent past and lead to making contact with some people and staying away from others. This is a form of decision making in which our feelings direct us on a certain course and away from other sources.

## UNCONSCIOUS FEELINGS

Even though feelings seem to play a clear-cut role in our lives, their effect is more complex than we suspect. Vital personal decisions are often made by unconscious feelings we don't even know exist (for example, History IX–1). An unconscious feeling is an experience that we would be aware of if certain *defense mechanisms* did not keep it from our consciousness. Generally, we defend against experiencing such feelings to avoid anxiety, because we believe our actions would lead to punishment or we would feel humiliated (low self-esteem).

Freud stated (1915a, 1915b, 1915c) that drives or emotions are represented by feelings (affects) and by ideas (images). Unconscious feelings may undergo changes with time, with harmful effects upon how we make decisions. They can become changed into their opposites, provoke additional anxiety, fuse with other feelings, or become displaced to the wrong person. Jung pointed out (1943; Hillman, 1970; Hall & Lindzey, 1970, pp. 81–82) that one idea can organize many different images, attitudes, and feelings into "a complex." The person with a "mother complex" relates to many different areas as though his feelings about his mother were the most important factor in his life. Let us look at some more examples of how unconscious feelings affect our emotional life and consequently our decisions.

## REPRESSION

Repression means that certain feelings, ideas, or meanings are kept from conscious awareness because they are too painful to experience, or because they represent activities which would lead to punishment.

*History X–4*: A man does not wish to admit that he feels emotionally deprived. It is more palatable for him to think of himself as a "giver." Consequently, he marries a woman who is not affectionate or warm. He continuously feeds her emotional needs, because he is unaware of his own, at least for a while.

## REACTION FORMATION

Another way of coping with feelings that would be troublesome to experience is to change them into the opposite, and then to act as though the transformed feelings are the genuine expression of our emotions.

*History X–5*: A woman is brought up to believe that it is bad to show hostility. She feels accepted by her parents and their neighbors only when she is friendly. In order to believe that she is really a good person, she involves herself with charity work while neglecting her family. Actually, her colleagues experience her as dominating, manipulative, and unpleasant when frustrated.

## AVOIDING ANXIETY

Many people avoid situations which are enjoyed by others in order to avoid feeling anxious or nervous. Through association, they are conditioned to be uncomfortable when expressing various normal emotions.

*History X–6*: A girl has been taught that sex before marriage is dirty and evil. To avoid temptation, she attends a women's college. She further decides to devote all her time to her studies. This has the further effect of keeping her from learning more realistic values, since she avoids new situations and people with attitudes different from hers.

## DISPLACEMENT

When we are afraid to express anger directly, we frequently find an innocent victim against whom to express our feelings. Such a person may superficially resemble the original source of our rage (Parker, 1972b).

*History X–7*: A man is married to a woman who harasses him unmercifully. Since he is emotionally dependent upon her, he dares not risk a confrontation. He fears that either she will abuse him further or she will leave him. He decides to release his feelings by pushing around a helpless youth who is entrusted to his care.

## FUSION

Feelings are frequently not expressed in a pure fashion. Different emotions can be combined without our being aware that this is happening, and we respond to what is essentially a new emotion. Sex and anger are frequently combined. Perhaps this is done easily because areas of the brain which are part of the neurological control mechanism (hypothalamus and amygdala) of these two emotions are close together (Adey, Lindsley, & Olds, 1974; Koizumi & Brooks, 1974).

*History X–8*: A man had a series of frustrating experiences with females, beginning with his mother and extending through early adolescent dating. He married a woman whose feelings of hostility to men required her to find a husband with a low boiling point, giving her an excuse to express her own rage. This couple solve their arguments with a combination of sex and violence. They decide that it is better to fight with each other than to present a model of discussion for solving grievances to their children.

## EMOTIONAL REACTIONS CREATING PSYCHOSOMATIC SYMPTOMS

It is possible, when under stress, to develop bodily reactions rather than appropriate experience of the feelings involved. This usually derives from childhood conditioning, for example, when a child is permitted to exaggerate illness in order to avoid school. When stress reduces our defenses, the preprogrammed bodily reactions which we call psychosomatic illness (Reiser, 1975, p. 496) are released. See also, Chapter 4 above.

*History X–9*: A woman awoke looking forward to having a good day. At that point she thought that she turned on a migraine headache. As she described her reactions: "I am the victim of the headache. I can't make it go away. I become destructive of myself. When my husband becomes caught in one of his moods, in contrast, he turns it outward. He gets angry with people. He cuts off all communication. You can't communicate with him." By implication, she is a problem to herself while he is a problem to those around him.

## DEPRESSION AND DECISIONS

Our discussion thus far has emphasized decisions which are bound to fail because the person was out of touch with his real feelings. However, there is a feeling which frequently brings all decision making to a halt. Depression (called in its extreme form *melancholia*) is one of the most painful experiences. Frequently it involves feelings of valuelessness, hopelessness, sadness, loss of self-esteem and loved ones, and misery; and it may include various medical complaints (Beck, 1973). Its origins may be both a reaction to real situations (exogenous depression) or obscure changes in the chemistry of the body, particularly the brain (endogenous depression). Both action and thinking are frequently slowed down, so that life seems to come to a halt. One kind of depression is related to loss of interest in life, whereas other types seem associated with anxiety and hostility (D. G. Klein, 1974).

We can say in conclusion that feelings are your way of signaling to yourself *how you appraise a situation* (Arnold, 1970). It is a kind of report from the front. Your feelings tell you whether you are succeeding in reaching your goals, or are meeting opposition, or are in a relationship which you believe is headed for trouble. Your feelings serve the complex function of giving you information. If they have been useful in guiding you, then you can "trust your feelings." If there are frequently mismatches between your feelings and an objective estimate of the people you deal with, your degree of success in handling important projects, your relationships, and so forth, then you must evaluate why you get wrong information. Perhaps reconsideration of the conclusions that you derive from your feelings are in order. Perhaps you may require psychotherapy to help you to more accurately deal with situations (Parker, 1973, Chapter 20).

In the next chapter we shall examine our values, which are one of the chief determinants of our feelings and moods. Values strongly influence whether we get the rewards in life which elevate our spirits, or whether we lead a life of frustration and despair.

# 11
# Values and
# Your Decisions

Values are an energizing force in a variety of vital human experiences. They guide our actions, influence our pleasure, create bonds or enmity between people, and influence social structure. In many ways they are like a magnetic field all around us: we are drawn in some directions, and repelled from others, by the nature of our own personal magnetism—positive attitudes toward some values and negative attitudes toward others.

Understanding your personal values is one of the most important goals in any effort to obtain emotional fulfillment through improved decision making.

I define a value as a particular kind of emotional reaction. Values are a readiness to experience pleasure or distaste for certain kinds of relationships, events, situations, feelings, and so forth. Therefore, values determine what we find rewarding or punishing in life. As a consequence, they guide us toward certain activities for the pleasures they promise, and away from others since we anticipate displeasure or actual punishment. In a sense values determine what is worth working for and what we seek to avoid.

The subjective quality of most values can be illustrated by the following news story from the *New York Times* (18 November 1974) :

WOMEN'S LIBERATION ABUSIVE, PRELATE SAYS

"Don't tie yourself to abusive movements like women's liberation; they destroy and distort woman's nature," the primate of the Greek Orthodox Church in North and South America told a reporter here.

"Women are more important to the church at home than on the altar," Archbishop Iakovos said at an informal news conference here yesterday.

"At home a woman is a true priestess," he said. "I see women on a much higher level."

The discrepancy between the attitude of this reverend gentleman and other prominent people concerning burning issues in today's social world is marked. For some people faith is a supreme value in its own right, going far beyond self-centered needs. Others experience religious devotion as "serving the motives of personal comfort, security, or social status" (Allport, 1966).

Freud (1923, pp. 44–50) felt that our sense of values (superego, ego ideal) evolved from many diverse sources. In part, our values as determined by our conscience, or superego, form as we resolve our sexual feelings and jealousy toward our parents. To some extent we please our father by becoming like him (positive values) and partially we forbid ourselves certain prerogatives which are his alone (negative values). This is the origin of the sense of guilt, that is, controlling our impulses in order to please father. Our sense of values, or "higher nature," is the adult representation of our relationship to our parents when we were little children. This "ego ideal" not only serves as the source of religious belief, but also sets up standards for our behavior. The discrepancy between our ideals and our "ego," or actual activities, can be the source of self-criticism or even self-hatred, which can ruin our good spirits for an indefinite number of years (see Parker, *Emotional Common Sense*, 1973, Chapter 9: "Alleviating Guilt, Anxiety and Worthlessness"). Thus, the guidelines for our adult life evolve (in part) from the child's struggle for security within the family.

When we reach adolescence, feelings of hostility and sexuality return in a powerful way. At that time, in addition to trying out a more secure and extensive self-image, we decide whether the parental values are worthwhile or if we must liberate ourselves from them (Mahl, 1969, p. 287). Curiously, despite the well-known adolescent rebellion, later in life our values seem to converge toward those of our parents (Buhler, Keith-Spiegel & Thomas, 1973).

Values are frequently derived from the characteristic attitudes of particular groups to which we belong (Wolman, 1965). We shall explore in detail (Chapter 12: "Group Influences Upon Decisions") how group membership creates values or generates conflict when our attitudes differ from those of the rest of the members.

How do values affect us in everyday affairs? Values alert us to particular events and stimuli in our world, as well as enable us to remember details which are consistent with them (Goldenson, 1970, p. 62). Thus, they reinforce what we already believe. In addition, they are generalized attitudes (predispositions to react in particular ways), in certain areas which are important to us (Lott, 1973). Furthermore, our values are sometimes determined by our needs, and we can make wrong choices in important matters if we misperceive what we really need (Wolman, 1965). People can distort their perceptions of definite objects, under the pressure of their values, even when these objects are so distinct that they can be measured objectively (Avant & Helson, 1973). You can see why effective decision making requires you to clearly understand your values and evaluate their relatedness to today's world.

Our identification with our values also contributes to our sense of self-esteem. We are Americans, or whatever kind of partisanship we were taught to believe in. In this way our values become part of our sense of self, and we experience life in some coherent way (Lott, 1973). Without definite values, we could not function in an integrated way. When our values are in conflict with each other, or with the environmental niche in which we find ourselves, our ability to have a constructive life is severely hampered.

It might be said that values actually define a culture. Societies generally have been more able to agree on negative values than on what is actually valued—they are more competent in outlawing certain kinds of behaviors than in rewarding particular kinds of actions (Nolan, 1974).

It has been pointed out that neurosis is a crisis in personal values (Yankelovich & Barrett, 1970). Sometimes circumstances make us doubt our own values, because qualities which we thought were important did not serve us well. Or we have been degraded by people whose opinion we found important (perhaps too important!). A frequent source of conflict is between the pressures placed upon us by our parents, to follow their values, and new attitudes created by different experiences, teachers, companions, and so forth. One of my patients has nightmares after group therapy. In the group she becomes aware of the conflict between her mother's pressure upon her to be a religious observer—and to marry—and the group's pressure in the direction of autonomy.

What are the advantages of understanding our values? Life's meaning becomes a lot clearer when we perceive what is rewarding to us and what is punishing. Discriminating between the events, people, and activities which are important and those which are trivial will leave time and spirit for what really turns you on. By understanding what you really care about, you will start to avoid people and situations which cause you pain and waste your time. As a consequence, there will be a significant improvement in your decision making.

You must remember, however, that people may feel vastly different about the same matter. What is valuable or rewarding to you may be trivial or repugnant to somebody else. Do not make the common mistake of believing that everybody shares the same values.

## Some Frequently Experienced Values

The following list of values is based upon a variety of sources, including career counseling and the practice of psychotherapy, as well as formal studies of human values by other authors. Among the objectives for studying it include: (1) becoming aware whether your goals and values are pulling you in the same direction; (2) clarifying your values, and therefore your motives in various activities; (3) determining the extent to which your values are similar or different to those of significant people in your life, namely, your mate, children, persons around you on the job, and so forth.

## SCALES OF VALUES

### Part I

TEMPERAMENT: Nonverbal emotional and energetic qualities

1. *Security vs. Excitement*: Some people value security above all. They make decisions and select activities according to whether reduction of nervousness or high levels of stimulation are important. Security can be a determining condition for some; for others the quality of stimulation and thrill is supreme.

2. *Stability vs. Variety*: For some people, it is possible to feel comfortable only in familiar surroundings. Others have considerable restlessness, and they experience a deep urge for change that affects their adjustment to all circumstances. One can contrast those who follow the traditional values of their family and community with others who want to change the established order, each feeling that their welfare and that of the community will be improved.

3. *Goal-directedness vs. Pleasure/Play*: For some people, life is meant for pleasure, play, and fun. For others, what we do ought to be directed toward long-range goals; otherwise we fritter our lives away and can be buffeted by unpredictable circumstances. Play is the quality which is most characteristic of children, and some people refuse to accept the poet's teaching: "Life is earnest, life is real." They want to laugh, to enjoy, and to ignore difficulties.

PHILOSOPHICAL VALUES: The significance attributed to life

4. *Grandeur vs. Simplicity*: Some people are exalted by observing or participating in events which are lofty, elevated, or

impressive. A deep sense of purpose is inspired by a high mountain, a Bruckner symphony, a solemn religious ceremony, or parades with flags and music. Alternatively, some people crave unadorned, generally more natural, plain, unpretentious surroundings to achieve their sense of fulfillment. For them, a day in the country, simple furnishings and clothing, chamber music, and other unpretentious stimulation are preferable.

5. *Spiritualism vs. Empiricism*: Many people feel that the most important meaning there is to life are qualities which are nonmaterial or mystical, and which go beyond the ordinary laws of science and experience. To them, intuition, meditation, altered states of consciousness, and other unusual means of understanding life teach certain values which are unavailable through usual types of experiences. To the empiricist, experience is the only source of knowledge. Hard facts, scientifically determined principles, personal contact, and verification are the determining factors by which decisions and judgments are made.

6. *Religion vs. Naturalism*: The religious, perhaps orthodox, person believes that there is a deity whose intent can be known through an organized church, or through some other type of revelation. As a consequence, the way we order our life ought to be determined by the values of faith and/or doctrine. Alternatively, nature is the only determinant of the quality of our life. What happens to us is the reflection of the unfolding of various levels of reality, according to the laws of physics, chemistry, biology, sociology, psychology, etc.

## Part II

PRODUCTIVITY: The urge to make something of value, either for our own material well-being or for that of society

7. *Economic*: Many people make decisions according to how much money they will receive, the benefits of spending it, and being with others who have lots of it. Money implies status and security. The materialist feels that the amount

of money one earns, possesses, or inherits is a measure of one's real value.

8. *Achievement/Career*: Professional accomplishment can be the chief value. It is possible to sacrifice family, friends, status, and advancement for it. This also implies pleasure in the results of one's professional activities. Fulfillment, maturity, and being worthwhile are represented by one's profession or occupation.

9. *Social Utility/Pragmatism*: This person insists that his employment, hobbies, and other activities must have some kind of importance to himself or the world. His/her endeavors ought not to be meaningless or without apparent consequence. What one does must have value. This is different from helping particular, known individuals, with whom one has a personal relationship.

HUMAN RELATIONS: The particular qualities which influence our relationships with other people

10. *Altruism*: This person believes that it is important to sacrifice one's personal welfare to do things for others. This may be expressed through one's profession, being a member of a religious community, charitable work, and so on. One ought to extend oneself beyond one's personal welfare in order to feel worthwhile.

11. *Authority*: This is the belief that our welfare depends upon the presence of a leader or organization which can provide guidance and direction. Leadership belongs to the elite. Some types of individuals cannot be entrusted with positions of responsibility. Furthermore, it is better for us to submit our individual needs to the general welfare of the community. Identification with particular parties or causes is a central factor in the lives of many people.

12. *Family*: To some people, the unity and well-being of their family, including cousins, in-laws, etc., is a driving and unifying force. All decisions, including marriage, job, location of home, etc., are made in accordance with the nearness and values of one's family.

13. *Personal Power*: It is important to have influence, to tell people what to do, and to determine the course of events. Power may be achieved without fame; therefore it is not important that the person pulling the strings be known to those who are affected, provided that he/she knows of his own importance.

14. *Personal Relationships*: Life is meaningless without close, intense, satisfying personal relationships. Relating to individuals or groups is the most stirring experience, so that certain careers, clubs, organizations, friends, etc., are the chosen activities. One feels most alive through social contact with other people, and it may not make much difference precisely who they are or what you are doing together.

15. *Prestige/Recognition*: Recognition, fame, acclaim, and honor represent a potent value for many. Recognition may be achieved as a scientist, politician, humanitarian, military leader, social welfare worker, artist, and so forth. A feeling of being well-known is necessary to one's image as a worthwhile person.

AUTONOMY: The enjoyment of one's own personality, uniqueness, and the capacity to function independently when required by circumstances

16. *Creativity*: The urge to bring something new into the world is an expression of one's individuality. It is a belief that one can create a work of art, a new product, a new kind of relationship, etc., in a way which has not been done before, and which can be appreciated for its advantages, newness, and uniqueness. Creativity implies belief in the new, dissatisfaction with the way things have been done, and the feeling that you are the motive force to bring about change.

17. *Culture/Aesthetics*: Many persons are devoted to the various arts, such as painting, music, photography, etc. Shared interests in cultural matters can make a couple's life more intimate. The person who has cultural and aesthetic values often feels that he/she is in contact with universal experiences which are timeless. Feelings stirred by works of art can be shared with others, regardless of cultural differences.

There is esteem for ideas and creations that have survived for generations.

18. *Learning*: Throughout history there have been men and women whose chief love has been knowledge and philosophy. They are interested in eternal values and in achieving a deeper understanding of the complex world in which we live. In addition, they value knowledge for its own sake. To own books or to belong to the community of scholars is a deep-felt value.

## WORKING OUT THE PATTERN OF ONE'S VALUES

### SCALE OF VALUES

Values may be defined as attitudes toward life which guide our actions. We are attracted or repelled by certain events, circumstances, activities, feelings, and so on. As a consequence, goals which are attractive to some people are repugnant or undesirable to others. People differ considerably in their values. Self-understanding in this area is extremely important in making prudent decisions with regard to career, personal relationships, handling money, and so on.

### Part I

INSTRUCTIONS: Only one value in each pair listed below is to receive a score. Among the three pairs of Temperamental Values, select the one value (in either the right or left column) that you experience as most attractive or important. Place a *1* in the space next to it. For the opposite value, place a — next to it. Now choose the next most attractive or important value (on either the left or the right) and place a *2* next to it. Place a — next to its opposite value. Then rank the third most attractive value as *3* and place a — in the remaining space. *Be sure you mark only one rank for each pair of values.*

*Note*: If both values in the same pair seem equally attractive, place a *C* (for conflict) between them. Try to keep *C*'s to a minimum.

### Temperamental Values
#### (C)

Pair 1:  Security                  _____  _____  Excitment        _____
Pair 2:  Stability                 _____  _____  Variety          _____
Pair 3:  Goal-Directedness  _____  _____  Pleasure/Play_____

Now follow the same procedure in ranking the Philosophical Values. Rank one value of each pair *1, 2,* and *3,* and place a — next to the opposite value.

### Philosophical Values
#### (C)

Pair 4:  Grandeur        _____  _____  Simplicity     _____
Pair 5:  Spiritualism    _____  _____  Empiricism    _____
Pair 6:  Religion         _____  _____  Naturalism    _____

### Part II

INSTRUCTIONS: Study the twelve values listed below, then rank them in order of their importance or attractiveness to you. First, mark the value most attractive to you as *1.* Then select the value that is least attractive—or most repugnant—to you and mark it *12.* Now select the second most attractive value and mark it *2.* Choose the second most unattractive value and mark it *11.* Continue in this way until all values have been ranked in order of their attractiveness to you. *Be sure the ratings reflect the way you feel now, not the way you would like to feel.*

*Note:* If certain values both attract and repell you, mark them *C* for conflict. Do not confuse relatively mild feelings of favor or dislike as conflict. In such cases, score these values slightly above or below the middle.

Productivity:        Economic                    _____
                           Achievement/Career   _____
                           Social Utility              _____
                           Altruism

| Human Relations: | Personal Relationships | _____ |
| | Family | _____ |
| | Prestige/Recognition | _____ |
| | Personal Power | _____ |
| Autonomy: | Authority | _____ |
| | Creativity | _____ |
| | Culture | _____ |
| | Learning | _____ |

After filling out Part II, try to form constellations or groups of values that you ranked relatively high or low. You may find that the way you score your values is significantly different from what you have been telling yourself. Or perhaps it will confirm that your self-image has been accurate.

## What Is It That You Really Want?

Now that you have determined the pattern of your values, take the time to consider your goals. Remember that a goal is some situation in the future which you think will be emotionally fulfilling. Generally, to achieve this might require the investment of considerable time, spirit, and perhaps money.

### MY PERSONAL GOALS

1.
2.
3.
4.

## Evaluating Your Goals

1. Are they my goals for me, or are they my parents' goals for me?

2. Can I achieve them? Do I have the intellectual, temperamental, and monetary resources to reach these goals?

3. How long will it take to get there, and do I care to invest the necessary time?

4. How old will I be when I have achieved these goals and how much time will I have to enjoy them?

5. Is there a match between my values and my goals? Are my values consistent with each other?

6. Can I achieve my goals through activities which I enjoy?

7. Am I willing to make the sacrifices necessary to reach these goals?

8. Will my negative values cause me grief or excessive struggle in achieving my goals?

9. Are my standards for success so high that the likelihood of success is minimal or the cost too great?

Let's consider how one individual is influenced by his values.

*History XI–1:* This previously married man entered psychotherapy because of a turbulent experience with his girlfriend. One cause of his divorce had been his inability to understand that his wife's needs and values were incompatible with his own. As a youth he thought that "everybody was the same, that we all have the same thoughts and attitudes."

He is ashamed of his occupation (blue collar) and the people in it with whom he must associate. He views his father as illiterate and says he wants to be couth, educated, and to go to the other side of the tracks. When he was asked to state his goals, he responded:

1. "I'd like to get myself together. I don't eat regularly. I'll starve for days and then I'll go on a binge. I'll spend a week drinking coffee, and then I'll get depressed and just eat. I cash my check, and just put the money in a jar. No savings, no planning, just buying something on a whim."

2. "I'd like to experience more. There are a million things I'd like to do. A lot of things I've missed out on, though there may be some things I can never reclaim. Going backwards is a step forward for me at times. Going back to school, for example."

3. "I'd like to have a family. I've never had a cohesive family. My father was a gambler and my mother, a bingo player. I've never seen a family relationship work in any way. I think I might want kids."

Let's consider his comments about his values, which he was asked to rate from +3 (favorable) to −3 (unfavorable). (These categories are slightly different from those in the previous list, which I now use.)

*Variety*: (+3) "It means being willing to take a chance on experiencing anything new. I'd rather let somebody else suggest a restaurant" (see also *People*).

*People*: (+2) "I'm experiencing people in a different way than I've experienced them before. I'm open to suggestions. People are something new in my life. The people I've hung out with were just the same as I was. I thought everybody was the same. I never realized people could think differently." (His craving for variety thus has to do largely with his new-found awareness of the richness and subtlety of human relationships.)

*Learning*: (+2) (This might be in the same category as variety): "There's new things to learn about, to feel, experience. Somebody told me it was strange that I said, 'I hate that shit' when he offered me an opera ticket, since I had never gone. It was judging something before I gave it a chance. I would do the same thing with people. If they didn't coincide with my thoughts I thought they were screwed up."

*Excitement/Adventure*: (+2) "I used to race a car, to steal hub caps. I used to screw in the park. Now, I'm looking for more structured excitement."

*Religion*: (−2) "I think religion exploits people. I don't disagree with anyone's feelings about it, just for myself. Just a handout, give me a few dollars and I'll say a prayer or perform a certain religious service. I don't see enough love in religion."

*Career/Achievement*: (−3) "Thinking or intelligence is frowned upon as far as my job is concerned. Having an idea is going over someone's head. For someone to show their intelligence takes away from whoever is running the job. The bosses have total control. I can't change my career because I don't have the education, or socialize well, or fit into other areas. Possibly in a few years I can."

This man is beginning to experience new possibilities in life. Basically, he is fighting against conformity to the standards of the gang he grew up with. Unfortunately, he is too pessimistic to apply his desire for variety and learning to his career. However, he is going to college, although he cannot yet see an advantage from this. One might also wonder whether the goal of getting himself together and the values of variety, excitement, and adventure are compatible.

Now let's consider how the values of another individual affect her decisions.

*History XI–2*: A young professional woman has come out of a long relationship with a man, and is reexamining her attitudes toward herself, her career, and her social life. Her chief goals are "self-awareness and being the captain of my own ship, making my own decisions and being responsible for myself." I asked her about conflicts and stresses in her life.

"I am going through many changes; it is unbelievable. I feel that I am being so bitchy to other people. I am cutting people out of my life. I find myself intolerant of people and situations that previously I was very tolerant of. Before (when she previously took the Scale of Values), I was interested in play and excitement. I think that my feelings now are contrary to the values I had before—variety, excitement, and change. Goal-directedness was boring. Play, pleasure, and enjoyment were all that I wanted.

"Now, I want to structure my life. Security isn't in the sense of being in a safe, cocoon type of existence. I want to have security in that I am secure in my own feelings, knowing where I am going, self-security, certainty that I know what I want out of life and where I am going. There is a conflict between stability and variety because I happen to like travel, and experiencing different types of knowledge. When I think of variety, I think of traveling to different places. I like to try differing things, but I want stability in my life."

In the philosophical value area, she favored empiricism, simplicity, and naturalism, in that order.

"I have always been deistic, I get comfort in nature. I enjoy grandiose events, getting dressed up; but when it comes to a consistent way of being, I prefer a barbecue with nice people and that sort of thing. My whole existence has been through trial and error, and through my experience the hard way. My values and ideas come through difficult experience and a lot of my knowledge is through delayed feedback. It has taken me a long time to learn some things about myself."

In Part II, she rated personal relationships no. 1, but family no. 7.

"I am still a people-oriented type of person. I still feel that friendship and my relationships with people are very important. I no longer know what love is, but I know that people and personal relationships, and personal involvement, are important. My family was in favor of my marrying H., but I feel that I am no longer vulnerable to parents, sister, and brother. I feel that I don't have to do everything that I think they want me to do. Also, I feel that I can be firm, yet warm and mature with them. I see a lot of unhealthiness within my immediate family. I have to do things for myself—and that's it."

Another constellation was authority (no. 12), personal power (no. 10), and prestige/recognition (no. 8), all on the low side.

"I am so sick of this bureaucratic situation that I work in; and I see the authority so far removed from the task at hand. Many people in authority are not intelligent, have come up through the ranks by apple-polishing, by being 'yes-men.' In a mature setting there has to be some chain of command, but I just see a lot of discrepancies. They don't handle themselves with authority; on the contrary, they are wishy-washy. As far as personal power is concerned, I would like to be in a position of leadership within my own professional specialty, but I don't have a driving need to be in a forceful position of power. I don't feel that I have to be well-known to have recognition. I don't have to publish books or do research to do my job well."

Although she is in a public service profession, altruism was downgraded to no. 11, and social utility was no. 9. "When I was in college, I used to enjoy working with obviously needy, 'culturally deprived' people. I was brought up in a nationalistic family, raising funds for the homeland, and for many years I cared so much about helping others and doing something for them. Right now it's very unimportant to me. I am rebelling. My values are in contrast to what they were.

"I am angry at everything, and I just want to be left alone. I am angry and I am going to cry. I am angry at being gullible, angry at making excuses for people, accepting things. I am angry at being nice. I am very much in tune with my needs. I want to be alone. I don't want men in my life."

This young woman agreed with my interpretation that she had been feeding others emotionally for a long time, and that she wanted to work on her own needs.

This chapter really represents a keystone of the entire volume. Decisions which are unrelated to your values and goals are self-destructive. Decisions which are based upon trivial values or false goals are inefficient. Let there be a consistency between your real goals, your important values, and your daily decisions.

Now let us see how social factors can influence us and subtract from our autonomy.

# 12

# Group Influences
# Upon Decisions

Up to this point, we have emphasized—perhaps overemphasized—the influences within a person's mind which influence decisions. However, this is an incomplete approach since being a member of a group will influence the kinds of decisions you make and the number of alternatives you consider as solutions to a problem; and it can even lead to self-destructive decisions which you would not make if you were acting alone. Groups make certain kinds of decisions, and they influence how decision made by others for them are carried out. It should also be recognized that groups can have extremely hazardous emotional consequences—depending upon the leadership, the characteristics of the group, and the vulnerability of individuals (Parker, 1976).

Consider what is known as a "social trap" (Platt, 1973). In colonial days the Commons, or public grasslands, were thrown open for any co-owner to permit his animals to graze. Anybody could have predicted that as the number of cows increased the grass would grow scarcer and finally the entire area would be overgrazed and thus destroyed for use. The "social trap" is that when one person does it, the entire community is tempted to do it. The social effect upon individual decisions is to destroy the common good, and thus the resources of individuals.

The most important characteristic of decisions made in groups is their emotional quality. Group decisions are frequently presented as objective and goal oriented. Actually, neurotic, unconscious trends are activated by the presence of several other people. When we are in a group, the Unconscious rules at least as frequently as in most other areas of life.

## GROUP ROLES

After a group has been in existence for a while, the members develop interlocking roles which fill each other's needs. Roles are predictable ways of relating to each other, and to the extent that each member is mutually useful it adds to the group's cohesiveness (Pedersen & Shears, 1973).

A paradox of groups is the interrelatedness of cohesion (or unity) and individual roles (or individuality). Group cohesion refers to the group's ability to function together to fulfill its needs and any assigned tasks. A role is a predictable, socially governed way in which people relate to each other. After a period of interaction in a group, the members set up roles which are locked into each other's expectations. This seems to have the function of satisfying both their own needs and those of the other members. Thus, the development of individuality forms an "interlocking" network which contributes to group cohesion (Pedersen & Shears, 1973).

What roles do people develop as they enter into groups? They are partially determined by preset *rules*, for example, chairman and participants. However, the most important determinant of the actual style of a person's participation is unfinished business from childhood, and the way of relating to others we developed while growing up. Group functioning is regressive because many issues formerly important in our lives become prominent though they are irrelevant to the real issues.

There is a difference between a group's *open agenda* (stated purpose) and *hidden agenda* (private reasons for participation). The open agenda is to accomplish a particular task, like how to get to the ball game, the design of a new torpedo, or discipline in the halls. More about that later. The hidden agenda is the consequence of the emotional factors in the group.

One of the most important qualities of group participation is the need to be *socially desirable* (acceptance, or the need to be liked). Furthermore, since all of us had problems of self-assertion within the family, the group becomes a continuation of a power struggle for which we may be well or ill equipped. In addition, we project our unconscious images on other people in the group, and then expect them to function according to our private script (*transference*).

Due to all of these *regressive* qualities, after a group has been functioning together for a while it begins to have the characteristics of a family. You can begin to assign family roles to the different members: mother, father, the boarder, the uncle, the visiting physician, or the ideal parent somebody never had. The unfinished business of everybody's personal life takes over. (You see, you never really leave home!)

If groups have the qualities of families, then some of the ways of describing the latter are relevant. I remember taking part in the staff meetings of a particular clinic which reminded me of nothing so much as a noisy and disorganized family dinner. Rivalry (staff), disobedient children (trainees), inadequate father (chief), overly protective mother (coordinator of training), landlord (head of clinic), and all the rest. Since my own hidden agenda is to avoid wasting time—not because of virtue but learned years before through the desperation of inefficiency—I probably played the role of efficiency expert or family shrink.

## STYLES OF GROUPS

What are some group styles? These are derived from the usual qualities of the households which the group leaders experienced, that is, their means of coping with emotional pain and dissatisfaction (Parker, 1972, 1973).

1. *Expressive*: People are permitted to express their feelings, which are considered to be legitimate. Therefore, emotions may influence the course of events.

2. *Nice*: You don't say bad things because it isn't nice. "If you don't have something nice to say, say nothing." Just let yourself go down the tube.

3. *Abusive*: Any kind of rottenness goes. If you are not strong enough to stand up to the bully or to the coarsest person present, don't expect the leader to protect you. You must act like a madman or a thug. Anything else is to invite a shove.

4. *Emotionally absorbing* (depriving) : You can express any kinds of feelings you like to the leader. It won't do any good because it will go in one side of the head and out the other.

Whether the group is family, therapy, social, or employment, it will be useful to analyze its style. If you find yourself in a group which differs from the one that you are accustomed to, look out. You are in trouble. It may be worthwhile to learn alternative reactions so that you can have freedom of expression.

Every organization has its style and its tradition. When I worked for the New York State Department of Mental Hygiene, I experienced more local autonomy than with the U.S. Veterans Administration. Although Albany (state capital) was closer than Washington, the local congressman's office was not. The Girl Scouts, U.S. Steel, and the supermarket all have their styles, traditions, and characteristic type of organization.

If you are going to use groups for your own purposes, to implement your needs, you will have to learn how they function and how decisions are arrived at. You must learn to recognize what really goes on.

Within this squirming mass, people play one of their characteristic roles. If you are trying to influence the group in a particular direction, you can find individuals irritating or helpful depending upon their role and whether it suits your purposes. If you can recognize someone who hampers an outcome satisfactory to you, then you can begin to isolate this person. It takes some skill to separate the ordinary warm-up period, when everybody gets acquainted and ready to go to work, from sabotage by a non-goal-oriented individual. The latter can prevent decision making. The next step is to discover the hidden agenda or *what is really going on*. Examples of the hidden agenda are a boss's need to get more work out so he can obtain a promotion, the desire to embarrass somebody under the guise of an objective report, transferring anger to a father figure, and so on. Members differ in the very reasons why they are there. You may be there to work, the next guy to come out of the rain, or that girl across the room to flirt with the leader. Among the other personal characteristics which influence the functioning of groups are the members' intelligence, experience, education, mood, and quality of social relatedness.

### INFLUENCES ON GROUP PARTICIPATION

When people participate in groups they can be described in three basic dimensions (Bales, 1973) : *dominant/submissive, friendly/unfriendly,* and *work-acceptant/work-resistive.* In addition, everybody has a certain unique quality of style.

Somebody's place on the dominance dimension can be detected by whom he addresses his remarks to in a group. People low in the dominance hierarchy address their communications to those higher up; they want to increase their influence and acceptance. The dominant members of a group speak either to God or to the whole group. Those with positive feelings are likely to be calm and trusting. The negative person is anxious and suspicious, and is perceived as unfriendly, isolated, and tending to disagree. Another way of looking at the dimension of attitude toward work is that some people accept authority and others tend to reject it.

*Individual style* or *personal role* also determines what part individuals play in the decision-making function of a group. They reveal our basic needs and training, and the images we utilize to manipulate other people. A role may be defined (English & English, 1958) as "an individual's characteristic kind of contribution to a group . . . or the behavior that is characteristic and expected of the occupant of a defined position in the group" (for example, chairman) . Each role influences the quality of the group's mood and of the decisions and actions which ensue. You can think of the effects upon a group of "the bright young man," the "know-it-all," "I'm from Missouri," or "I'm stupid, don't bother me." Many of these roles are *transferences* from unresolved earlier experiences and conflicts.

Other factors also influence the kind of role people play in group processes. Sometimes they cooperate because the authority has the legitimate right to give orders. At other times we decide who has the most clout, and what punishment will occur if we do not perform well (Lichtman & Hunt, 1971). Roles have been divided into three types (Lifton, 1972, pp. 4–5). *Group task roles* involve facilitating and coordinating the group problem solving activities. This includes giving information, energizing, seeking clarification, offering opinions, and so on. Another kind of role is *aiding the group to grow and become vital*. This includes encouraging, harmonizing, setting standards, and offering compromises. The last role is *antigroup activity,* which includes the Playboy, Dominator, Aggressor, Recognition Seeker, and Help-Seeker.

The particular role which will get you ahead may be defined by the open or hidden agenda of the leaders of the groups in which you participate. However, as a group leader yourself, or member with an agenda, you should learn to recognize which activities are consonant with your welfare, and which must be exposed and eliminated.

## LEADERSHIP

What are some of the ways that leadership affects the decisions made in a group? There are basically two kinds of decisions that a leader must make, and leaders tend to emphasize one or the other of the appropriate characteristics.

*Instrumental* leadership is task oriented, because it is directed toward achieving group goals, coordinating with the institution, and initiating new ideas and solutions. This maintains the system toward the *external* world. *Social-emotional* leadership is directed toward the *internal* system, that is, maintaining morale (Schichor, 1970). One may consider the quality of leadership from the point of view of its attitude toward the members of the group, as well as the nature of the task performed. Thus, leadership can be autocratic or democratic. Each kind of leadership has advantages and disadvantages according to the situation and the expectations of group members (Lichtman & Hunt, 1971). Authoritarian leaders can bring a group to the best or worst solutions, compared with democratic leaders, when some outside criterion of accuracy is available (Cammalleri et al., 1973).

There are various combinations of these characteristics which make people successful or unsuccessful as leaders or participants in groups. When a leader shares his power (Wood, 1973), not only do the members achieve increased autonomy, responsibility, and achievement, but they develop their own creative skills. Furthermore, the leader's interactions are increased, and I would suspect that he enjoys his position more. He does not have to feel like he is sitting on the spout of a boiling tea kettle to keep the pressure within! Since there is evidence that those at the bottom of an organization tend to have poorer mental health, less job satisfaction, less self-esteem, and greater feelings of inferiority, compassionate leadership would tend to share authority in the hope of gaining information and cooperation to alleviate these conditions (Argyris, cited by Lichtman & Hunt, 1971).

If you are a supervisor of a group, you will be interested in creating working conditions so that decisions can be implemented (Argyle, 1972).

1. *Active interest* means a supervisor's presence, with hints from his experience and general guidance, but without excessive direction concerning the details of a task. This leads to improved quality and reduced cost while increasing subordinates' feelings of autonomy and job satisfaction.

2. *Consideration* or personal interest aids subordinates in obtaining rewards and avoiding punishment, and includes warm, friendly support. This seems to reduce absenteeism and labor turnover.

3. *Democratic-persuasive skills* are the processes of motivating people by explanation and persuasion rather than by giving orders. It allows subordinates to participate in decisions which

affect them through using group discussion and decision making. In a variety of circumstances it was shown that this quality of leadership increases output and reduces interpersonal tension.

## INTELLECTUAL QUALITIES AND COMMUNICATION

Groups also have kinds of intellectual qualities influencing their effectiveness. The first is their *ability to perform the stated task*. This will vary according to the group's size and experience, as well as the quality of leadership. The second kind of quality refers to the *inner functioning* of the group. A group thinks in ways which are characteristic of the collective intelligence of its members. It has a *memory*, so that when one person is gone somebody else will remember an event or prior solution.

Lilly (1972, p. 88) has described the functioning of several people together as follows: coalitions develop with linkages having particular characteristics. "Agreements are reached and thus the sources of new information from each member are reduced. ... Each human to human interlock is unique; but also each interlock is a function of other current and other past interlocks of each member and of learned traditional models." The communication is unique for each group, but it is limited compared to the total exchange which might be expected when the number of separate individuals is considered.

One of the chief determinants of a group's mood and effectiveness is the quality of communications. This is the area in which much damage is done to group productivity and morale. The stupidity of some administrations is considerable. I have worked in many large organizations in which directives came from the reigning boobs without any consideration for the facts. The orders did not consider the actual events they were intended to control. They were sabotaged from the beginning because the "troops" had no intention whatsoever of obeying these orders or implementing them in their daily activities. A sensible administration would have had some meetings or sent representatives around to find out what was going on, and then tried to gain cooperation.

Communication in a group is *vertical* (different levels of command) or *horizontal* (people at the same level). The older style and theory of management emphasized the vertical, authoritarian manner, with people considered to be so many pawns, or perhaps faceless gears that moved the wheels and were interchangeable (Lichtman & Hunt, 1971). Today's vast organizations sometimes attempt the same degree of centralization, but the real leader is no longer the Chief Executive Officer or Chairman of the Board. These gentry are so isolated from the real world that they frequently don't even know what products they're selling. Those divisions were sold a long time ago. The real director of operations is the guy who programs the computer. When I was doing career counseling, I was told horror stories of vast companies with the computer on the West Coast and operations everywhere else.

What about horizontal communications? Due to the speed of current industrial and business life, and the large number of levels of command, more communication today tends to take place horizontally. There is no time to waste letting the supervisors know what is happening. Foremen, engineers, and workers make immediate decisions through consultation with each other. Any attempt to hamper this through administrative decisions is paid for by wasted time, energy, and materials. In the long run, you, the consumer, pay for unnecessary hierarchical levels of control, particularly those which function in only a downward direction. Inadequate communications tend to decrease the liking of members for each other, and then the rate of participation is reduced (Lichtman & Hunt, 1971). In contrast, *excessive amounts of communication* interfere with the ability of a group to filter out and select information relevant for their functioning (M. T. Wood, 1973). As a group leader, one of your most important tasks would be conveying enough information to aid in the performance of a task, but not so much as to create a traffic jam at the coffee machine.

Group effectiveness in decision making is also affected by whether there is open or closed communications with the surrounding environment. We can ask whether there is feedback from the people and institutions functioning with or controlling the group which is then used to modify internal operations. An ideal "open" system obtains information concerning dangers or requirements for change, matches it against predetermined criteria for security or acceptance by supervisors, consumers, and so forth, and also has the capacity to make significant changes in the outside environment subsequent to this evaluation (Pedersen & Shears, 1973).

## EFFECT OF NUMBERS OF PARTICIPANTS

The number of individuals in a group affects the kind of decisions which will be made. In determining whether a decision should be made by one party or by a group, there are several considerations. Although one person may have prejudices and other limitations, single individuals whose ideas are cumulated generate more total solutions to a problem when it is necessary to create alternatives for consideration (Street, 1974). Although brainstorming (group-generated ideas, with evaluation suspended for a while) has become well known, it is believed to be inferior in quality of ideas created than is the case of individuals working alone. After individuals are given the task of creating alternatives, a group can be formed—with its greater range of information and experience—to evaluate these ideas and select among alternatives (Argyle, 1972, p. 131; Street, 1974; London, 1975). Groups outperform individuals in the quality of decisions made (Schoner, Hoyt, & Rose, 1974; Street, 1974), particularly if a wide variety of information is required, and if group members deliberate before they vote.

Group decision making has certain defects, however, because (1) it is possible for individuals to disclaim responsibility or accountability (Cooper & Wood, 1974); and (2) a group may be "incapable of fully utilizing the contributions of individuals who have high-quality decisions" (Schoner, Hoyt, & Rose, 1974).

Peter Drucker (1967), one of America's most influential management consultants, raises the question of who should be part of the group, that is, *who should be invited to meetings?*

He defines an executive as somebody who gets things done. In today's world, executives include "knowledge workers" as well as those who manage other people. Decision making is no longer confined to those at the top of the organization. Different individuals may have skills or knowledge relevant to separate decisions. He uses as an example of an effective executive one who invited his staff to participate in meetings in the following way: he circulated the names of the people invited to a meeting. Anybody else was invited to attend who felt that he needed the information or could make a contribution, but everybody was promised a summary in any event. As a result, fewer people showed up, and the business was expedited quickly.

### Social Desirability and Conformity

After this discussion of the structure and quality of formal communications in groups, we can look at how groups motivate themselves as a function of the needs of their members.

Two of the most important facts influencing group decisions are the need to *conform* and the need to be considered *socially desirable*. People have a great need to belong to a group, and frequently can't stand being excluded. Not only do they lose the positive advantages of membership, but they feel worthless and devalued if not accepted, isolated, or asked to leave. As a result, they tend to conform to group norms. *Sanctions* are the punishment meted out by a group for deviations from its norms. They include hostility and loss of influence. Therefore social desirability is an important facet in understanding the dynamics of a group. Many individuals react by conforming with group expectations in order to make them more socially desirable. There is evidence (Maddi, 1970) that people who are high in the need for social desirability want to appear competent, attentive, acceptable, and conforming. They tend to have only a superficial interest in others. Further, they seem to feel controlled more by external influences than by their own reactions. No wonder that their decisions are determined by a popularity contest!

The *conformist* believes that his relationship with other

people is on a *contractual* (defined) basis, rather than an intimate one. He worries whether he is considered to be conscientious and nice. Perhaps he even believes that his basic drives (sex and anger) can interfere with his ability to play a correct role (Maddi, 1970). The conformist sees himself as little more than a player of social roles. This is too high a price to pay for social desirability.

Another facet of social desirability is the relative *status* of people. By this I mean how well they are esteemed and what power comes to them because of the opinions of others. This is in addition to whatever influence is officially given to them or other people by the structure and definition of the group. Status may be related to the prestige of one's occupation, rank, or pay (Wahrman, 1972), or it may be related to seniority, friendship with the owner of the business, willingness to share one's cookies or other significant qualities relating to productivity. High status generally protects a person from sanctions, or punishment for deviations from group norms.

*High status people* seem to have less tendency to conform to these norms since they do not fear punishment. Even at the end of a disastrous war, Hitler was excluded from blame by the majority of the German people. In relatively infrequent cases, high status people are punished excessively when violation occurs (Wahrman, 1972). When we expect much of people we either forgive them or become vindictive. Mr. Nixon has received little sympathy for his numerous personal problems after his fall from grace.

## GROUP MOOD

Just as the characteristic feelings of a person can be described, so can those of a group. Some groups are angry: when I walk in the street and I hear a lot of people screaming at each other, I assume that it is a particular kind of therapy group! Other groups are warm and congenial. I have had therapy sessions in which the group could be described as depressed. The underlying theme of loss and hopelessness brought all present (myself included) to tears.

The mood of a group can determine the effectiveness with which it will reach decisions. You can evaluate in advance the likelihood of an outcome which will meet your needs by the feelings which you observe around you. Since groups have profound effects upon the mood of the individual, you can also learn to recognize which groups are counterproductive to any value you can obtain from them because you leave with a headache, feelings of depression, anger, futility, and so on. You have now learned how to identify the negative-antiauthoritarian or non-goal-oriented individual whose role in the group may be counter to yours. You should have the courage to confront these people directly, or if not, to discourage the leadership from inviting them to participate. Satisfactory group decisions occur when individuals are motivated to present their ideas. Openness is dependent upon encouragement of group acceptance of a variety of ideas. Nevertheless everybody should be committed to closing ranks at the end of the discussion when a conclusion is reached.

## RISK TAKING

An important emotional quality of a group is its attitude toward independent thinking, danger, need for conformity, and safety generally. The opposite pole of the dimension of conformity is risk taking. Both conformity and risk taking can evolve from the need for acceptance or social desirability. While groups (such as committees) have a reputation for making "safe" decisions, research shows this is not so. "When subjects make individual decisions and later reconsider their decisions in groups there is often a so-called 'risky' shift to a less safe decision" (Argyle, 1972, p. 133). This may be due to a diffusion of responsibility so that individuals do not feel accountable for their actions. The "risky shift" away from safe solutions is considered a source of unwise decisions of which chairmen and other leaders should be aware.

What is the origin of risk taking in groups? Some people recommend a greater degree of risk taking after group participation than before (Clark, 1971), since they do not wish to appear less able to take risks than their peers (or less courageous) (Clark & Willems, 1972). Increased encouragement to take risks depends upon the consequences of failure not being severe (groups are notoriously cowardly), and the presence of particular people actually encouraging the taking of a risk. Of course, the greater risk can be supported if somebody has sound information (Vinokur, 1971). Curiously, there is no correlation between the propensity to take risks and having dogmatic attitudes. On the contrary, there is a significant correlation between intelligence and dogmatic attitudes (Taylor & Dunnette, 1974)!

## Conflict Between Risk and Acceptability

The offering of a new idea to a group represents a conflict between the desire for acceptability and status, and the fear of rejection and loss of status. Simultaneously, accepting somebody else's idea is offering them more status relative to yourself. It can be inferred that people who are fearful of rejection will be particularly careful to test out ideas privately before they present them for public appraisal. In fact, it is possible that certain individuals go into special pursuits (for example, pure science or classical studies) in order not to have to "confront and persuade others in order to succeed" (Rickards, 1974).

## Need for Power

Group decisions involving risk are affected by the *feeling of powerlessness* or the wish to overcome it. Adler felt that this was the condition with which we start life. Fear of *seeming to be weak* influences many people, and causes them to try to appear more self-assertive than they really feel. It is also likely to cause some people to take excessively great risks (Vinokur, 1971; Clark, 1971). In the American culture, *the daring person has high social esteem*. To involve the group in risks may be one way of becoming an influential member. The individuals hope, by taking greater risks, to demonstrate their willingness to assume responsibility and become leaders, and to take credit for success

(Vinokur, 1971). There is no evidence that successful leaders are necessarily those who advocate the greatest risks. However, as members of a group, individuals may utilize their power to perform acts (sometimes atrocious ones) which they would not dare to perform individually. Dicks' (1972) study of German mass murderers shows clearly how they utilized the violence of the Third Reich to express unconscious hostility, and then claimed that they acted under orders (cadaver-obedience).

## STAGES OF PROBLEM SOLVING

A group has to go through several stages before it is ready to generate decisions which are solutions to a problem (Argyle, 1972, p. 116).

During the *forming* stage, the members find out the task, the rules, and which methods are appropriate. They experience anxiety and depend upon a leader. At the *storming* stage, group structure has begun to form, with subgroup conflict, which polarizes opinions, and there may be a rebellion against the leader. This results in emotional resistance to the demands of the task. Next comes the *norming* phase, during which cohesion develops, with resistance overcome and mutual support taking the place of conflicts. Cooperation is manifested through an open exchange of views and feelings. Finally, in the *performing* stage, with the resolution of interpersonal problems, the exchange between people becomes the tool of achieving the task at hand, and roles become more flexible. Energy is available for effective work, and constructive attempts to complete the task lead to the emergence of solutions to problems.

## GROUP NUMBER AND PROBLEM SOLVING

The actual decision goes through several phases. These are generating alternatives, evaluating alternatives, and choosing between alternatives (Schoner, Rose, & Hoyt, 1974; London, 1975). During each phase, the number of individuals involved for optimal results may vary. Therefore, although individuals get the greatest sense of satisfaction in their work when they can participate in all phases, or find satisfaction in choosing among alternatives generated by others (Cooper & Wood, 1974), a prudent supervisor will control the interaction among members of his staff according to the progress of the project. The quality of group decision making need not depend upon the feeling of involvement, although morale will be reduced by the belief that one's influence is limited (London, 1975).

Certain kinds of solutions benefit from privacy or anonymity of response (Street, 1974). As the number of individuals increases, group dynamics begin to shape the process of making decisions. When two people are involved (*dyads*) a majority vote cannot determine the process, so gentle persuasion is required by the two parties involved in order to avoid splitting the group with each person becoming isolated. However, when the group gets as large as three, the third party can be isolated (without destroying the group), or can be the target of competitive efforts to obtain his allegiance by the other two. As the group gets even larger, it becomes more of a vehicle to release tension than with smaller groups. There is a pattern of members offering more information and fewer suggestions (Pedersen & Shears, 1973).

## ATTITUDES TOWARD SUCCESS AND FAILURE

The success of any group enterprise can be determined (as in individuals) by the balance between *desire for success* and *fear of failure* (Zander, 1974). These are separate dynamic factors in both individuals and groups. However, the effect of participating in a group can change the characteristic attitude of persons when they function alone. This ties in with the requirement that the leader create working conditions which enhance group cohesion and other factors which make for successful implementation of decisions.

It has been discovered that a strong motive for success leads to selection of goals which are challenging. Neither success nor failure is certain. However, where there is a strong desire to avoid failure, both groups and individuals choose either very easy or very hard goals and then don't work hard to achieve them.

Research indicates that *emphasizing the negative consequences of failure reduces performance*. A study of an organization which had been unsuccessful in reaching its goals showed that it did not lower them to realistic levels. Rather, they yielded to pressure to maintain high goals to meet the needs of the sponsoring group. As a consequence, they could not meet their quota, motivation dropped, efficiency decreased, and another cycle of failure began.

Since groups develop aspirations of their own (apart from the supervisors), it is useful to include workers (those who implement decisions) in the goal-setting process, and get them emotionally involved in the group's capacity to succeed. Even those who wish to avoid failure become more realistically oriented when they are given positions of responsibility.

We can see that when a group is involved in the formulation or implementation of decisions, an additional degree of complexity determines how effective the process will be. In Chapter 14 we shall discuss the steps by which group decision making can be enhanced, as part of a general presentation of using people effectively during the implementation of your goals.

# 13

# Self, Adaptation, and Decisions

Now we can begin to pull all the material together. We shall try to present a comprehensive view of how people adapt to life through a series of decisions. This is one of the most difficult and controversial areas in psychology, and philosophy. There are questions about whether our mind functions as a psycho-physiological unity (*monism*) or has separate material and spiritual components (*dualism*). This is an ancient theme in the history of philosophy (Murphy, 1949, pp. 5–8). Other unresolved questions concern contradictions and polarities in our mental life, for example, free will versus materialistic determinism (Thomsen, 1974); orientation toward past, present, or future; the tie between me and you; conscious versus unconscious experience; emotional versus rational expression; verbal versus nonverbal, and so forth.

## INTEGRATION AND DECISIONS

I consider the self as the integrator of all of our experiences. The self is like a conductor of a large orchestra which is performing a complex polyphonic score with both familiar and unfamiliar harmonies. While the conductor is unravelling a rhythm and balancing several choirs of instruments, a critic is offering his opinion, a dissatisfied subscriber is propelling in his direction an overripe egg, the principal horn player burps during an exposed passage, and the memory of his dissatisfied Professor of Conducting is haunting him. It is true, "Life is hard, and dying is not easy."

We can consider the self to be the organ of decisions, which is a reflection of intellectual-emotional-neurological-biochemical reactions of our bodies. The integration between mental processes and autonomic, vital bodily practices was a secret of mystics for a long time. According to Western physiologists, brain waves, muscular tension, blood pressure, heart rate, and so on were largely involuntary, reflex responses to internal changes and external stresses. Today, we are more aware of an intimate connection between our moods and these bodily processes. Through biofeedback (utilizing instantaneous information concerning our bodily processes), we can actually learn to control these processes in order to achieve relaxation and undo a variety of psychosomatic illnesses (B. B. Brown, 1974). *Our self is considerably more extensive than had been imagined.*

The question has been raised as to the nature of our responsibility for the choices we make. After all, "decision making is not the act of some private creature, 'the mind,' acting upon the brain." Rather, "choosing" or "willing" is a description of an underlying decision process (Young, 1971, pp. 605–606). Actually there is evidence that the brain processes accompanying activities evolving from previous experiences differ from those accompanying mere sensory responses to stimulation. These are considered to reflect actual decision-making processes (Begleiter & Porjesz, 1975).

## Consciousness

One cannot discuss decision making or human adaptation without considering the nature of consciousness or self-awareness. One can regard consciousness as alternating among alert attention to the external world, self-awareness, emotionally colored imagery or fantasy, goal-directed thinking (evaluating, setting ideas in order, and problem solving), planning, anticipation as to what the future holds, and memories (which can be more or less complete and accurate). It appears that it is difficult to be effective in more than one of these activities simultaneously, although all of them can leave some permanent record in the stream of consciousness (engram).

The process of knowing involves separating our experiences into the knower (self) and the known (object or environment) (Edinger, 1975). Our awareness of self has a number of components (Fenigstein, Scheier, & Buss, 1975). *Private self-consciousness* is attention focused upon our inner thoughts and feelings. *Public self-consciousness* is awareness of one's self as a social person with an effect upon others. *Social anxiety* is the experience of discomfort in the presence of others.

Our fantasy life reflects either self-acceptance (the feeling that we are worthwhile people) or low self-esteem (unworthiness and self-hatred). Some people overcome low self-esteem through complex daydreams of heroic achievement, while others experience scattered thoughts about failure, without attempting to overcome them by planning for achievement. They seem to rely upon the outside world to build up their spirits (Singer, 1975). Fantasies may also intrude upon ongoing activities if we have excessive amounts of unfinished business on our minds while attending to something else.

One difficulty in realistically evaluating a real-life situation is that events, people, and situations rarely occur in a clear-cut, meaningful fashion. On the contrary, people and situations are generally ambiguous, or susceptible to a variety of interpretations. We differ in our *tolerance for ambiguity*. Available information can be sparse, excessive, or contradictory (Norton, 1975). This affects our functioning in many areas, including the nature of decisions we make and the occupations in which we can function effectively. In fact, many people experience vague situations as uncomfortable or even threatening.

Yet, to adapt adequately requires us to process information accurately, whether the source of such information is one's self or the outside world. Attaching meaning to experiences occurs only after sensations and fantasies have become organized. The nature of awareness is affected in part by the amount and intensity of simultaneous or rapidly changing data which come into awareness. The brain selectively screens information reaching consciousness according to its intensity or our state of alertness, prior experience, and so forth. Intense amounts of sensation can cause altered states of consciousness, for example, fainting or dizziness from pain, confusion from rapid change or excessive unfamiliarity, or the "high" of blasting discotheque music.

## MEMORY

One danger of the "information explosion" existing in today's society is the possibility that "memory storage will become excessively cluttered. . . . Much greater demands are put on the retrieval system, as well as on the storage capacity" (Bellak, 1974, p. 134). In short, we can no longer count on our memory to maintain and offer for use much of the detail of the events and stimulation to which we are exposed. However, without conscious attention, there would be no memory or record of our activities (Penfield, 1975, pp. 74–75). Curiously, in the relaxed state of hypnosis, in which conscious attention is focused simultaneously on the instructions of the hypnotist and on oneself, memories which seemingly were not attended to very clearly can be recovered.

Memories appear to have varied origins. They have been categorized (Penfield, 1975, p. 63) as *racial* (exemplified by the unlearned behavior of animals), *new* (e.g., skills, conditioned reflexes, and nonverbal concepts), and *experiential* (recall of the stream of consciousness). The relative balance of these in influencing our behavior (decisions) is a source of controversy. The behavioral geneticists and Jungians show great interest in hereditary, preprogrammed patterns of the nervous system; the behaviorists, in the conditioning of our attitudes and values; and the existentialists, in the meanings which we have attributed to life and its varied events.

## OTHER ASPECTS OF AWARENESS

One of the important dimensions in consciousness is the balance between inner life (introversion) and attention to the outer world (extraversion) in the Jungian conception (1943, 1945). These are not opposites; rather, they are potentials, both of which can be developed. Nevertheless, from the viewpoint of adaptation, "persons who daydream a good deal sacrifice some accuracy in attentiveness to the external world in order to attend to their own fantasy material" (Singer, 1975). Their concentration on what they are experiencing is greater than on the external world. On the other hand, people who are largely reality-oriented tend to be experienced by others as unemotional or cold.

One of the important functions of consciousness is prediction, followed by decisions about how to handle what we anticipate about the future. Creating new images so that we can more clearly conceptualize alternatives in the future has been called "lookahead," and is an important distinction of human beings (Kaplan, 1972). Images, in the form of memories of past events, act as positive or negative reinforcers. By this is meant that pleasant or unpleasant memories influence our decisions, as well as our appraisal of the current situation.

## NEUROLOGICAL CONTRIBUTIONS TO THE SELF

The functioning of our body must be considered in any intelligent approach to decision making. It is useful to be receptive to learning more about the physiological background of human behavior, since decision making appears to be a quality even of single brain cells (neurones) —insofar as they integrate electrical input and actively control their responses (Dunn & Bondy, 1974, p. 198).

Electrical and behavioral changes indicating awareness and responsiveness to new or changing situations are called "arousal" or "activation." An optimal state of arousal permits efficient levels of awareness and the probability of memory formation (engram storage). Sensory overload produces cognitive deterioration. Excessive or minimal arousal is deleterious to a number of central nervous system functions, including metabolism and behavioral performance (Walsh & Cummins, 1975).

Decision making requires that we process information into usable portions, refer it to relevant areas of the brain, match it against information (or perhaps misinformation) already in storage, and then evolve a course of action. We have already seen that stored information may be genetic in origin, formal learning, or prior experience. In addition, hormonal influences in early development sensitize our brains so that particular subsequent events (e.g., sexual characteristics of people) are much more interesting than others (Hamburg, Coelho, & Adams, 1974). We become conditioned even before we are born to react positively to some kinds of situations.

## BRAIN MECHANISMS AND DECISIONS

One of the important areas regulating sleep, arousal, and attention is found in the core of the brain stem called the *reticular formation* (Curtis, Jacobson, & Marcus, 1972). This network of brain cells seems to provide "direct access to the brain mechanism which interprets sensory events ... (and even) stimulates the activation of specific memories" (Kleinman & John, 1975). Most information from the world (except, significantly, olfaction—a very primitive source of knowledge) enters our brain on branched pathways: one path proceeds directly to the *cerebral cortex* (gray matter) and one to the *reticular formation*. When the latter is inactive, damaged, or anesthetized, then we are unconscious—regardless of the amount of stimulation reaching the cerebral cortex. When information is forwarded by the reticular formation to the cortex, simultaneously with direct stimulation, we become aware that something significant is occurring around us.

A very interesting hypothesis concerning the cerebral mechanism of awareness has been stated by Penfield (1975), after decades of study of the responses of awake human beings to electrical stimulation of their cerebral cortices during brain surgery (Penfield & Roberts, 1959). He describes the activities of three regions of the brain (whose functions are additional to that of the reticular formation) : the *"interpretive cortex"* (primarily of the temporal lobes), the *"highest brain-mechanism,"* and the *"automatic sensory motor mechanism* or *computer"* (both of the latter in the brain stem).

According to Penfield, the computer carries out stereotyped patterns of previously learned behavior. It generally does not make decisions for which there is no precedent; nor, when functioning alone, does it permit recording the stream of consciousness. It coordinates relatively separate activities of the brain that are usually performed automatically: reading, writing, driving, and so forth. When the highest brain-mechanism is inhibited, as in some instances of epilepsy, automatic states without awareness, and so forth, previously learned activities take place under control of the computer, but without our being aware of or remembering the events ("blackouts").

The highest brain mechanism reflects a person's attention to a particular matter. Alertness is enhanced because this mechanism inhibits unrelated inflow of information. It does allow relevant data to enter consciousness, together with interpretations such as familiarity or danger, and memories. "The function of this gray matter is to carry out the neuronal action that corresponds with action of the mind" (p. 63).

The interpretive cortex relates the individual automatically and subconsciously to his immediate environment. It offers such signals as "familiar," "frightening," "coming nearer," "going away," and so on. It also is capable of "bringing back a strip of past experience in complete detail without any of the fanciful elaborations that occur in a man's dreaming" (p. 34).

Penfield places greater emphasis upon activities in the brain stem than upon those in the cerebral cortex, the usual site to which consciousness and related intellectual activities have been attributed. He refers to the entire series of circuits that integrate sensation and activity as the *centrencephalic system.*

Intellectual functioning of the brain does not take place in isolation. It requires input from the environment for adaptive functioning (Delgado, 1969). Unless we are in contact with the world, our thinking becomes disorganized and primitive. Total freedom from distraction is actually counterproductive: we need some distractions in order to be fully awake and reality-oriented!

Inhibition is an important property of the nervous system. Many activities occur only during other activities or after others are held back. Basch (1975, p. 515) points out that some actions require prior inhibition to permit matching of incoming messages against previously formed patterns. This assures that basic functions such as self-preservation and reproduction can occur effectively. This task is performed by what he calls the "associational cortex."

## ASYMMETRY OF THE HUMAN BRAIN

This distinctive quality of the human brain creates problems of integrating feelings with rational considerations as well as a neurological basis for the unconscious (Chapter 9). The dominant cerebral hemisphere is generally the left one. The result of this is right-handedness, since many controlling nerve pathways partly cross over to the opposite side (as do most sensory inputs). This is a very early development, as demonstrated by the finding that newborn infants look spontaneously to the right about four times as often as to the left. They show electrical brain activity (EEG) on the left side to verbal stimulation, and on the right side to nonverbal stimulation, long before the development of language skills (Kinsbourne, 1975).

In adults, the left hemisphere specializes in processing information which can be subdivided and rearranged, or addressed to particular questions; while the right hemisphere perceives complete relationships or creates a new organization of data (Bever, 1975). It has been demonstrated that as our understanding of complex data proceeds—that is, as we shift from seeing it as a whole (e.g., a musical passage) and learn to break it into parts (components of the music)—brain activity shifts from the right to the left hemisphere.

Effective decisions require integration of complex information absorbed at different times with different qualities. This occurs on opposite sides of the brain. Disharmony in our emotional life occurs in mental illness, brain damage, illness, or other stress. It can be dramatically illustrated by the case of an unfortunate person whose left and right cerebral hemispheres were separated surgically to prevent the spread of epileptic seizures from one side to the other. (The enormous connecting band of nerve fibers called the *corpus callosum* was severed.) In this case, "his right brain took a severe dislike to his wife. His left hand was continuously making obscene gestures at her and once tried to strangle her. Only by using his right hand to break the grip of his left could the man prevent an unfortunate result" (Thomsen, 1974).

This separation of feelings, skills, and attitudes from one side to the other is one cause of the conflicts which occur within ourselves, between individuals with different values, and between the rational and moderate versus the fantastic and excessive (Keen, 1974). As we understand the function of the central nervous system, we advance our knowledge of ourselves; we learn to avoid mysticism and subjectivity, and we turn toward more profound, objective understanding.

## THE MIND-BODY PROBLEM

The relationship between the vastly different properties of mind and body may be the oldest philosophical and scientific problem mankind has confronted. How the different energies interact and become transduced into each other is still obscure, although some of the conditions leading to the exchange are becoming known. Yet the difficulty of finding an answer can be illustrated by the different reactions to this question by two distinguished neurologists:

Penfield (1975, p. 85) : "For myself, after a professional lifetime spent in trying to discover how the brain accounts for the mind, it comes as a surprise now to discover ... that the dualist hypothesis (separate existence of mind and body) seems the more reasonable of the ... possible explanations."

Delgado (1969, p. 61) : "While (psychic energy) ... depends

on cerebral physiology (and indirectly on the health of the whole body), its actual source is extra-cerebral because mental activity is not a property of neurons but is contingent on the received information which activates stored information and past experiences, creating emotions and ideas." In short, mind is a reaction to stimulation.

## SELF AND ADAPTATION

*The self is also the organ of adaptation.* By adaptation I mean the way in which we act in accordance with our own nature as we are confronted with reality. To accomplish this, the self utilizes all of the external and internal events of our lives. A well-adapted person functions as a unity. All of his memories and capabilities are functioning toward reaching cohesive, reasonable goals. The unintegrated personality (in some instances) is called a schizophrenic, or split brain, because his feelings, talents and thoughts frequently function in contradictory ways.

Our self involves knowledge of our strengths, weaknesses, feelings, historical past, and goals. It also includes our unconscious, and our tendency to misperceive and to form preconceptions and to behave in stereotyped, inappropriate ways. It represents the continuity of our experiences, and as such it is our identity. It is also the connections that we draw between events, and the conclusions about life or the philosophy that we form.

Harry Stack Sullivan, the well-known psychiatrist, describes the self as "the only thing which has alertness, and which notices what goes on, and needless to say, notices what goes on in its own field..." (1940, pp. 21–22). "The self is primarily a very elaborate bundle of memories, processes, perceived relationships, and past experiences, understandings of the course that events follow in hanging together—all in the interests of making one feel competent to deal with other people without becoming aware of the myriad threats to one's self-esteem that are implicit in almost any interpersonal situation" (1956, p. 15).

Rollo May (1967) puts it another way: "What interests me

is what makes people strive for something." Freedom of choice is related to that which does or does not have meaning.

Our self is also the process of experiencing and organizing our feelings. It is also our decisions, actions, and the course of life.

## HISTORICAL CONTINUITY

Part of your self is the memory of your life, and those events which are there but which you cannot remember. Part of our self is stored away, but sometimes we do go into the attic.

*History XIII–1: Repressed feelings of worthlessness keep a woman in her role of being a substitute mother.* A woman was considerably older than her younger siblings. Both parents went to work, and she assumed the responsibility for taking care of them. As the material develops, you can see her initial memory was being overburdened by responsibility. Hidden behind the socially useful role is the perception of herself as ugly.

*Hypnotic session #1*: I regressed her to her twelfth birthday: How old are you? "I'm twelve, I have to take care of the two children." Tell your parents that you want to be alone. "I can't." After much urging. "I don't want to be bothered, so I can go out and play." Tell something to your mother. "You will have to learn to be a mother so that I can be a little girl."

*Hypnotic session #2: Age twenty-five*: To her mother: "You stink." To her father, "You're self-centered." To her sister: "You poor little baby. I know what you feel. I can see all the nice things in you. I wish I could make it better for you." *Age eighteen:* "I don't know what I want. I want to be a lady. I feel rough, vulgar, and stupid. Too stupid to go to college." To father: "You are terrible. You like us ladies to work for you. You don't treat them like ladies. You feel them up, you terrible man." To mother: "How could you marry such a terrible man; you yourself don't know what it is like to be a girl." *Age fourteen*: "I was very smart in junior high school. My parents were always fighting; there was no time for anything. My father treats me like a piece of dirt. I'm not entitled to anything except working for you. Mother, why don't you protect me? I wanted to be a nice little girl that people loved to be pretty and taken care of. I didn't want to be used. I didn't want to be responsible and watch out for myself and everything. My boyfriend [whom she subsequently married] was safe. He wouldn't overpower me. He was kind, and he took care of me. At fifteen I felt like a monster, ugly and fat. I don't have pretty clothes. I don't speak quietly like a lady should. I only feel comfortable with boys in throwing ball. I miss being young and pretty, feeling soft."

Later on, she said: "I wish I was young. It all came too late. No one ever helped me."

Although she has developed into a fine mother and very feminine woman, she still feels used by others. She has difficulty in giving up her role of the young girl who gains self-respect by taking care of her siblings. Perhaps her deepest feeling was of being ugly, so that only through this burdensome task could she get some sense of value. She agrees that under the same circumstances some girls run away or rebel. These solutions would not help her to overcome the deepest unconscious feelings of being unfeminine: "I want to be a lady." She reports that others, not her parents, had to tell her how to dress, to sit, to use deodorants, and so on.

When this woman could vividly recall events of years past, she was able to see how they affected the way she related to her present life. This kind of experience can also be brought back with electric stimulation when a conscious person is undergoing brain surgery (Penfield & Roberts, 1959, p. 35).

## SELF-AWARENESS

Just as our self has a historical dimension, it also experiences who we are. Our self-awareness can be considered from various angles: *body image; body boundary; identification; role; self-esteem;* and *feelings.*

*Body image* is "the picture of our own body . . . the way our body appears to ourselves" (Schilder, 1950, p. 11). It is so persistent that even when there is a radical change, for example, the loss of a limb, we create a "phantom." "The individual still feels his leg and has a vivid impression that it is still there. He may also forget about his loss and fall down" (p. 13). "The experience of one's own body (particularly in early childhood) is the basis for all other life experiences. . . . Anything that has happened in one's life can never be completely lost" (Schilder, 1964, p. 51). Even some mental symptoms of the adult are believed to have developed from the characteristic attitude of the person toward his body when younger. When there is damage to the parietal and temporal lobes of the brain, opposite to the side that controls handedness, not only is there a defect in the concept of one's body, but perception of outer space is also hampered (Curtis et al., 1972, pp. 502–503). Thus, our perception of the world and of our own body occurs within the same area of our brain.

Our body image affects the style of our decision making. However, it is slow to change. Our image of our appearance causes us to expect social rejection or acceptance. I have noticed, for example, that many lovely women who were obese as children or adolescents still regard themselves as fat as though they had never changed.

## IDENTIFICATION WITH OTHERS

Part of our self develops from our wish to be like others, or from the ways we unconsciously take on other people's characteristics. Strangely enough, anger toward somebody may influence us toward becoming like them!

I believe that *anger is more important than sex* in determining character (Parker, 1972b). It is experienced earlier and more often. We must defend ourselves from abuse and accidental misuse from the very beginning of our lives. In addition to accepting the positive qualities of our parents, their nurturance, and model of competence, we also become like those who create anxiety in us through their aggression and criticism (Anna Freud,

1946, Chapter 9). Sometimes we even carry on the characteristics of those who have created much emotional pain in us. Then we pick a fight with those who have the characteristics which we share with our parents. This is "identification with Pain-Inflicting Parents" (Parker, 1972). In short, in our self is the historical continuity of our lives, that of our parents, and also those who shaped them—an emotional chain, if not a neurological archetype!

*Fear* also plays an important part in our learning to identify with others. Freud (1933, p. 62), not an admirer of human nature, put it concisely: "Parental influence governs the child by offering proofs of love and by threatening punishments which are signs to the child of loss of love and are bound to be feared on their own account." This is the motivation behind much identification and the formation of our conscience (super-ego).

*Body boundary* is a less familiar concept. There must be some defense against being constantly assaulted by the outer world. Without this, we would be constantly vulnerable. The barrier we use can be social distance, muscle tension, or in an overly alert (paranoid) attitude toward threats. Freud (1920, p. 53) pointed out that we need a protective shield to cope with "the enormous energies at work in the external world." When our barrier against emotional danger (defenses) fails, we are subjected to trauma, for example, in the neuroses of war or continued stress (Niederland, 1972). This barrier, also, serves to keep us from becoming aware of punishable excitation from our own drives (Freud, 1920, p. 56, although this point was denied later, 1936, p. 21).

Wilhelm Reich (1945, p. 44) extended the concept of the stimulus barrier to that of the "character armoring." The way we carry our body, the manner in which we relate our dreams, speak, and so on are considered part of our defense against sexual and angry impulses from within, and also against becoming aware of events in the world which stir them up. This resistance serves first to prevent change in insight, and then causes an inability to obtain gratification or enjoyment (pp. 114–130).

Our awareness of the body boundary, and other boundaries such as those of our car and house, becomes more acute when we feel threatened (S. Fisher, 1972). Thus, the body boundary serves to reduce our feelings of vulnerability and to help us cope with threatening stimuli from ourselves or the world around us.

*History XIII–2: The model of her mother's lifestyle created a problem in a wife's marriage.* A married woman reported to me that one of the few sources of conflict with her husband was that she would grudgingly get out of bed at 7:15 A.M., when she had to go to work. She could not relate to him at that time, feeling that it was only later in the day that she could get started. In addition, she had a variety of self-doubts and compulsive actions, and felt unable to make decisions. She evaluated herself as cleaning the house excessively.

Her mother was a housewife, who was described as a guilt provoker and also a late sleeper. She set no goals for her daughter, except that she should go to college. As a child, her day was quite unvarying. Her father would come in without fail at 6 o'clock and the family would have dinner. "It was the same every day." Her own husband's schedule is changeable. When her daughter, playing with some creative toys, asked her whether she did this when she was young, she realized that she was not encouraged to do anything distinctive. In fact, my question to her during our initial interview about *whether she was permitted to make decisions* when she was young surprised her. Upon consideration, she said that she had been told by her mother that she was encouraged to be independent, but actually she doubted it.

We can see in this history her *identification with her mother.* Despite all the years that have gone by, she kept the image of the mother as someone who gets up late. So, even though it causes conflict, she acts as though she were her own mother and gets up late because this is obviously how mothers act! Another significant fact, though not immediately related, is her lack of awareness that her mother stifled her initiative, but pretended to do the opposite. Women had no autonomy outside the household, and she herself never formed clear-cut goals for herself.

## Role

There is a difference between the part we play in society, our *role,* and the labels we place on ourselves, our *identification.* This distinction can be blurred in people who have little self-awareness. They tend to identify themselves by their social role —as husband or wife, or physician, engineer, and so on.

The earliest and most persistent form of identity is *gender* or sexual identification. The identification of one's self as belonging to a particular sex is called "core gender identity." It is defined by Stoller (1968, pp. 19–20) as the awareness of being male or female, produced by the infant-parents relationship, the child's perception of its external genitalia, and a biological force. The person's sexual identification is quite fixed at an early age, perhaps around two years (Money, Hampson, & Hampson, 1957). Sex roles are learned through relating to the parent of the opposite sex as well as identification with the parent of the same sex (Money & Ehrhardt, 1972, p. 13). In most cases, the gender identity is so firmly set by puberty that it cannot be changed (p. 23).

Our role is partially determined by the expectations of other people and the part which is assigned to us to play in the social world. This is different from the belief that we belong to one sex or the other. An indication of how the sexual roles are changing was obtained in a study of the projection of human figures (M) into Rorschach inkblots by my former teacher, Fred Brown (1971). He observed that the proportion of male patients referred for psychological examination increased over the years. Further, patients earlier in his professional career tended to see a higher proportion of male figures than those in later years. He related these facts to the changing role of women in our society, and to male rejection of an aimless competitiveness. Thus, sexual identification changes with social forces.

Some of my own research sheds light on this (Parker, 1963,

1965, 1969). Identification (including gender), tends to be pretty stable, even among people who have been hospitalized for severe mental illness (schizophrenia). I compared the human figures projected by college students on inkblots with those of hospitalized schizophrenics. Different phases of the subjects' personality were revealed by the *identification* of the figure or image (what kind of person—Actor—was perceived) as contrasted to the *role* (the kind of activity—Action). It appeared that the acceptability of the Action depended upon how closely they could identify with the external characteristic or identity of the figure they perceived. The normal group (college students) enjoyed activities in fantasy figures which were like themselves. The mentally disturbed (schizophrenics) enjoyed the activities of figures which were unlike themselves. Part of their disturbance was their inability to accept impulses which they experienced as part of their own personality. The nondisturbed group (students at my alma mater, of course) felt that activities they didn't like were associated with images unlike themselves. In this way they maintained their self-esteem.

There was also a tendency to attribute attitudes we don't like to persons of the opposite sex. The Actor in our fantasy is frequently the person with whom the most vital or turbulent relationship was formed when we were children. This, of course, may be the parent of the opposite sex. Returning to Brown's study, his finding that patients whom he studied years ago tended to see a larger proportion of male figures may be related to the stresses experienced by fathers and the effect upon their sons during the Depression and also during wartime absences. This illustrates the continuity from past to present, in which the experiences of our childhood are relived in contemporary images, influencing our feelings, actions, and decisions.

## SELF-ESTEEM

Self-esteem is the value that we place on ourselves as satisfactory or unsatisfactory. It is one of the most important factors which affects our well-being.

The basic attitude which we have toward our self is an intimate, impossible-to-separate mixture of how others regarded us in the past, our reaction to their feelings, and our identification with them. Our sense of identity is influenced by aggression (A. Freud, 1946), humiliation (Parker, 1972), fantasies about the parent (M. Klein, 1929), and castration anxiety or the Oedipal complex (Freud, 1923, pp. 40–41). Abraham (1924) pointed out the relationship between severe depression, or melancholia, and identification with somebody with whom we are angry for leaving us. Sullivan (1940, pp. 21–22) summed up well the question of the association between development of a sense of identity and our self: "The self ... is built up out of this experience of approbation and disapproval, or reward and punishment (creating our sense of self-esteem or self-hatred). . . . For the expression of all things in the personality other than those which were approved and disapproved by the parent and other significant persons, the self refuses awareness. . . ." Now we can understand why any feelings we have of worthlessness are so hard to overcome: they have developed out of the most vivid experiences of childhood.

One must consider the connection between self-esteem and repression. When our feelings about our self are painful, memories of events and of ourselves as being inadequate or humiliated are likely to be buried. This unhappy part of our self-concept will affect our decisions and our self-esteem. We will not ordinarily be aware of it except under such special conditions as dreams, hypnosis, or hallucinogenic drugs. Thus, there is some parallel between our awareness and feelings of self-esteem. We tend to remember success. However, the failure we do not throw away. We store it and then use it self-destructively.

Feelings may really be the essence of our self. After all, what is more important to us? I really disagree with Descartes' assertion, "I think, therefore I am." It is more characteristic of our human condition to say, "I feel, therefore I am." Those who have difficulties in experiencing deep feelings (affect-block) often describe themselves as not alive, or like being dead, or living in shades of gray. It is our feelings which either make life worthwhile, or drive us to suicide, or give us warning that we don't like the way the world treats us. Our feelings guide our decisions by granting us courage or by discouraging us from taking those steps which would expand our world. It is feelings which help us to have a long memory of a happy life, or make inaccessible a painful past. Feelings and living are inseparable.

## ADAPTIVE FUNCTION

Adaptation can be considered to be the change in our self as we improve the fit between ourselves and our world to ensure survival (Gilula & Daniels, 1969). Rapid change in our environment can make previous adaptive patterns actually maladaptive. We can think of adaptation as the actions we take (within our inner world, and in manipulating the outer world) which meet our needs, prepare us for future eventualities, and improve our mood. Adaptation involves both active adjustments and a passive acquiescence or acceptance to facts as they are. They may be fulfilling or self-destructive.

The way in which we cope with life will determine whether we fulfill our needs. If we grow up with a crippled self, we behave inadequately; this causes us to experience further deprivation or be unable to experience satisfaction as do people with normal childhoods. Particularly, the infant must have his psychological needs met. The deprived infant is apathetic, immobile, and unreactive. The earlier and the longer that there is no loving person to care for him, the greater the subsequent emotional crippling (Provence & Lipton, 1962; Malmquist, 1972). However, as Adler pointed out (cited by Malmquist), a child can use his tears manipulatively. Thus a feeling of depression may be adaptive if it brings fulfillment of emotional needs which would otherwise be ignored. However, the maintenance of an unhappy mood could also be considered maladaptive, if other activities would relieve it. We see here the adaptive connection between deprivation, feelings, and subsequent actions.

Adaptation also means preparation for the future. Our goals, skills, plans, tendency to hoard or to squander, are all part of our self. The person who has developed self-confidence will cope differently with new situations and opportunities than he who can only anticipate defeat.

We are always enmeshed in one situation or another, and our characteristic mode of reaction reveals our adaptation. To our employer's pressure we may adapt by working harder or passively sabotaging; to financial strain by changing jobs or economizing; to our loved one's distress by controlling our temper. Each of these changes in our actions is really a modification of our self.

In addition to processing information for our choices, a successful adaptation requires an adequate internal organization of our body and mind, as well as freedom of action (White, 1974). Not only must our bodies be sturdy enough to support our choices, but also we must avoid being overwhelmed by self-destructive attitudes of guilt, incompetence, and worthlessness. We must also preserve enough options that we can avoid dangers and select alternatives.

Nor can we avoid the importance of using our intelligence (Wechsler, 1975) in order to achieve a worthwhile adaptation to life, since it is "the capacity to understand the world . . . and resourcefulness to cope with its challenges." No, feelings are not all!

To obtain the quality of life we call emotional fulfillment requires maximizing decisions which lead to a constructive lifestyle, and recognizing and then changing circumstances which are degrading.

It is necessary to start by evaluating your personality and above all your frame of mind. The emotional condition in which you find yourself is a complex product of your basic nature, the world in which you have played a role, and the kind of adaptations which you have used in order to survive. As a consequence of your experiences, you develop a certain quality of self-esteem or self-hatred, emotional fulfillment or deprivation, social competence or inadequacy, and so forth. When you appreciate that you must make changes, you will then have to evaluate what kind of change is necessary. I recognize at least three kinds of adaptive changes.

## FORMS OF ADAPTATION

*Internal changes*: Changes in our personality are one form of adaptation. These may be constructive or self-destructive. When we improve our skills, control our temper, compromise our needs with those we love, we are building an emotionally fulfilling future. If we learn to see ourselves as vile or inadequate, or never express love or anger, or always yield or fight with authority, and so forth then the result is self-destructive.

*External changes*: This refers to changing your environment. If you are working hard and are in financial need, asking for a raise is a constructive example. Influencing others to behave differently to us is another. Provoking people into being angry with us, or rejecting us, would be self-destructive kinds of influence.

*Exploratory*: This follows the example of our primitive ancestors. It means making major changes in the way we live, not merely in the details of our personality (internal) or the world around us (external). Examples would include going from one city to another, leaving our parents, terminating relationships or engaging in new ones.

With this intimate information about the self and the way it integrates experiences, let us look directly at ways to improve the quality of your decisions.

This has been a long passage about the complex and numerous byways which the mind passes through between an impulse or wish and a decision. Now we can start the pleasant task of applying all of this information to your life and emotional fulfillment. In the next chapters I will summarize many of the critical factors which you will have to take into consideration in order to make effective decisions.

# 14

# The Foundation for Effective Decisions

Decision making is a basic characteristic of all living organisms. Even bacteria, one of the simplest forms of life, engage in this process, as stated by the prestigious journal *Science* in an article entitled " 'Decision'-Making in Bacteria" (Adler & Wung-Wai Tso, 1974). As the authors point out, this one-celled creature must sometimes choose in the "conflict" between pursuing something attractive when it is in the general region of something repellent. What's more, they do it successfully! "Apparently bacteria have a processing mechanism that compares opposing signals from the . . . receptors . . . sums these signals up, and then communicates the sum . . ." to the swimming organs. You too engage in this evaluating process. This chapter and the next are designed to help you increase the balance of constructive to self-destructive decisions.

What is a decision? A decision is the intention of taking action in order to change the world in which you live. Every day we make decisions. Even the most inconsequential ones begin to have a cumulative effect on your style of life and emotional well-being.

You can improve your effectiveness in any significant area which requires that you plan and then coordinate the activities of many people. Some examples are moving your home or buying another, having one constructed for you, getting married or divorced, organizing a business, carrying out a project or somebody else's instructions, changing jobs, and so on.

Every major change in your life creates alternatives for you to consider. Sometimes they force you to cope with significantly different circumstances. A systematic way of evaluating a situation, considering different courses of action, and analyzing the likely events which follow from your decision, leads to better decisions and ensures that the results are in accord with your intentions. Effective decisions include gathering information so that if circumstances should occur which are unpredicted or beyond your control, you will be aware of them as they take place, and you can modify your decisions or substitute new ones for those which are out of date. You will not be taken by surprise.

Here is the sequence of events and/or controls you must utilize to become an effective decision maker.

*What is an effective decision?* An effective decision is one which changes your life by bringing you to your personal goals in a timely way without excessive cost. By applying these procedures you will be able to use what you have learned up to now.

## WHEN ARE DECISIONS NECESSARY?

*In a crisis:* A crisis may be defined as a situation in which an abrupt change for the worse can be expected. During or after a crisis the usual way of doing things becomes changed because we are swept up by events. In personal affairs, crises can be created by illness, unexpected deaths, antagonism of mates or business partners, catastrophic events, and so on. If we don't cope successfully, we may make poor decisions, or even fall apart and have others make decisions for us. Fortunately, in many crises, the onset of a setback or serious disaster can be predicted, so that by proper decision making, the worst results can be avoided, or perhaps the situation can even be turned to our advantage.

*To reach realistic goals:* It is not generally realized, but the goals which we set for ourselves are a specific form of decision.

Since goals are among the most emotional of all decisions, we must remember what we have learned about impossible dreams (Chapter 6), and how groups influence goal setting (Chapter 12). Goal setting is related to our self-esteem (Greenhaus & Badin, 1974). People with high self-esteem wish to maintain their self-image of competence and become motivated to perform well. Those of us with low self-esteem may not be motivated to perform well because a poor performance is consistent wtih our self-image of incompetence. Moreover, our expectations of how well we can perform may be a result of how others have evaluated our performance and what they expect of us.

The effectiveness with which we implement our decisions (or others perform for us) is also a function of fear of failure, fear of success, and concern over the consequences of advancement in our profession. This is particularly true in the case of women according to current research (O'Leary, 1974). Because many of them have been raised on self-destructive stereotypes, they fear that success (effective implementation of decisions) may result in social rejection because they may be considered unfeminine and abnormal. It is believed that men are more likely to have developed autonomy, or motivation to achieve, because of their own standards. Female children seem to become more conditioned to reliance upon external reinforcement as standards for behavior. Sometimes successful women become anxious when they deviate from a conventional female role. We can conclude that setting realistic goals requires that we clear our heads of all factors not related to our real talents and other important considerations.

*In changing conditions*: We all undertake actions based upon particular assumptions. However, unless we are realistic, and ready to be in tune with new information, we can find that our knowledge is totally out of date. This can be true even in the case of big business which presumably can afford to hire people to bring important facts to the attention of management. Consider the industries which have been plagued by the oil shortage —to the public's detriment: automobile, housing, air transport, and so forth. The American public was sold on the idea that energy was limitless and cheap. Apparently even hard-headed business types began to believe this pap, until the realities of geology and *realpolitik* caught them with goods and services that couldn't be sold, or manufactured economically. Huge cars, planes, and houses now have become uneconomical because decision makers did not anticipate that the previous conditions were changing.

*When your needs are unfulfilled*: It is possible to drift along for years in a state of suspended dissatisfaction. Nothing is going right, and yet there is no specific source of pain, no rapidly deteriorating relationship or business venture which forces you into activity. You are simply in a low state of grumble-grumble. Only a major change will bring you toward a more fulfilling existence. A decision to live your life differently can change the balance from dissatisfaction to activity and constructive change.

*To improve present conditions*: It is one thing to be dissatisfied, but it is another to be satisfied and yet see that your life could be far better. Many people decide to drop out of psychotherapy when an emergency is over. Others wish to stretch their emotional potential to the utmost and continue their work in calm times. The owner of a business who decides to expand or open up a branch is improving his situation. The woman who decides in middle age to return to college may already be earning a satisfactory living but not be satisfied with the nature of her job. The family who lives in a suitable home, but feels that it needs more space is also acting to improve conditions but not out of any serious distress.

*To achieve long-term goals*: This requires the most careful kind of planning. The intention is to work toward a goal which may take years to fulfill, and whose effects are intended to be far-reaching. When you plan a career, or a family, or a major change in the way you run your home or business, then most of your resources, time, and emotional energy may become involved with the carrying out of your intentions. The consequence of failure will be frustration, wasted resources, and wasted years of effort.

## Making a Personal Assessment

Having decided that an important decision must be made, you must remember that you will be the one to carry it out. Your personal characteristics become a part of the decision-making process since you will guide events to their proper conclusion and be the focus of any change. Unless the decision is relevant or fulfilling to you, the entire matter can be wasteful or self-destructive.

*Assets*: Most people do not have a clear idea of their real strengths (or liabilities). Even if they should be successful, they cannot determine which of their qualities would make them attractive to a *new* employer, mate, and so on. Strengths can be in the area of interpersonal relationships, general intelligence, specific abilities or skills, education, and experience. Prior to making many kinds of decisions it would be useful for you to obtain a professional assessment from a qualified counseling, industrial, or clinical psychologist. In addition to knowing your assets, you must also take into account your motivation and goals. I had a young man in my office recently who was told he would make a good lawyer. The only problem was that he didn't want to be a lawyer. Every important decision must include a personal assessment of whether you want to, and are capable of, carrying it out.

*Liabilities*: A characteristic can be a strength in one situation and a liability in another. The quality of self-assertion might be marvelous if you are running your own business, but a decided weakness if you are under the supervision of a domineering boor. However, not every characteristic can be treated in such a relativistic manner. There is definitely age and sex discrimination in some areas of life. You might really be too old or not bright enough to benefit from certain kinds of training. Your interpersonal relationships can be poor, so that many activities which are otherwise feasible are excluded to you. You may be wasteful of time, lack self-discipline, be in poor health, have a drug or alcoholic habit, and so forth. All of these may be liabilities which must be overcome before major decisions can be made which change your style of life.

*Personal necessities*: You probably have particular qualities which affect the possibility of your enjoying the results of particular decisions, or developing the motivation to carry them out. The young man who had the pattern of abilities to become a lawyer was not interested in this profession. A lawyer might prefer to work in one specialty rather than another because his particular values would be violated in certain activities but rewarded in others. Some other person might prefer to marry rather than enter long training for a profession because the goal of family life was more important than professional success. A woman could decide to enter the private practice of medicine rather than go into a research project because her style was that of a "loner" rather than of collaborating with others. All of these somewhat subjective qualities will affect your success in carrying out decisions. They must be taken into account when alternative courses of action are considered.

*Temperament and constitution*: Each of us has certain personality traits which originate in our bodily structure and functioning. These are frequently ignored when people make decisions or have decisions made for them. These basic ways of reacting enhance or detract from your effectiveness in carrying out particular decisions. A calm person might make an effective psychoanalyst, sitting behind a couch attending closely to a patient's free associations and offering an occasional interpretation. However, another psychotherapist whose temperament was directed toward action and variability might do better as a group therapist or encounter group leader. The surgeon who must concentrate and make rapid decisions for hours at a time or literally kill somebody has a different temperament than the industrial physician evaluating compensation cases, or the obstetrician caring for anxious pregnant women, or the pediatrician treating sick children.

Therefore, the enduring qualities of your personality must become a part of the decision-making process. They dictate how you deal with new or ongoing events, how you channel your energy and perceive your world, how much effort you can expend, and how you concentrate your efforts. They limit your choices.

*Self-discipline*: No decision is a suitable one unless you have the willingness to make sacrifices to carry it out. The would-be writer who would rather go "on the town" at night than stay at his desk merely ends up hating himself. Self-discipline affects many different areas of life. As a student, parent, business executive, brain- or hand-worker, traveling salesman, and so on, there are always distractions and temptations to take us away from our immediate tasks. Sufficient deviations from a path lead to the destruction of our long-range goals. A few less-than-adequate performances on the job or in school can cause our careers to be retarded or aborted. Therefore, you must make a careful assessment of your capacity to exercise self-discipline before making final decisions. Everything else can be "go," but if you can't concentrate your efforts there will be serious or disastrous consequences.

*Motivation*: Motivation and movement are related. Unless you truly want to go in a certain direction, it is foolish to start a trip when there are other choices available. Motivation must absolutely be considered as a factor in deciding which of several alternatives is best for you. If your parents tell you about all the advantages of having a medical career, and how much it would please them if you became a physician, there is no point in planning to enter medical school unless you like the idea of becoming a practicing physician. Poor motivation eventually leads to lack of self-discipline, rebelliousness, indifference to quality, and all the other emotional garbage which puts an inglorious end to great decisions. It is essential that you recognize lack of motivation once a decision has been made. Since I recommend setting up a schedule to aid you in evaluating your progress, serious deviations from your schedule may be a sign that you really don't want to do what you have decided to accomplish. Finding other things to do, getting involved with details, spending hours agonizing over something but leaving it unfinished and finding yourself full of self-hate are all signs of poor motivation. Having this experience frequently is a sign of passivity and is an emotional problem to be corrected.

*Self-assertion*: Whose decision are you carrying out? We have seen the many reasons why the true origin of a decision is obscure. When you look carefully at the preliminary stages of making a decision, you may discover that you are working on somebody else's program (your parents', for example). Perhaps you have been seduced into carrying out a plan which you think is yours but really meets somebody else's needs. Another way of looking at the question, "Why carry out a decision?" is to ask, "Whose needs does it really meet?" Even though you do all the creative thinking, take responsibility for carrying it out, sacrifice spirit and opportunities, you may discover that somebody else is benefiting from your efforts. (I do not refer here to making sacrifices for children.) In relationships with friends, family, and employers, others may reap the rewards; and you may or may not receive even a "thank you." It frequently happens that an undue burden falls on one person. There may be many children, but one of them takes the responsibility for an elderly or disabled parent. It is quietly agreed who is the "good child" and the financial cost and all efforts are borne by him or her. You should insist that everybody involved share in the decision and be around to carry it out. They will be there with their hands out when it comes time to read the will!

*Self-confidence*: Many decisions require both courage and ability to carry out. *Practically all fears in the social world are neurotic.* However, even if the disaster that you anticipate will never come about, the mere fact that you experience fear will have an effect upon the outcome. You may take less initiative, make less daring (or too daring) decisions, handle yourself poorly in face-to-face contacts, choke up in groups, let yourself be eliminated from competition, or permit yourself to be dominated or cheated. Therefore, your degree of self-confidence determines the likelihood of success in a particular venture. It might be necessary for your future for you to improve your self-esteem and confidence through some form of psychotherapy. When you have eliminated the encrusted fears and doubts and self-hatred, there are new opportunities which will open up. You will handle them in a forthright, efficient way.

Many people try to overcome fear or weakness recklessly. They plunge into an area which they fear in the hope that they will come out with a stronger character. Some examples I have come across in my clinical practice include entering the marines, becoming a salesman, and marrying. It is true that occasionally success is achieved. I think that more often it is not, and there is more stress and failure than is necessary. The success rate in forcing oneself to do that which one fears is poor. It might be better to make decisions out of necessity, when the goal is meaningful, and then try to master each situation as it arises. This is less reckless than having as a primary goal the direct increase of self-confidence by courting danger.

*Integrity and reliability*: Occasionally somebody comes into my office and asks me to engage in some hanky-panky in order for them to collect insurance fees or something of that nature. I politely tell them that I do not care to risk either my license or my freedom. I then pontificate that people pay me fees in order to relieve themselves of anxiety and I do not propose to do anything which will increase my own. There are many situations in life where honesty, keeping one's word, and being reliable are the essentials of a job properly performed. Not to function in this way means violating the law, disappointing clients, creating ill feelings, and all the rest. It may be that you have been requested to take a bribe, have a conflict of interest, or give favors to friends. If this sits poorly on your conscience, avoid it. Be prudent.

You might, however, be in a situation where you are being unjustly treated, where you have assumed integrity on the part of a contact or contractor. I give people only one chance to lie to me or cheat me or fail to keep their word. Emotional well-being is generally enhanced by treating others with integrity and reliability. It is also important in carrying out your decisions that you expect the same from those on whom you depend. However, since this section refers to a personal evaluation, you must assess what will be expected of you when you agree to carry out a decision. If there will be temptations or an unwilling-ness to participate, you would be better off to refuse.

## PERSONAL FACTORS IN POOR DECISION MAKING

There are numerous ways in which your personal character-istics can sabotage your decisions before they even get off the ground. Part of a personal assessment is determining whether you have any of the following self-destructive traits:

*Secret pleasure from the present situations*: Many of us moan and groan about how life is treating us, and yet, to every-body's astonishment, we do nothing to change it. A classic example is the spouse of an alcoholic. Upon closer examination, we see that she may enjoy playing a martyr's role and fears independence. The employee who feels mistreated on the job may not take any action because of a lifelong dependency and unwillingness to risk unemployment.

*Neurotic doubts*: The inability to make decisions may be a deep-rooted character trait. Emotional problems in growing up may have crippled a person's capacity to be forthright. Perhaps a parent always criticized him for any action he took, so that an imaginary voice is saying: "Do it," "No, don't do it." Con-flicting feelings or values also prevent a person from taking sen-sible, necessary steps.

*Dependent attitude*: You or others upon whom you rely may have been brought up not to question authority because of religious training or authoritarian parents or teachers. The humble person does not step out decisively. The inadequate person has been taught that he is incompetent. In these cases as well the fear of taking a risk hampers effective decision making.

*Not knowing who you are*: If you don't know who you are, then you don't know what you want. You have no sense of values to guide you or to provide rewards. You will end up by being a satellite in the lives of people who are more forceful and self-determined than you.

## WHAT RESOURCES ARE NECESSARY?

Most decisions require more than mere will power to carry out. As you consider alternative means of reaching your goals, it may be that the resources which you command will determine which decision is realistic and which are too costly or impossible in terms of available assistance.

*A proper work atmosphere*: A good working environment enables you to function efficiently and retain control over any project throughout its entire operation. You ought to be able to function efficiently, without losing track of your thoughts, and have access to those people and things which are necessary for your plans.

Some students do well in dormitories with rock and roll blaring and pandemonium all around them. I would rapidly go berserk. Each of us has a certain optimum environment in which we do our best work. A struggle is often necessary to obtain this. Whether we make financial sacrifices to have a separate office at home or request that other workers not play the radio, demand supplies, facilities, and amenities in our office, our emotional well-being and ability to function creatively and productively depend upon a suitable work atmosphere. It might even be worthwhile for you to change jobs when you cannot obtain this. However, whatever you are doing, you should work toward a proper environment so that you function effectively. It may mean having a telephone, or disconnecting the telephone. When something important is at stake, creating the proper circumstances may mean the difference between success and failure. It will certainly mean the difference between good motivation and daily frustration and/or distaste for what you have to do.

There are so many different kinds of working environments that it would be time-wasting to try to describe all the possibilities. In general, I think that conducive working conditions for the purpose of planning and implementing effective decisions (except for field inspections of progress) can be described as quiet (or as nearly so as possible), interruption-free (or some control over visitors), accessible storage space (divided according to your own requirements, with some personal time invested for orderly classification of materials), suitable communications, accessible library (even if it is only a telephone book and a good dictionary), and supplies on hand.

Your own requirements may be somewhat different, but at least you should review in your mind whether the time, space, and facilities help or hinder you in planning and carrying out your projects.

I would like to make a special comment about noise, perhaps because I am particularly irritated by unnecessary noises. I distinguish between those which are inherent to a situation and those which are created by insensitive people. When I am doing something which requires concentration (therapeutic sessions or writing), I can stand the noises of the metropolis, for example, fire engines and construction. However, the noises of radios, dogs barking in a confined courtyard, and so on are very disorganizing. Noise is an irritation which may cause emotional responses, physiological changes, health problems, and loss of sleep. It certainly reduces our efficiency to perform certain kinds of tasks (Theologus et al., 1974). Noise affects our efficiency where several kinds of information must be integrated so that we can form a judgment. Perhaps under noise conditions we reduce the number of cues that we can pay attention to simultaneously (Weinstein, 1974). You must be firm about removing noise and other distractions.

*Correct assumptions*: The first procedure in examining a situation is to make explicit your assumptions. What are your beliefs? Which are the conditions which require a decision? What will affect any decisions you carry out? What situation do you anticipate during the time span that you are planning for? What will be the conditions when the plan is finally carried out? Do you expect certain kinds of assistance, or particular political or economic conditions, or opposition? Do you have the prerequisites for a particular training course you need? You are going to move to a new city. Do you know whether there will be housing, employment, and suitable entertainment opportunities? You are going to order the construction of a new house, or obtain services, or get supplies. What are the laws pertaining to construction, licensed builders, the price and credit terms of your suppliers? Take nothing for granted!

*Current information*: Obtaining the right kind and amount of data is the next step after eliminating prejudices and false preconceptions. Nothing is more stupid than not knowing the obvious or not getting easily obtained data. The next most stupid thing is assuming that you know it all. I know one man, who considers himself a genius at marketing, who got upset when I called to his attention a newspaper article which revealed unfriendly public reaction affecting his industry. He assumed that people's prejudices could be disregarded. In actuality, even "soft" information like the climate of opinion can affect the outcome of our important projects. This man assumes that all that is necessary for him to sell his product is a clever advertisement. Actually, the attitudes of potential customers are the key issue. If the demand is right they would beat down the doors of any company, even those with mediocre advertisements. Information is like milk: it rapidly gets out of date, becomes sour, and can make you sick.

There has been a change in how business can be carried on effectively. It has been pointed out that every choice a (large) corporation makes "... affects thousands of people who had no voice in the classical marketplace but who are increasingly creating new market conditions through social pressure, moral suasion, and law.... (This creates a new job for management which) may be the most complicated.... Before acting, managers must weigh a multitude of interests" (Burck, 1975).

It is easy to get too self-confident concerning your capacity to process information. One of the world's biggest banks is led by a man whose very name is synonymous with handling vast sums of money. This bank became a symbol of poor management (Robards, 1976). A government memorandum stated: "There appeared to be poor communication between the lending and support staff, poor credit files and lack of knowledge of the borrowers' current status." To illustrate how poor information-gathering and -utilizing techniques led to a serious condition—after its chairman was informed of the proposed strategy to cope with the large flow of money to the Near East during the energy crisis—he asked, "Who are we going to send there?" His subordinates expected him to ask, "How much are we going to make on it?" or "What is the rate of return?" These would be questions related to the process of running a bank; they would invite discussion of prudent banking risks. Instead, he simply accepted the plan as proposed. This prominent banker was described as a man who "needs people to tell him what he wants to hear. Anybody who does the opposite loses his favor. He's not an operating guy or a detail man." In short, although responsible for the operation, he is seen as somebody without grasp of the details and who lacks interest in finding the right questions.

Some managers use informal techniques for staying in touch (Meyer, 1975). They are interested in providing lower-level executives with a sense of participation. Not only do they acquire additional information which does not arrive through the usual channels, but they make sure that "orders from on top are reaching the troops intact." Techniques which are effective include letting subordinates know they can reach you, chatting with people when you deliver memos personally, playing tennis with the staff, leaving your office to go to the production areas, eating in the company cafeteria rather than the private one, taking a local elevator rather than the express to encourage casual contacts, and so forth.

People have peculiarities in asking for and using information. Early in a situation, when the ultimate solution is indefinite, they may ask for more information than they do later when the goal can be rapidly clarified (J. M. Levine, 1973). Furthermore, as the situation becomes clearer, so that earlier apparent conflicts no longer exist or information is clearly more relevant to the final goal, they do not increase their requests for information. It has also been observed that when information which is objective is supplied, there can be wide disagreement as to how it should be evaluated. People differ considerably between the way they think they reach their conclusions and the process they actually follow (Valenzi & Andrew, 1973).

It is a misconception that once a decision is made, it is final. There are examples of multibillion dollar corporations which wasted vast sums and the talents of geniuses because their information was out of date. The Ford Edsel sold poorly because, by the time it was in production, market tastes had changed. General Motors had to shut down whole auto plants because they assumed that fuel would always flow like water. These people had both money and talent to obtain correct industrial intelligence. If they can misallocate resources because they closed their eyes to reality, you, who are hanging on by the skin of your teeth (in a lot of instances), cannot afford to ignore pertinent facts. Indeed, it might be more difficult for a private person to obtain relevant information concerning situations which influence his decisions.

Whether you are functioning as part of a company or institution, or making a private decision, get the facts. And remember, some of the facts concern the attitudes of people upon whom you will rely to carry out your decisions. Some of the facts might only be available to your subordinates who presently carry out assignments and deal with the public or with contractors, suppliers, tradespeople, and so on. Correct facts include changing needs for your services or product, weather, geography, transportation, and the population and characteristics of those who will be affected by you, or can affect your chance of success—all of these facts are part of your resources as you implement your decision.

Nevertheless, good decision makers may proceed even when the situation is vague, or the facts are in conflict (Feinberg, 1971). Excessive need for facts may be merely a way of stalling.

I quote from D. C. Hilary, of Don Aux and Associates, Organizational Development Consultants of New York City:

> The small businessman must recognize that every decision he makes today will affect his activities and profits in the future. One of the questions I always ask a new client is: "What do you see ahead for your industry, and in particular for your

individual company?" If he tells me he hasn't thought about it, it is safe to assume he hasn't thought about a great many other things that he should have.

Sometimes the situation is reversed and there is a heavy information load. Then it becomes urgent that you learn to select and simplify the facts (and semifacts and downright irrelevancies and misinformation) which are flung at you. Unfortunately, excluding from consideration less relevant material, or even ignoring certain classes of information, biases the options open to us. Perhaps only information pertaining to positive (or negative) outcomes is utilized. This information will have a greater impact upon judgments than a more balanced approach (Wright, 1974). Perhaps the answer is to sample carefully important information *known* to be negative or positive so that both dangers and opportunities can be evaluated simultaneously.

*Capital*: Many people get into trouble because they do not estimate correctly the amount of money they will need to carry out a decision, where they will get it, how much interest they will have to pay, and at what rate they will have to pay it back. Check your assumptions. It is a typical experience that the cost of a project is usually much more than was anticipated. Whether it is inflation, inefficiency, poor planning, or change of plans before completion, inevitably there are unanticipated expenses. Although these sound like considerations for major industrialists, the principle holds true for anybody who spends money to carry out a serious decision. The price of a belt is not going to change while you are looking at the merchandise and wondering whether to buy it. However, these days there is often a serious delay between ordering a high-priced item and its delivery.

Sometimes one phase of an operation cannot proceed until some material or service has been delivered and is operational. Most people are ashamed to ask for return of their money or penalty clauses for nondelivery or nonperformance. They permit their capital to be tied up with large down payments, payment-in-advance, or deposits. As a consequence, suppliers of goods and services use their money without interest, their own free capital is at a minimum, and they are forced to go to banks for money at usurious rates. The principle is clear: estimate what you will need, provide a reserve, assume that the project may not be ready on time and that you will need further reserves, and take vigorous steps to prevent being used as a patsy by unscrupulous businessmen and consultants.

We have laid the foundation for considering the actual process of formulating and implementing effective decisions.

# 15

# Creating and Implementing Effective Decisions

We have now reached that stage where you can integrate all of the information you have learned up to now into effective decisions. It must be emphasized above all that to be effective, a decision must be timely. Events do not cease simply because you cannot make up your mind. My friend D. C. Hilary points out that: "Bankruptcies don't happen overnight. Every bankruptcy that I have analyzed was caused by a businessman who feared making a decision more than he feared the consequences of his indecisiveness."

A good decision is preceded by these steps:

1. Deciding why and when the decision must be made;
2. Evaluation of your personal characteristics, such as needs, values, and temperament; and
3. A preliminary estimate of the resources available to you.

Evaluating your personal needs, and also the resources available to you, will determine the limits of the reasonable alternatives from which you will select the ultimate decision. It is foolish to go into the final stage of decision making without having some general idea of the kind of solution you seek and of whether you can carry it out with your access to services, people, and capital. You might as well remember to examine your assumptions about conditions which will affect the success of your decision.

## Making the Decision

*Select Several Alternatives.* It is rare that any decision is so clear-cut that there is only one possible course of action. In this case it is a matter of doing something or doing nothing at all. There may be some compulsion, that is, "take it or leave it." Thus, what appears to be a decision is really acting under the force of panic or other circumstances.

Some mistakes managers make in decision making include emphasis upon routine, "programmed" problems, while avoiding those which involve unfamiliar, unpleasant, or challenging ones (Burck, 1975). This way of decision making is a fine way of ensuring that your solutions will be inadequate or irrelevant to the real world.

According to Peter Drucker, prominent management consultant, an "effective executive" (1966):

1. Decides whether he is dealing with a special case, or with a general problem which may recur. In the latter eventuality, he creates rules dealing with this kind of situation.

2. Determines the conditions or facts which a decision must satisfy: present or future.

3. Decides on the right solution, before making any compromises.

Let us assume that genuine alternatives are possible. Then, it is useful to make explicit your assumptions concerning the facts. One way of approaching the decision would be like this: if Assumption A is correct, then the best course of action is A'; if Assumption B is correct, then B' follows. For example, if you or somebody you care about are considering a career, and the choices have been boiled down to law or accounting, you have obviously assumed that:

Assumption $A^1$: In four years there will be a need for accountants;

Assumption $A^2$: Scholarship funds are available for accounting studies;

Assumption $A^3$: My grades are good enough for accounting studies;

Assumption $L^1$: In seven years there will be a need for lawyers;

Assumption $L^2$: Scholarship funds are available for law studies;

Assumption $L^3$: My grades are good enough for prelaw studies.

When you look into each of these assumptions, it might turn out that the projected need for members of one or the other profession, available funds, and grades make one decision the logical choice. Let us imagine that neither of these alternatives can be pursued. In this case, a vast amount of effort, perhaps funds, and motivation have been saved because *future difficulties have been anticipated.* There is still time to consider other alternatives. The only loss has been some delay. In fact, as you study the conditions influencing the first two alternatives, new ideas may evolve. In any event, you will have gathered considerable information which makes the choice and evaluation of the next set of alternatives more efficient.

Let us assume that examination of the situation suggests several alternatives. You will want to analyze each possibility as follows:

1. What are the advantages of this course of action?
2. What are the disadvantages of this course of action?
3. Can this decision be supported by my available resources?
4. Are there any "red lights," that is, any aspects of the situation which make this alternative impossible regardless of any advantages?

Let us assume that you are planning to buy a house or rent an apartment. As you consider the alternatives, one type of residence may have a balance favoring it. Nevertheless, it would take only a single characteristic—for example, lack of transportation, schools, excessive cost, neighborhood—to rule it out completely.

What should you do if there are no "red lights," and several alternatives remain possible?

*Choosing the right alternative*: There will be many occasions where a particular decision cannot be made on the basis of objective or quantifiable advantages. The proper decision is one which takes into account subjective, qualitative features of your personality. This will be particularly true where you will have to carry the decision personally or if it is designed to satisfy your needs, or help you to reach particular goals.

*What characterizes an effective decision?* An effective decision takes into account your personal qualities, as well as those of the world in which you function.

1. *It maximizes your strengths.* Since certain decisions will be carried by you on your back, you must ascertain that you have the particular qualities to carry them out. There must be a match between you and the requirements of the situation. The model of the round peg in the round hole is suitable for more situations than just planning a career or looking for a job. It must be utilized wherever your motivation and capacity to function are critical over long periods of time. For example, in choosing to rent an apartment or buy a house, you or your spouse's capacity for household repairs would make a significant difference in costs. If your strength is in social relationships, your employment choice of an entry level position as a receptionist would be more advantageous than as a secretary or an administrative assistant, even if slight salary and other conditions favor the alternatives.

2. *It minimizes your weaknesses.* A certain characteristic which is a strength in some circumstances could be a weakness in others. Also, certain personality qualities may be an invitation to built-in failure under most conditions. Any decision requiring a lengthy time span to carry out will maximize the chance that weaknesses will be exposed. Lack of persistence or self-discipline, disinterest in continuing your training, dependency, inability to get along with people, alcoholic or drug problems, educational deficits, extravagance, problems of anger, inability to assert yourself, excessive devotion to sexual exploits, and so on could have devastating effects upon your functioning and capability to obtain what you want in life. You will have to learn to avoid long-term projects which you would sabotage through self-destruction. If you cannot overcome these, you should obtain psychotherapy to

change toward a constructive lifestyle. (See Chapter 20 of my book *Emotional Common Sense*, Harper & Row, 1973, for aid in selecting a therapist.)

3. *It sustains motivation.* Anything worthwhile requires a vast amount of effort. However, no decision is worth anything if we become bored, indifferent, or actively hostile to pursuing it. We really have to *enjoy* the activity while completing the project. Years can go by before we have reached our goal. At certain stages of life, reaching one goal may mean that we have to set yet another goal to avoid stagnating or falling back. This means that for long stretches of our life we might be working toward distant goals. Unless we like what we are doing, we may waste our lives or consume time, spirit, money, and opportunities in a series of projects which are started and never completed.

*Monitor changing circumstances*: Nothing gets out of date faster than facts! If this weren't the case, there wouldn't be annual revisions of the almanac, encyclopedia, and so on. It is hard to imagine any decision that isn't affected by the cost of living, employment factors, foreign affairs, economic considerations, and technological change. I don't care whether it is marriage, furnishing a home, or opening a business. You name it, any plan that you are contemplating will take place in a world that is different from the day you decided to do it. Therefore, you have to be on the alert to changing circumstances and alter your procedures as you get feedback from the world "out there." Since certain events are out of your control, you will have to compensate in other areas. If you are planning to refurnish part of your house, and the bedroom set that you are determined to get has just risen in price from $700 to $850, either you go $150 in debt or you cut back in some other area. People who do not compensate find themselves unexpectedly short of funds or in debt. Remember the physiological concepts of homeostasis and adaptation. Apply them where appropriate to your life. Our body adapts to changing requirements until stress is over. The same model of monitoring the world and then changing direction and instructions to others applies to any decision you make.

*Anticipate difficulties*: The first thing a new chess player learns, after mastering the moves, is not to underestimate his opponent. We may think we are making a great move, only to have it countered in some humiliating way. Worse than that, *he* may be making plans for *us* that we never dreamed about. It is a valuable lesson. Think ahead. Do not assume any plan can be carried out without confronting some major obstacle. Whereas our advice to "monitor changing circumstances" refers to becoming aware of events as they occur, to "anticipate difficulties" points out that sometimes we can predict what will happen. We can benefit from future events, or avert danger, through proper planning.

## IMPLEMENTING THE DECISION

You can be a good executive even in the privacy of your own home. In fact, you are an executive at all times. The only question is, "Are you a good or bad executive?" Management consultant Peter Drucker (1966) states that the effective executive *plans, organizes, integrates, motivates,* and *measures.* If you have any control over your own destiny, you too can follow this standard.

*Divide the project into parts.* Separating a project into parts is necessary for several reasons. First, you can determine who is the best person to carry out each part and where each unit fits into the entire scheme; you can also monitor progress. Second, you can evaluate each part or objective as to how it affects the other segments and how they affect it. Finally, you can pace your own work more effectively.

*Improve personal efficiency.* Everybody has a certain span of attention. Different people have different capacities to move from one kind of work to another and to overcome distractions, as well as different requirements for fun. Therefore, in order to maintain your most efficient flow of work, you have to estimate a reasonable output for yourself according to the way you use your time—so much work per day or week. When I write, I can function effectively for about five or six hours at a time, so I have learned to allocate at least that much time. Then, when I have other things to do, I do not object to putting the manuscript aside and returning to it later. To estimate what you can do in one day, and then do it, is a fine way to avoid discouragement. I have observed that, when people working on their own are suffering from a work block, they can frequently function for one hour. I tell them to work an hour in the morning and an hour in the afternoon and to enjoy the rest of the day. Put frustration and guilt out of your mind. Gradually, encouraged by working effectively during the brief interval, they increase their output until their productivity is satisfactory.

*Decide what you must do personally.* There are parts of any project which only the leader or decision-maker can carry out, including supervising others, gaining information, and directing service. You should evaluate the cost of what you contribute directly, versus the cost of service which you expect from others. Time versus money is one way of looking at it. However, when you have decided what your personal duties are, then you have defined the next part of the process of planning.

*Decide what others must do.* Having a clear idea of how others will participate in carrying out your decisions and projects is a major point in success. You must know exactly what you expect, make provisions to gain information about progress, and not assume that anything will be done properly unless you or somebody you trust checks on it personally. Furthermore, you may have every reason to believe in advance that your superiors, colleagues, subordinates, and consultants are competent and reliable. However, as information comes back to you, you may learn otherwise. It may be necessary to provide further training for some people working under you. Others might have to be replaced. You might also learn that some of the conditions which you personally set up are unfulfillable. Therefore, your instructions will have to be modified.

*Decide priorities.* Every complicated task can be divided into parts: those that should have been finished yesterday, those that must be done today, and those that can wait until tomorrow. There are probably even portions that need not be done at all. It is the person who is hiding his incompetence who becomes involved in details which, although conspicuous, are valueless.

D. C. Hilary describes trivial activities consuming the time of important people as "toilet paper decisions," that is, deciding on the quality of toilet paper while million-dollar projects wait. He tells of one conference with a client concerning long-range corporate planning. They were interrupted by an inquiry as to whether a 60 or 75 watt bulb should replace a burnt out bulb. This was not only wasteful in terms of the comparative salaries paid the porter and the executive, it was distracting to both consultant and company president. Keep your eye on the ball!

Therefore, whether you are carrying out a job personally or supervising somebody else, you must establish priorities. This involves evaluating both the importance of a section and when it must be finished. Remember that when one part is incomplete, frequently other parts dependent upon it cannot be finished. You can't install a boiler in a house until the foundation is in. A job campaign depends upon having a good resume, but the resume can't be submitted until you have your records in order. A positive offer may not come until you have permission from former employers to use their names as references.

*Establish a schedule.* From a certain point of view, time is all that we have. To achieve our goals late takes something from our lives which can never be returned. Therefore, to establish a schedule is not only efficient (and good business), it represents an effort to bring you to your goals while you are young enough to enjoy them. A schedule will be based upon:

1.   What tasks have to be performed before others can follow
2.   What parts of the project are most important
3.   What parts of the project must be coordinated with other people, who may be available only at certain times
4.   Target date for completion
5.   Sufficient leeway to compensate for errors and unexpected obstacles

*Set reasonable standards.* For many products, there is no objective standard of right or wrong or of excellence. You may have one standard, the company purchasing agent another, and the consumer a third. For qualitative work, as art or writing, probably the best standard is one which uses most of your abilities, but does not interfere with your capacity to be productive. Nobody ever had higher standards than Beethoven. He revised his compositions over a period of years. Even his final manuscripts were a mess from last minute revisions. But Beethoven produced. And so did Rembrandt, Da Vinci, Michelangelo, Edison, and most of the other creative people of history. At a certain point they said, "This is good enough." The usual perfectionist does not produce. In his mind the work has not reached a certain mystical quality. As a result he either completes nothing, or is afraid to submit his work to the market place. This is a conflict I am in currently with a client who has a creative block. I tell him that he cannot be the ultimate judge of the value of his work. The reader can't be ignored. When he finishes something, then it will be valued or rejected, but no one will have any idea of his ability until he risks presenting his material for sale.

## ANALYZING USE OF YOUR TIME

This checklist concerning the effective use of your time will aid you in carrying out major decisions and in other areas of your life. Effective use of time leaves you more of it for fun or for the main arena. Nothing in this book is more important.

*Do you scatter your efforts?* Keep your eye on the ball. The function of a schedule and of priorities is to help you to decide what is important and what is not. Remember that there are only a limited number of projects or activities that you can personally attend to or supervise at one time. Learn to allocate responsibilities and duties to others. If too much work comes to you, you have not learned to say "no," or perhaps you are being exploited.

*Do you allocate enough time for a task?* I consider myself reasonably efficient, and yet invariably it takes me longer to do something than I anticipated. Therefore, it is necessary for me to set up schedules which take into account unexpected delays. It is also important to allocate sufficient time to warm up, do what has to be done, and then straighten up your work area so that you can do the next task. Portions of time which are too small are wasteful because nothing gets done. If you can't get going until you have a cigarette or a cup of coffee, then this warm-up must be built into your schedule. Similarly, time for breathers has to be built into the schedule.

*Are you alert to ways in which you waste time?* Time wasting is a way of concealing disinterest or incompetence. You owe it to yourself to determine the ways in which you fritter away your precious time. Then decide what you would be doing if you did not do these particular things. You might discover that without them there would be duties which you do not want to do or which you cannot do. By being aware of this you can come to grips with a dangerous situation. You should always question the reason for, and the importance of, any activities which take your eye off the ball.

*Are you alert to ways in which others waste your time?* When I taught at college on a part-time basis I told the students they had to take their final exams on time. Even if they didn't take a final exam regardless of college rules I was going to submit a grade for them at the end of the semester. They were told that by the time they got to the dean's office to complain, I would have received my final check and would be on the high seas cruising. It was effective in getting the students to prepare their work in the time allocated for it. One of them did not do so. Because of low pay I did not continue teaching at that college. When the department informed me eight months later that one student was "entitled" to a make-up exam (one day after I had decided to throw out all the materials) I made myself unavailable. They had exploited me sufficiently by then through low pay. I decided to let one of the full-time tenured faculty worry about the delinquents.

There are many situations in which poorly motivated or inefficient people seek company in order to cover up the fact that they are not doing what they are supposed to. Avoid getting caught up with them. If they sink, it's their problem. If they have already accomplished what they must do, don't fill time as their "break." Do not let others waste your time. Overly dependent people are particularly guilty of this. As I was writing this, by coincidence, somebody called. In the course of our conversation this vastly overworked executive reported that he was taking an employee and his wife to the ballet, in order to motivate her to participate in his employee's affairs. This seemed to me a great time waster: the executive was assuming responsibilities that were properly those of the employee.

*Do you eliminate unncessary tasks?* Many duties are performed simply because of traditional reasons ("We have always done it this way") . This includes such areas as household tasks, business, and relationships between friends and the family. Use the principle of being alert to the ways you waste time: determine what does not have to be done, then don't do it.

*Do you throw out what you don't need?* The biggest time waster is having to plow through files, objects, and garbage of all sorts which is not necessary. I had a professor once who said "If I don't need something in a year I throw it out!" To collect unnecessary materials is a neurotic trait. It is believed to be related to infantile resistance to premature toilet training. The child learns to retain feces as a marvelous way of irritating Mommy. Think of your own retentive qualities in this way and your desk will be clear and your files easily accessible.

*Do you handle something only once?* It is wasteful to have something to do, put it aside, have it in the way when you need something else, take it out, put it back, and so on. There will be more hours in the day if you complete it the first time.

*Do you leave time for fun?* If there is no joy in your life because of the extra pressure of duties, you are doing something wrong. It is true that unexpected pressures arise which extend the working day. However, sometimes these can be avoided or reduced by saying "no," by not being overly ambitious, and by not letting others be needlessly dependent upon you. Excessive time spent on projects can also be an indication that important personal decisions are being avoided.

## USING OTHERS EFFECTIVELY

Almost anything you set out to do will require some input from others. Here are some guidelines to increase their ability to serve your purposes.

*Try to deal with motivated people.* You may get more effi-

cient service from a professional person, service station, or tradesman, if he/it is not the most prominent, busy, or prestigious
provider of service. I have seen a prominent law firm rip off
thousands of dollars from a hard pressed institution because the
principals didn't choose to assign the most aggressive, hard-
working lawyer to the task. They used the name of a formerly
prominent politician whose reputation was supposed to open
doors instead of suing some malefactors. Deal with hungry people;
they will work for a reward.

*Show appreciation for others.* A gracious smile, a thank you
note, or a tip can work wonders. Let people know you are pleased
with what they have done for you. Create an atmosphere in
which people enjoy dealing with you and serving you.

*Recognize conflict of interests.* Make sure that the people
upon whom you rely have your interests at heart and are not
double dealing with somebody else. Be particularly wary when
this person or firm has any contacts with adversaries, competitors,
enemies, and so on. In addition, make certain it is to their advantage to render good service to you. It could happen that one
of your business contacts could benefit from your failure through
buying you out at crisis prices, or competing. Perhaps through
intermediaries your salesman is skimming off business or giving
trade to a low bidder for a rake-off. Make sure your employees
and representatives *are working for you.*

*Disseminate information.* Often executives and people-in-the-
know hold on to important information as though it were military secrets! The proper functioning of any organization (even
a family) depends on information being available to everybody
who needs it to carry out their assignments. As you find out what
is happening, you must let everybody know who will be affected
by it. This gives them the opportunity to change their plans to
accomplish your purpose.

*Set realistic requirements.* Be certain that what you demand
is something others can produce. I did not go to a certain psychoanalytic training institute because the schedule they set up
for me did not take into account my other responsibilities. When
I indicated there was plenty of time to make a switch, I was told

to wait until the last minute. I know one chief of clinic who announced that the clinic would be open on a particular evening, but he did not ask his staff whether they would be free at that time. One way to set realistic requirements is to discuss a proposed plan before putting it into effect. Ask those who have to carry it out if they think it is possible—a simple procedure but one frequently ignored.

*Create a trustful atmosphere.* Allow people to tell you the truth. Some executives receive only the information they want to hear because their employees fear they will be penalized for telling unpleasant truths. Some people do not want to hear bad news or others' reactions to their faults; they vent their irritation on the person who tells them. Resisting the truth is a serious error; it will impair your ability to carry out your decisions.

*Evaluate your effect on others.* You probably have certain characteristics which enhance or reduce your ability to gain information, cooperation, favors, and so on. Since you are the most important tool in implementing your decisions, you had better find out how well you work!

*Expect results on time.* Don't accept weak excuses. You will have to pay the penalty for others' inefficiency. Part of being self-assertive is determining that others must do what they are being paid for or have promised to do.

*Get rid of unreliable people.* It is my experience that if somebody has failed you once, they will fail you again.

*Learn how to say "no."* One of the most important social lessons is to distinguish between real and unreal obligations. Not everybody who asks you to do something has a right to expect you to do it. If you have a strong ego, self-confidence, and a set of priorities, you will be able to select those occasions when you must give in to others' requests and avoid those which are wasteful of your time and effort.

*Do your own work on time.* The best way to antagonize others and interfere with important projects is to cause unnecessary delay. Don't expect others to exert themselves if you are tardy.

*Make certain your instructions are carried out.* No matter

what you want, those on whom you are relying may have different ideas. The world is full of people who say one thing and do another, and who are indifferent to contracts, promises, and the welfare of others. Perhaps their intentions are good, but they become ill or die, have personal problems, family distractions, or legitimate inability to deliver goods or services. They may be unable to let you know something is wrong, or have insufficient goodwill or intelligence to do so. The decisions you make and the policies you set can be valueless unless others are working effectively under your direction. You must be able to travel to observe progress, or get reliable people to report to you directly. These should not have a conflict of interest between you and the party from whom you are expecting some service. Above all, they ought not to be employees or allies of, or indebted to, the person on whom you are dependent. They can then be expected to lie and misinform you if this is convenient to them or to their superior. You must use as your informants people who are personally loyal to you. Use reliable representatives whose allegiance is to you. Do not trust reports from afar that all is going well, when the reporting party would benefit from covering up failures.

*Don't make promises you can't keep or don't want to keep.* This follows from the principle of learning how to say "no." By making unnecessary promises you can either find yourself resentful because you are working for others, or find others resentful of you because they are counting on something you will not do. I have trained myself generally not to accept invitations to anyplace without thinking it over for twenty-four hours. If I am out of my office, I say that I must consult my schedule (even if I know that the time is clear). Since I never carry a schedule I can wait until later to decide what I want to do. If I am in my office, I invent a "cockamamie" excuse so I can decide if this expenditure of time is in my interest.

*Choose consultants wisely.* Aides can make or break you. Whether you are seeking legal, medical, business, technical, or other advice, the quality of your consultants will be an asset or a liability. It can be a mistake either to overemphasize your own abilities or to put too much credence in the abilities of your consultants. When a new auditorium for the New York Philharmonic Orchestra was being planned, the acoustical consultants asked all the famous conductors about the characteristics of the best halls they had ever conducted in. The results differed from one maestro to another. Finally somebody concluded that the best hall was the one in which a conductor heard the loudest applause. When the building was complete, it actually proved to be acoustically deficient and required years of effort and large sums of money to make it acceptable. It was subsequently largely torn down and rebuilt. Since even experienced, dedicated, talented consultants can make mistakes, the least you can do is guard against unscrupulousness.

The most frequent complaint about consultants that I have heard concerns lawyers. (However, the problem could apply to other services as well.) After giving considerable sums of money in advance, clients find they do not have access to their attorneys or that the preparation of documents is delayed. Ill-mannered treatment from professionals in many areas is common. The solution for this problem depends on your self-confidence and self-assertion. It is important that you get a clear estimate in writing in advance concerning the cost of the service. Then, obtain a definite commitment about the schedule at which it will be rendered, with the understanding that if it is not performed on time, this will be a breach of contract.

Many professional people are very busy, and like the traditional physician, permit as many people to come into their office as there are seats and standing room (figuratively speaking). They serve themselves by taking your funds, which they then use for their own purpose, and serve you at their convenience. When you surmise that this is the case, you will be in a better position to defend your interests if you have an agreement in writing. However, even without a written agreement, you still have recourse. You can sue, complain to the local bar or ethics committee of the professional association, or to the state board that licensed your consultant. If you have paid for services which you are not receiving, then make a nuisance of yourself in order to get your money back. Unfortunately, planning a suitable campaign to accomplish this is expensive in time and spirit, and it could add to your expenses. In any event, absolutely insist that your consultants render timely and efficient service.

*Encourage cooperation from others.* The most neglected resources are the casual bystander, the humble assistant, the neighbor, the tradesman, and all the seemingly insignificant people who are peripheral to any activity. If you have opened up a new office, newcomers may not find it without the cooperation of the elevator starter. If you are expecting an important parcel, cooperation from the mailman or a neighbor could save a time-wasting trip to the post office. Congenial relationships with the people you meet in daily life will prepare the foundation for the success of your decisions and projects.

## LEADING GROUPS TO EFFECTIVE DECISIONS

Sometimes you may be the leader (executive) of a group of individuals carrying out a program for which you are responsible. Here are some considerations which summarize the experience of some consultants to big business and other major organizations (Avis, 1973; Drucker, 1966; Feinberg, 1971; Lamb & Turner, 1969; Schaffer, 1974). They include the procedures which are known as Management by Objective.

## SUMMARY OF EFFECTIVE DECISIONS IN GROUPS

1. As leader, you must function in such a way that you are seen as functioning in the interest of your subordinates.

2. Nevertheless, you should set high standards for performance. If these are not met, you must steel yourself to the necessity for changing or disciplining personnel.

3. In planning sessions, have the agenda known in advance, so that individuals can submit proposals separately evolved. Remember, "brainstorming" does not create the best solutions.

4. Keep extraneous issues from interfering with the vital parts of the agenda.

5. Distracting or destructive individuals must be prevented

from censoring others or raising unnecessary conflicts or false issues.

6. Only people really required to take part in a decision should be invited.

7. All members of an organization who have relevant information, or whose cooperation will be needed to implement a decision, should be consulted.

8. When there is sufficient information to make a decision, the discussion should be closed, and then plans made to implement the decision.

9. All decisions must include some means of obtaining information concerning progress, changing conditions, and new requirements (feedback) .

10. Goals should be related to facts and previous achievements, or to realistic estimates of the causes of failure, rather than to emotionally determined wishes to avoid failure or please others.

11. While you cannot give up responsibility for the ultimate result, responsibility should be delegated clearly to others who are carrying out segments of the project.

12. The risks of any project should be evaluated from the point of view of payoff to the organization, not the social standing of the risk-recommender or those whose views are put aside.

In the next chapter we shall consider the overall pattern of a good lifestyle, so that your decisions can be integrated into an emotionally fulfilling pattern.

# 16

# Improving
# Your Lifestyle

The purpose of creating effective decisions is to open your life up to new opportunities, in particular a more satisfactory lifestyle. Decisions make up the difference between a life of drudgery, with the constant risk of disaster, and one of emotional fulfillment.

Lifestyle was introduced by Adler to describe and explain the unity in a person's personality (Ansbacher & Ansbacher, 1956, Chapter VII) i.e., how we achieve our goals and cope with anxiety. I see lifestyle as both the person's characteristic way of adapting to society and also the quality of the environment which he creates around him. The way in which we relate to other people, are productive, and achieve autonomy represents the dynamics of our lifestyle. The world that we create around us, including people, residence, travel, and material possessions, are the visible forms of our lifestyle. The balance between stress and enjoyment is the *outcome* of our lifestyle, or the degree of fulfillment.

Let us look at *relatedness, productivity,* and *autonomy* in turn.

## RELATEDNESS

We start our lives with absolute physiological and emotional dependency. We would immediately die if someone didn't take care of us. Most people develop the competence to maintain their physical needs, but we vary tremendously in how we cope with our emotional needs.

Unfortunately, the chief barrier to emotional satisfaction is the effect of previous emotional life rather than our current situation. Everybody has experienced some frustration, neglect, and hostility. We differ from each other in the amount of this mistreatment and our vulnerability to it. Those who have had both encouragement to mature and emotional support are fortunate. Most people have had significant emotional deficits which leave a craving for the missed emotions. The unfulfilled needs cause a kind of chronic emotional deficit which ordinary family life doesn't fill. Current emotional satisfactions are used to pay off old debts. As a consequence, we feel unfulfilled and blame those near us for being unsatisfactory.

This kind of resentment and frustration has a counterproductive effect upon our partner by driving him or her further away. As a consequence, chronically frustrated people either crave relatedness or avoid close contact with other people because of fear of further disappointment.

One of the worst ways of attempting to achieve fulfillment is to define one's entire existence in terms of a relationship with a loved person. Some men and women expect their mate to supply richness, variety, and love without taking emotional initiative to supply their own needs.

What is a practical program for turning the balance in your emotional life away from neurotic cravings and toward emotional fulfillment?

*Admit that the past is gone and irremediable.* Continued attention to past slights, injustices, deprivations, injuries, misconduct, and so forth on the part of our parents, relatives, and society will keep us from getting our share of the emotional wealth in the world around us. We should understand what shaped our personality, but reach the philosophical conviction that some events are unalterable and only harm can come from ruminating about them.

*Have a frank exchange of feelings with your partner.* This includes sharing your own emotional past as well as your feelings about today. You ought to recognize that emotional neediness is not a license to get fulfillment totally from your mate. On the contrary, by admitting that your emotional hunger started in childhood, you are alerting him to the fact that you may be hard to please and relieving him of needless guilt and obligation. The results are not predictable. It may encourage your partner to be more attentive to your needs, or it may be an invitation for criticism. Expressing your needs directly may be a healthy change if the way you have trained yourself is to conceal weakness; for then you will be able to observe whether your partner is responsive to you or not.

*Let go; avoid clutching.* Among the most destructive ideologies perpetrated by the mass media was that of "togetherness" invented by some foolish magazine writer. The goal of complete emotional fulfillment within the family is ruinous. There is even serious discussion of the advantages of child-free lives (Peck, 1971). No human being has the depth or range of interests and feelings to totally satisfy another. It is an unreasonable demand to expect another person not to have pains of his own, and therefore always to be there when we ourselves hurt. We must assume that our partner cannot totally meet our needs, and we cannot meet his. Let go, let the other person get out of sight. If you resist clutching you have the right to feel that filling some of your own needs outside of a current marriage or friendship is legitimate.

Furthermore, there are deaths, illnesses, absences, or entire periods of our lives when there is no mate with whom to relate. Thus, we must seek some appropriate people with whom we can talk it over, gain solace, cool off, or just have fun.

It is also important to have activities to enjoy when no one is available.

*Make friends.* In addition to being a positive experience, friendship is a balance wheel, or a reserve, against the trials of life. It is an important kind of relationship which many people neglect. There are frequently significant intervals during which we are not married or are emotionally estranged from our spouse. But at any time, there is the opportunity to have friends.

In rain or shine, there is a use for friends in our lives. This may sound cynical but it is down-to-earth. Certainly I am not speaking about exploitation, although many people enter into exploitative "friendships" on one side or the other. It is possible to make the same mistakes in the area of friendship as in marriage. One can be demanding or cold, crave exclusivity, be overly sensitive or insensitive, and display the whole range of self-destructive emotions. One of the signs of a friendship is the opportunity to be open, and to be able to express intimate experiences. I can imagine that some friendships might be limited in this regard but have other values such as companionship and shared interests. You can have some friends to talk to, others to go to concerts with, still others to play cards with, and so on. Since it is not always possible to have one friend available when you need him or her, it is important to cultivate many people. In this way the benefits of companionship are maximized, without placing excessive demands upon one person.

Many people who do not know how to make friends may be precisely those who need them the most but cannot get them because of their social anxieties. Perhaps the capacities that you should work on are (1) accessibility, (2) mutual interests, and (3) initiative. Be accessible. Unless you are out there nobody will find you. Go to places where you want to be. Leave your usual rounds and indulge your interests. Finally, take initiative. If there is somebody you want to meet, say "hello."

*Express your feelings.* What are the feelings whose sharing is likely to lead toward emotional fulfillment? They are companionship, love, and compassion. You can see that these are largely generous ones—we give them away. I assume that the capacity to love would be developed by anybody with some warmth in his background. The inability to express love and tenderness, to make another person feel accepted or better when distressed, is certainly a dark cloud in an emotional life. A problem of giving and sharing is a cue to the necessity of gaining professional aid. You needn't have the effect that these people had on each other:

*History XVI–1*: In group therapy a man attacks somebody else for having the same tendency to hold back feelings that he has:

M: I wish I could be myself without having to watch myself come out and then go back into myself. I wonder what people think of me.

L: You want more of me. At this moment I'm not ready to give that much.

Therapist: She is to you the chronically frustrating good woman.

M: I'm getting more and more angry and sad at these types of men and women. I was upset when I met my goody-goody friend who does the right thing. It hurts me when I see him. He is hunched over and has a corpselike handshake. He thinks a nice guy has to finish last.

Therapist: You're upset by him. What do you want?

M: I want somebody to open up, to be fulfilled.

Therapist: What about you?

M: I don't understand.

R: If he wasn't mopey he would have something to give you. Why can't you say if he wasn't so wrapped up in himself he would continue to have a social relationship with you?

## PRODUCTIVITY

I believe that a life is not complete without being productive. I cannot empathize with those who want to engage in pleasure indefinitely. It is quite possible to invoke moral or philosophical values in this discussion, but since I am not learned in these areas, I will discuss productivity only from the viewpoint of the psychologist.

Mankind has a drive for new experiences and variety. As a species we are naturally curious. In addition people also have a need for mastery—over both things and people. We want to express our influence upon the world, to put our imprint out there, to make something, or to be a part of a group that is important in affairs of the world.

*Developing natural aptitudes*: Each of us has a pattern of natural aptitudes which enable us to fit better into one kind of environment than another. This includes the world of work. Therefore we must find out which capabilities are worth developing and which ones are likely to be handicaps. Our temperament (as well as some combination of brain and muscle) defines our greatest potential. However, there are many roads to success even within the same occupation. One could hardly think of more diverse personalities than Babe Ruth, Joe Di-Maggio, and Ted Williams. Their combinations of strength and coordination are shared by few, but their attitudes toward people, training, and teamwork were notoriously different from each other.

If you are at a fork in the road of your career, or dissatisfied with it, it would be useful to get vocational counseling to determine how your abilities fit into today's labor market. I would recommend consulting directly a vocational, counseling, or industrial psychologist. Having worked for several executive counseling companies I feel that their fees are excessive. Even when the service was good, I sometimes had to struggle to ensure ethical treatment of clients when company profits were at stake.

*Goal orientation and decision making*: A suitable lifestyle cannot be achieved without establishing clearly your values and goals. This will avoid the hazards of drifting. Among the basic decisions to be made are the amount of money you need and whether you want to get your "kicks" on the job or off it. Be prepared for some sacrifices and plenty of disappointments.

*Parental standards and job satisfaction*: The ability to enjoy productive work—of some kind—seems to be related to the attitude our parents had toward our future. The person who could never please his parents might go to one extreme or the other: either reaching for unobtainable goals, or simply not getting any pleasure at all from work and other activities. Some people had parents who set no standards for them or never made any predictions as to the kind of career or profession they would attain. These individuals are often perplexed as to how to obtain fulfillment in the world of employment. Apparently it is better to have wrongheaded standards imposed upon us— against which we rebel—than to have none at all!

Work is one of the most underestimated areas of emotional stress. Most people are frustrated in their jobs, and they ought to make decisions for mobility. Why is work so harrowing? Because a high proportion of supervisors and owners are technically and/or emotionally inadequate to do their jobs. Let me share one of my favorite fantasies. I daydream about millions of people quitting their jobs because they have been mistreated by the institution or supervisor (note, I avoid use of the word "boss"). My fantasy then has these superior beings fired or demoted because they couldn't motivate their staff to work for them.

What would be the realistic consequence of people quitting because of mistreatment? As individuals they would improve their own well-being. As a society, many individuals would be transferred to other duties since they were unable to maintain an effective work force. People with qualities of leadership would have better opportunities. The entire economy would benefit from improved productivity, cost effectiveness, and all the other factors to which contented employees contribute.

What is job satisfaction? It includes developing your natural talents, being able to utilize them, having dignified working conditions and wages, receiving recognition because of the value of what you contribute to the team, and making some contribution to society.

*Preferred style*: It is necessary for you either to find a job which accommodates your style (temperament and constitution), or modify your present position so that it is suitable. If you cannot, you may be in a completely wrong field. You cannot have enjoyment from your position unless you work within your preferred style. As one study pointed out, "administrators would apparently rather do all of their tasks sacrificing a bit on quality, while professors would rather sacrifice on quantity and do a high-quality job on a smaller number of tasks" (French & Caplan, 1972, p. 53).

One of the chief attributes of style is how much structure and personal direction you require. Are you a self-starter, or do you need personal contact with a supervisor to get moving? Do you need order, or can you function in chaos? People who work for large companies frequently underestimate the amount of support they receive from other departments. As a consequence, they find themselves to be incompetent when they move to a comparable position in a small company. They were not aware of the gaps in their knowledge. They may be basically structured types and not used to solving the problems inherent in less structured or supporting situations.

Why do people stay in miserable jobs? Self-destructive anxiety usually keeps us frozen in stress-producing, heart-attack-risking positions. Our belief that nobody else will hire us is a frequent reason offered. Foolish expenditures which make it impossible to take risks or to be briefly unemployed is another. If you are in debt over your neck, then you must control your own extravagant habits or those of your family. Are you keeping up with the neighbors, spoiling your children, making up for your wife's dissatisfaction with you through spending money, building up your ego through lavishness, gambling? All these truly marvelous activities could have the self-destructive effect of keeping you in your present position!

Low self-esteem also keeps people in miserable jobs. The decision toward self-evaluation is the initial step toward emotional fulfillment. If you are in the habit of downgrading yourself, then take the steps necessary to improve your self-esteem including psychotherapy.

Nevertheless, there is no substitute for courage.

*Competence*: You have probably heard about "separation anxiety." This is the belief that we are incompetent when we are away from momma so that we promptly become a nervous wreck. Well, some of us are that way, but it isn't natural. Here is what some psychologists have to say about the normal feeling of self-confidence displayed by children before they are taught how incompetent they are: "The human infant, unlike many other mammals, separates himself from his mother at the first moment any mode of locomotion is possible. He does not wait until he can creep or walk efficiently...." (Rheingold & Eckerman, 1970). Now listen to this: by separating himself, the infant increases his opportunities to relate to the world and to learn its nature. While in contact with his mother, he learns only about her and what is near her. "There are limits to what the most attentive mother can bring to him." These writers are courageous!

Curiosity is a characteristic of children. Unless they are hampered, they will learn a great deal through their own initiative. Competence is our natural condition, and social disability (Vance, 1973) must be the result of a crippling influence. There is an interaction between our beliefs about our self (self-esteem, wish for achievement), the world (helpful or hindering), and our belief about where control of our destiny really lies (external or internal). If we believe that the real events of our life are beyond our control, regardless of our wish to achieve something worthwhile, we will not get moving. On the other hand, if we believe that we can influence life, then we will try.

The combination of competence and belief in ourselves is the key to using productivity as a source of emotional fulfillment. If we are constantly being criticized because our work is inadequate, or secretly believe that this is the case and must cover up, then our employment probably causes intolerable stress. Belief in one's competence is frequently the difference between success and failure, because the self-confident person will try to be promoted, take risks concerning new procedures, and make his presence known to the power structure.

The competent person has better social relationships because he can express his opinions without doing so at the expense of his colleagues. You must learn the difference between the goal-oriented response and the snide comparison! Further, the competent person frequently has superior communication skills.

His oral comments lack the vagueness, mumbling, hesitancy, and self-imposed restraints of the person who feels that others reject him.

How do we develop professional and interpersonal competence? People who feel competent in interpersonal relationships make it a habit to be aware of themselves and the people around them (Seeman, 1973). They also avoid becoming promoted to positions for which they know in advance they aren't qualified (Peter & Hill, 1969). It is important that you make the sacrifice necessary to complete or further your education. For example, an engineer's skills are generally believed to be obsolescent after about five years. You might consider moving from company to company or job to job so that you add to your experience and go where it is valued. Above all, to avoid the barrenness of a frustrating, stressful job experience, save money so that you can take risks and make choices. The decision of self-sacrifice may be the only proper one to avoid disaster.

There are several related factors which will influence your performance as you struggle to achieve your goals:

1. What are the standards of success? (Heckhausen, 1968)
2. What are your expectations of success?
3. Are you really achievement oriented?

*Standards for success*: We have already seen that setting impossible standards is foolish. Nevertheless, you will have to decide what criteria you will use to determine your success. You must also ask whether your criteria of success will meet the standards of those who are paying your rent! Further, as you struggle toward your goal, will you be doing something which is enjoyable? Do you have some control over how your success will be judged, or are you putting yourself under the domination of somebody else who will determine your value?

People perform more satisfactorily when there are definite goals. Their motivation improves. Those with high self-esteem work more effectively toward difficult goals than those whose self-esteem is poor.

*Expectations of success*: I cannot totally agree with the

famous psychologist B. F. Skinner (1971, p. 39) that behavior is shaped by its consequences. We do not always repeat that which is successful and avoid that which makes us feel bad. Sometimes we accumulate the memories of bad experiences. One woman, successful as a dress designer, said, "My failures were me but my talents were not me." You will have to break out of the box of defining yourself in terms of the other person's expectation of you (Seeman, 1973). Instead, define yourself in terms of the rewards you wish to receive for your services. Our definition of success may derive from parental standards we are taught in childhood or adolescence (Buehler et al., 1973). Unfortunately, while we give ourselves credit for being independent thinkers, we are all too often copying somebody else's values.

There are substantially different reactions to the outcome of efforts by those who inherently hope for success, and those whose chief motive is to avoid failure. Those who are motivated to succeed tend to take the credit for success *and* the blame for failure. Those who are most afraid of failure do not usually believe that they have personally achieved any success. However, they accept the blame for failure. The sense of expectancy—what we think will happen—ties together present and future, and also past because this is where it all began. Success breeds success (Hinrichs, 1970). Failure invites failure. You must change your pattern of thinking to that of a success story. This is not pap at all! There is evidence that thinking positive thoughts and having successful people as models really improve performance (Heckhausen, 1968).

*Achievement motivation*: There does seem to be a type of person who is more motivated to accomplish something than most other people. One way you can tell whether you are one of these is by your persistence. Achievement-minded persons are persistent because they see the connection between what they do and the results. They do not see themselves as controlled by fate (Miner & Dachler, 1973). They also don't pay much attention to the critical voices within telling them that they are incompetent snot noses.

## AUTONOMY

Autonomy may be defined as the experience of yourself as a separate but adequate person. It is characterized by a vivid sense of personal identity and role. The autonomous person has clear values, realizes which of his needs require fulfillment, and integrates his efforts into a beneficial lifestyle. He balances initiative with capacity to be a follower, and takes responsibility without assuming others' obligations. He can relate to others but does not clutch nor let someone else's demands rule his life. While he is aware of his social image, he is not excessively swayed by others' opinions. To be autonomous is to be self-assertive because you know your own mind and you have learned how to look after your own needs.

A recent scientific study (Kurtines, 1974) has compared the autonomous person with those who are nonautonomous. You can see that the issue of autonomy relates to many of the factors making for efficient decisions.

*The autonomous person:*
1. Is self-reliant, forms independent judgments, and thinks for himself
2. Does not have work inhibitions, and tends to be efficient, capable, and able to mobilize his resources easily and effectively
3. Is persistent in working toward his goals
4. Derives pleasure from his work and values productive achievement
5. Tends to take a stand on moral issues

*The nonautonomous person:*
1. Is suggestible, that is, overly responsive to other people's evaluations of a situation
2. Conforms to social expectations
3. Is submissive and overly accepting of authority
4. Is concerned with making a good impression
5. Is unable to make decisions without vacillation, hesitation, or delay (Kurtines, 1974).

Perhaps the most interesting finding is the connection between autonomy (or independence) and definite moral standards. Perhaps the truth about ex-President Nixon's associates is that they had only the *illusion* of competence and success. They were so impressed by being immersed in presidential glory that they could not perceive that they had undertaken an immoral, dangerous, and therefore imprudent route for themselves (and the country).

Many people complain that their inability to know what they want and who they are causes them to yield to the wishes of others. On the other hand, it is possible to exaggerate your autonomy. The symptoms of this are making no decisions which are affected by the wishes or feelings of others, disregarding social value in the pursuit of your goals, and being indifferent to the welfare and companionship of others. Thus, while autonomy is an extremely important aspect of emotional fulfillment, it needs to be balanced with relatedness and productivity. Nevertheless, some advantages of autonomy are the ability to enjoy one's own personality, to participate in activities which are fun without needing a companion, and to function as a self-starter without supervision or support.

What is the most frequent kind of emotional conflict in today's relationships? The conflict between one person's desire for relatedness and another person's need for autonomy seems to be the most common source of difficulty that I observe in my therapeutic practice and human relations workshops. When an individual who experiences autonomy meets someone who needs an excessively close relationship, there is a struggle because the dependent person's demands for companionship, affection, and stimulation are draining. As a result, the autonomous person either pulls away or feels resentful. In any event, the clinging person's demands are self-destructive because they have the opposite effect upon his needs: demanding too close a relationship creates emotional distance. More women than men experience an overwhelming need for relatedness because they have been trained by their parents to look forward only to marriage. Consequently, they have not developed significant parts of their personalities. However, I have observed the opposite as well: the husband clings emotionally to his wife, who wants to be moderately independent and to function by herself outside their home.

## TOWARD CHANGING YOUR LIFESTYLE

One of the greatest changes in the industrial world today is the variation in lifestyle from one generation to the next, and even enormous changes made within one lifetime. In most of the world, a person's lifestyle was pretty much determined by who his parents were. Even in this country, with its development of social mobility, I suspect that the average difference between the status of father and son was relatively small until recently. Today, upward and downward mobility is extensive. You can get into college with bad grades through open enrollment. On the other hand, we see people deliberately giving up the advantages of their birth and rejecting their parents' hard-earned money and materialism because they prefer the hippy style of life. We have unisex, gay liberation, beards in low-ranking troops, civil rights demonstrations on aircraft carriers, judges refusing alimony to competent young women, legal abortions, fuel shortages encouraging ownership of unpretentious cars, young people backpacking all over the world for long periods instead of entering the work force, and all the rest. In fact, there is even an organization devoted to those who wish to avoid parenthood (National Organization for Nonparents—NON).

It will be helpful to you to know the reactions of others when they became dissatisfied with their lifestyles. Many shared their experiences with others at my human relations workshops in New York City. You may be able to identify with their problems and gain confidence from the fact that you are not alone. Some of their solutions sound pretty courageous to me.

A man said: "I had no identification. I was a chameleon. Anything went. I was afraid to have an identity because then I would be assertive, and there would be two people in conflict. However, it wasn't bad at all."

Another offered the following: "My mother has always seen

me as a five-year-old child. She talks to me by telling me to sit up straight. I went along with it. Now I've decided not to permit it. A new identity required much effort."

Here is how a woman phrased her change of identity: "I was a mother, wife, and teacher. Now I'm a person in my own right. My children resent my new self, my going out alone. But I decided I would do what I wanted to do, not what my fifteen-year-old daughter wanted."

A man had this to say about attaining his goals: "I had wanted money. I was not satisfactorily employed or married. I just had money to spend. I wondered who I was and what did I want to do. I'm in the process of changing my lifestyle. Now I am a volunteer counselor. I'm helping people. I don't have to be affluent any more. My family consisted of three separate people, myself, mother and father. There was no communication. I learned my values from other families."

A woman is satisfied with her lifestyle: "I came from a poor background. I wanted to get out of it. My parents wanted me to go to work. A guidance counselor advised my achievement-oriented sister to go to college. She influenced me to go to college. I have middle class values and don't want to give up the way I am living."

How do you get started in changing your role? The first task is understanding yourself and the effect you have on other people. Are you satisfied with it? Are you getting what you want, or giving what other people want? Only an hour ago I had in my office a woman who spent most of her life taking care of her husband and children. Now, under some stress, she wants her husband to be far more attentive; she needs him. He is not used to this, and is having too great a time enjoying his own newly achieved independence. She (and perhaps you) will have to unlearn the role of giver and learn a new role, that of a needy, frustrated person. In consequence, her husband will have to learn to give more of himself.

In changing their roles, different people have made the following points. Change is stressful, and one will have to give up many familiar ways of doing things. One woman, who left a suburban life to come to the Big City, said that she had to learn new social attitudes and struggle with being alone. She had to be willing to burn her bridges behind her. As you change your role, you will have to consider making changes in employment, residence, and maybe even sexual adjustment.

Changing your role should cause you to think in terms of *forming new relationships* and *changing the ground rules* of old ones. This involves the right to express your feelings. It means looking for people with whom the communication is two-way and comfortable. As you become better able to share (not compulsively to give or to clutch) your standards for friends and mates will change radically.

One way of starting, as a woman suggested, was to *"think in terms of images. The way you think will make you happy."* The gloomy, pessimistic person must discipline himself to have pleasant thoughts to imagine functioning without anxiety, to daydream of being competent. This will drive out the ghosts of past failures.

Perhaps the most cheerful way to start a new life is to *give up your old burdens.* One man stated that he "could not imagine a life without obligations." Another man is depressed every time he takes his son to see his ex-wife since he can't figure out a way of avoiding this pain despite the termination of his marriage. Other people take an extreme solution. One man was so dissatisfied with his family life that he joined the army and got rid of everything he owned. Another, having lost his identity as the family breadwinner, formed an affiliation with a particular special action group to obtain fulfillment.

## EMOTIONAL FULFILLMENT

It is with some reluctance that I approach the topic of emotional fulfillment because people vary so much in their needs and the ways in which they meet them. Therefore my comments are first of all subjective, and only secondly from the vantage point of one who has been privileged to share the feelings of many people.

I think that emotional fulfillment (within Western society) has some of these characteristics: (1) capacity to enjoy life; (2) feeling that life has some meaning, that one is connected to some larger scale of events and groups of people; (3) the achievement of one's personal potential, emotionally, socially, and intellectually, and (4) ultimately, that peace of mind which we call self-acceptance. Another student of highly talented people has stressed that the most self-actualized were open in the expression of their feelings, were concerned with others, and struggled to be creative (Gowan, 1973).

To accept yourself means to have tried your best, to have tried to live without doing harm to others, and to have evaluated yourself according to your own scale of values.

To have reached this point in the manuscript has been a labor of love for me, because it meant doing something that I value very much: engaging in scholarship, thinking, and then organizing and setting down my thoughts. I trust that you will have gained considerable perspective on how you can create effective decisions and through them improve your emotional life.

# Appendix

SELF APPRAISAL FOR CAREER ADVANCEMENT

Today's Date _____

*Frustrations and difficulties in present (or recent) position*: State those frustrations and difficulties which have caused you to seek a change. Include anything which jeopardizes your present position, blocks suitable advancement, or otherwise causes you to be dissatisfied:

CAREER GOALS: (Please be specific)

Immediate:    1.
                     2.
                     3.

Long-Range:   1.
                     2.
                     3.

Personal Goals:    1.
                          2.
                          3.

## LIST PERSONALITY CHARACTERISTICS WHICH AFFECT THE ACHIEVEMENT OF YOUR CAREER GOALS

### CAREER GOALS:

*Strengths*: List the personality characteristics which enhance your efficiency and make you valuable to an employer. Include those for which you have been commended or complimented and those which add to your enjoyment of the job or positively affect the people with whom you have contact. Give a brief illustration of each, if you can:

1.

2.

3.

4.

*Weaknesses*: List the personality characteristics which reduce your efficiency, create situations in which you function poorly or are uncomfortable. Include those for which you have been criticized or which seem to affect negatively the people with whom you have contact. Give a brief example or explanation of each:

1.

2.

3.

4.

ANY FURTHER COMMENTS:

### Attitudes Toward Supervision

*Helpful Supervision*: What characteristics of a supervisor create conditions in which you can function efficiently and with satisfaction?
1.

2.

3.

*Troublesome Supervision*: What characteristics of a supervisor are particularly troublesome to you?
1.

2.

3.

Do you have a preference for or against supervision of others?

Describe the job which included the greatest number of people you have ever supervised.

## Attitudes Toward Further Training

Indicate any area in which your education is deficient that would hamper your career advancement.

When was the last time you received any training suitable to your career advancement? In what area was the training?

## Performance Profile

People vary considerably in their requirements for structure needed in order to perform effectively and comfortably. They also differ in the amount of initiative which they will assume under varying conditions.

A *structured* position is one in which there are company/institutional policies and regulations affecting the way in which a job is to be carried out. The goals and procedures are precisely defined, and the criteria for success are very clear. In an *unstructured* position, the worker devises his own procedures, which may vary from time to time; the means of carrying out the job are left to the worker's initiative; and the goals and criteria of success may not be clear at all times.

Rate yourself in the following areas on a scale of 1 (least) to 10 (most).

| | | |
|---|---|---|
| *Highly Structured*: | Comfort | _____ |
| | Effective | _____ |
| | Initiative | _____ |
| *Moderately Structured*: | Comfort | _____ |
| | Effective | _____ |
| | Initiative | _____ |

*Loosely Structured*:  Comfort      _____
                      Effective      _____
                      Initiative      _____

## OFFER SOME DETAILS:

_____ *Self-Interest*: Is your time occupied with tasks which relate to your own goals, values, needs, and interests, or are you working for others? Rate yourself on a scale of 1-10 (10 representing self-interest).

_____ *Use of time on your job*: Do you generally spend your time on activities which are productive or wasteful? Consider whether your activities on the job lead to promotion, increased income, deeper involvement, etc. Rate yourself 1-10 (10 is good use of time).

_____ *Use of personal time*: Do your off-job activities increase your education, meet your personal needs, leave you sufficiently refreshed, advance you toward personal or career goals?

_____ *Attention to overall plans/concepts/goals of your position*: When you do your job, do you try to become aware of the overall scope of the operation, or do you pay attention only to assigned details? (1-10).

_____ *Attention to necessary details*: Do you do your job carefully, following instructions, and following through to make sure that your instructions are carried out? (1-10).

_____ *Promptness*: Is your work performed on schedule (so that others can coordinate with you, and so that you have sufficient time to check for errors, make last minute changes, and modify it according to new conditions, etc.)? (1-10).

## ADDITIONAL DETAILS

1. *Attitude toward structure*:

2. *Self-interest*:

3. *Use of job-time*:

4. *Use of personal time*:

5. *Overall scope*:

6. *Necessary details*:

7. *Promptness*:

## MODELS OF PREFERRED WORK ACTIVITIES AND RELATIONSHIPS

There are a number of interpersonal work relationships with individuals whom you do not supervise and who do not supervise you but to whom you may relate while on a job. Please list first three preferences in order (1, 2, 3).

> *Committee*: Exchanging ideas and sharing responsibilities with several others.
>
> *Loner*: One who has primary responsibility for carrying out a delegated task without requiring substantial aid from others.
>
> *Consultant/Trouble Shooter*: Serving as an expert to help others carry out tasks assigned to them.
>
> *Liaison/Coordination*: Conveying information, instructions, problems, etc., from one department to another without having responsibility for actually carrying out the task.
>
> *Teacher/Trainer*: Educating others on how to carry out assigned tasks with greater skills without direct responsibility for performance.

*Sales*: Internal and external contacts necessary to the development of satisfied customers (new and old).

*Public Relations*: Internal and external contacts to promote corporate image.

*Industrial Relations*: Developing employee morale, interpreting company policy, etc.

*Direct Service to People*: Face-to-face activities in which you offer individuals some service or knowledge while representing your company/institution/profession (nonsales).

*Creating Concepts and Ideas*: The world of intellectual creation is very satisfying: thinking, writing, inventing, designing, and research are examples.

*Working with Tools and Equipment*: Manipulating and changing objects and materials ("working with my hands," "hands-on experience") is a chief source of vocational pleasure for many people.

*Managing*: Integrating ideas, people, materials, and money to carry out the functions of an organization.

*Entrepreneurial*: Preference for working for oneself, i.e., running and/or owning one's own business or profession.

*Staff Work*: In support of an association, executive, or other officer—finding information, coordinating ideas, creating alternative plans for him or others to carry out.

*Aesthetics*: Earning one's living by creating beautiful things, e.g., art, music, interior design, creative writing.

*Please Rate Yourself in the Administrative Areas Listed Below.* Compare yourself to those businessmen, professionals, executives, teachers, etc., you have known and against whose performance a comparison is reasonable. Remember that individuals vary in ability, so that in every group not everybody can be above average; some are definitely below average. Furthermore, the ratings of different abilities of a particular person may vary considerably. To help you form an accurate self-evaluation, imagine that your rank among 100 individuals is to be determined. Then decide where you rank for each of the abilities listed below.

| Rank in 100 | Highest 5% | Above Average (76-95%) | Average (25-75%) | Below Average (6-24%) | Lowest 5% |
|---|---|---|---|---|---|
| Conceptualizing | | | | | |
| Planning | ___ | ___ | ___ | ___ | ___ |
| Organizing | ___ | ___ | ___ | ___ | ___ |
| Administering | ___ | ___ | ___ | ___ | ___ |
| Delegating | ___ | ___ | ___ | ___ | ___ |
| Negotiating | ___ | ___ | ___ | ___ | ___ |
| Supervising | ___ | ___ | ___ | ___ | ___ |
| Leading | ___ | ___ | ___ | ___ | ___ |
| Training | ___ | ___ | ___ | ___ | ___ |

#### ADDITIONAL AREAS TO EXPLORE?

1.

2.

3.

#### ARE THERE ANY SENSITIVE AREAS TO BE DISCUSSED PERSONALLY?

Just indicate by a check _____

# References

Abraham, K. The first pregenital state of the libido (1916). The influence of oral eroticism on character-formation (1924). *Selected Papers.* New York: Basic Books, 1953.

————. A short study of the development of the libido, viewed in the light of mental disorders (1924). *Selected Papers.* New York: Basic Books, 1953.

Abramowitz, S. J. Internal-external control and social-political activism. *Journal of Consulting and Clinical Psychology,* 1973, *40*: 196–201.

Adey, W. F., Lindsley, D. B., & Olds, J. Ontogenetic development of brain and behavior. In W. R. Adey, et al., *Brain Mechanisms and the Control of Behavior.* London: Heineman, 1974, pp. 274–325.

Adler, A. *The Science of Living* (1929). Garden City, N.Y.: Anchor Books, 1969.

————. *What Life Should Mean to You.* New York: Grosset & Dunlap, 1931.

Adler, J., & Tso, Wung-Wai. "Decision"-making in bacteria: chemotactic response of *Escherichia coli* to conflicting stimuli. *Science,* 1974, *184*: 1292–94.

Allport, G. W. Traits revisited. *American Psychologist,* 1966, *21* (1) : 1–10.

*American Almanac.* New York: Grosset & Dunlap, 1973.

Ansbacher, H. L., & Ansbacher, Rowena L. (Eds.) *The Individual Psychology of Alfred Adler.* New York: Basic Books, 1956.

Argyle, M. *The Social Psychology of Work.* New York: Taplinger, 1972.

Arnold, Magda B. Perennial problems in the field of emotions. In M. B. Arnold (Ed.), *Feelings and Emotions.* New York: Academic Press, 1970, pp. 169–85.

Associated Press Almanac. New York: Almanac Publishing Co., 1973.

Avant, L. L., & Helson, H. Theories of Perception. In B. B. Wolman (Ed.), *Handbook of General Psychology.* Englewood Cliffs, N.J.: Prentice-Hall, 1973, pp. 419–50.

Bakan, D. *Disease, Pain, and Sacrifice.* Chicago: University of Chicago Press, 1968. Reprinted, Beacon Press, 1971.

Bakwin, H., & Bakwin, R. M. *Clinical Management of Behavior Disorders in Children.* Philadelphia: Saunders, 1960.

Bales, R. F. Communication in small groups. In G. A. Miller (Ed.), *Communication, Language, and Meaning.* New York: Basic Books, 1973, pp. 208–18.

Basch, M. B. Toward a theory that encompasses depression: a revision of existing causal hypotheses in psychoanalysis. In E. J. Anthony & Therese Benedek (Eds.), *Depression and Human Existence.* Boston: Little, Brown, 1975, pp. 485–534.

Beach, D. N., & Mahler, W. R. Management by objectives. In A. J. Marrow (Ed.), *The Failure of Success.* New York: Amacom, 1972, pp. 231–40.

Beck, A. T. The phenomena of depression: a synthesis. In D. Offer & D. X. Freedman (Eds.), *Modern Psychiatry and Clinical Research.* New York: Basic Books, 1972, pp. 136–58.

————. *Diagnosis and Management of Depression.* Philadelphia: University of Pennsylvania Press, 1973.

Beck, A. T., Weissman, Arlene, Lester, D., & Trexler, L. The measurement of pessimism: the hopelessness scale. *Journal of Consulting and Clinical Psychology,* 1974, *42*: 861–65.

Begleiter, H., & Porjesz, B. Evoked brain potentials as indicators of decision-making. *Science,* 1975, *187*: 754–55.

Bellak, L. *Overload: The New Human Condition.* New York: Human Sciences Press, Human Sciences Division, 1974.

Bernstein, I. S. Principles of primate group organization. In A. B. Chiarelli (Ed.), *Perspectives in Primate Biology.* New York: Plenum, 1974, *9*: 283–98.

Bernstein, I. S., & Gordon, T. P. The function of aggression in primate societies. *American Scientist,* 1974, *62* (3): 304–11.

Bernstein, I. S., Gordon, T. P., & Rose, R. M. Aggression and social controls in rhesus monkey (macaca mulatta) groups revealed in group formation studies. *Folia Primat,* 1974, *21*: 81–107.

Bever, T. G. Cerebral asymmetries in humans are due to the differentiation of two incompatible processes: holistic and analytic. In D. Aaronson & R. W. Rieber (Eds.), *Developmental Psycholinguistics and Communication Disorders.* New York: Annals of the New York Academy of Sciences, 1975, pp. 251–62.

Bohannan, P. Beyond civilization. *Natural History Magazine,* special supplement, February, 1971.

Brace, C. L. The origin of man. *Natural History,* January 1970, *79*: 45–49.

————. Neanderthal: ridiculed, rejected, but still our ancestor. *Natural History,* 1968, *77*: 38–45.

Brown, Barbara B. *New Mind, New Body.* New York: Harper & Row, 1974.

Brown, F. Changes in sexual identification and role over a decade and their implications. *Journal of Psychology,* 1971, *77*: 229–51.

Bruner, J. S. *Toward a Theory of Instruction.* Cambridge: Harvard University Press (Belknap), 1966.

Buehler, Charlotte, Keith-Spiegel, Patricia, & Thomas, Karla. Developmental psychology. In B. B. Wolman (Ed.), *Handbook of General Psychology.* Englewood Cliffs, N.J.: Prentice-Hall, 1973, pp. 861–917.

Buettner-Janusch, J. *Origins of Man.* New York: Wiley, 1966.

264     Effective Decisions and Emotional Fulfillment

Burck, C. G. The intricate "politics" of the corporation. *Fortune,* 1975, *914*: 109–12.

Cammalleri, J. A., Hendrick, H. W., Pittman, W. C., Jr., Blout, H., & Prather, D. C. Effects of different leadership styles on group accuracy. *Journal of Applied Psychology,* 1973, *57*: 32–37.

Campbell, B. C. Man for all seasons. In B. Campbell (Ed.), *Sexual Selection and the Descent of Man.* Chicago: Aldine, 1972, pp. 40–58.

————. *Human Evolution: An Introduction to Man's Adaptation.* Chicago: Aldine, 1966.

Carmill, M. Rethinking primate origins. *Science,* 1974, *184*: 436–42.

Carr, A. T. Compulsive neurosis: a review of the literature. *Psychological Bulletin,* 1974, *81*: 311–18.

Cattell, R. B., & Scheier, I. H. *The Meaning and Measurement of Neuroticism and Anxiety.* New York: Ronald Press, 1961.

Cavalli-Sforza, L. L. The genetics of human populations. *Scientific American,* 1974, *231*: 80–91.

Cervantes (Miguel de Cervantes Saavedra). *Don Quixote* (1605–Part I; 1615–Part II). New York: Signet Classics (New American Library), 1964.

Clark, R. D. Group-induced shift toward risk: a critical appraisal. *Psychological Bulletin,* 1971, *76*: 251–70.

Clark, R. D., & Willems, E. P. Two interpretations of Brown's hypothesis for the risky shift. *Psychological Bulletin,* 1972, *78*: 62–63.

Cooper, M. R., & Wood, M. T. Effects of member participation and commitment in group decision making on influence, satisfaction, and decision riskiness. *Journal of Applied Psychology,* 1974, *59*: 127–34.

Curtis, B. A., Jacobson, S., & Marcus, E. M. *An Introduction to the Neurosciences.* Philadelphia: Saunders, 1972.

Dallett, Janet. Theories of dream functions. *Psychological Bulletin,* 1973, *79*: 408–16.

Darlington, D. C. The origins of agriculture. *Natural History Magazine,* May 1970, *69*: 46–57.

Darwin, C. *The Expression of the Emotions in Man and Animals* (1872). Chicago: University of Chicago Press, 1965.

Davis, K. The migrations of human populations. *Scientific American,* 1974, *231*: 92–107.

Delgado, J. M. R. *Physical Control of the Mind: Toward a Psychocivilized Society.* New York: Harper & Row, 1969.

Dicks, H. V. *Licensed Mass Murder: A Sociopsychology Study of Some S. S. Killers.* New York: Basic Books, 1972.

Dobzhansky, T. *Genetic Diversity and Human Equality.* New York: Basic Books, 1973.

Dollard, J., & Miller, N. E. *Personality and Psychotherapy.* New York: McGraw-Hill, 1950.

Downing, R. W., & Rickels, K. Mixed anxiety-depression. *Archives of General Psychiatry,* 1974, *30*: 312–19.

Doxiadis, C. A. Ekistics, the science of human settlements. *Science,* 1970, pp. 393–404.

Draper, Patricia. Crowding among hunter-gatherers: the (!) Küng bushmen. *Science,* 1973, *182*: 301–03.

Drucker, P. F. *The Effective Executive.* New York: Harper & Row, 1966.

Dumond, D. E. The limitation of human population: a natural history. *Science,* 1975, *187*: 713–21.

Dunn, A. J., & Bondy, S. C. *Functional Chemistry of the Brain.* Flushing, N.Y.: Spectrum Publications, 1974.

Dunner, D. L. Recent research on classification, genetics, and treatment of depression. *Journal of Clinical Issues in Psychology,* 1975, *6* (2) : 14–16.

Early, Kathleen. Silent discourse. *Sciences,* 1975, *15* (8) : 19–23.

Edinger, E. F. The meaning of consciousness. *Quadrant,* 1975, *8*: 33–48.

Ehrhardt, Anke A. Maternalism in fetal hormonal and related syndromes. In J. Zubin & J. Money (Eds.), *Contemporary Sexual Behavior: Critical Issues in the 1970s.* Baltimore: Johns Hopkins Press, 1973, pp. 99–116.

Eidelberg, E. (Ed.). *The Encyclopedia of Psychoanalysis.* New York: Free Press, 1968.

Eisenberg, L. The human nature of human nature. *Science*, 1972, *176*: 123–28.

Ekman, P. Face muscles talk every language. *Psychology Today*, 1975, *9* (4): 35–39.

English, Horace B., & English, Ava Champney. *A Comprehensive Dictionary of Psychological and Psychoanalytical Terms*. New York: Longmans, Green and Co., 1958.

Fawcett, J. Biochemical and neuropharmacological research in the affective disorders. In E. J. Anthony & Therese Benedek (Eds.) , *Depression and Human Existence*. Boston: Little, Brown, 1975, pp. 21–52.

Feinberg, M. R. The powers and pitfalls of the clinical and industrial psychologist as administrator. In L. E. Abt & B. F. Riess, *Progress in Clinical Psychology, IX. Clinical Psychology in Industrial Organization*. New York: Grune and Stratton, 1971, pp. 106–14.

Fenigstein, A., Scheier, M. F., & Buss, A. H. Public and private self-consciousness: assessment and theory. *Journal of Consulting and Clinical Psychology*, 1975, *43*: 522–27.

Fisher, C., Byrne, J. V., Edwards, Adele, & Kahn E. REM & NREM nightmares. In E. Hartman (Ed.) , *Sleeping and Dreaming*. Boston: Little, Brown, 1970.

Fisher, L. E., & Kotses, H. Race differences and experimenter race effect in galvanic skin response. *Psychophysiology*, 1973, *10*: 578–82.

Fisher, S. Experiencing your body. *Saturday Review of Science*, July 8, 1972, pp. 27–32.

Flavell, J. H. *The Developmental Psychology of Jean Piaget*. New York: Van Nostrand, 1963.

Fleagle, J. G., Simons, E. L., & Conroy, G. C. Ape limb bone from the Oligocene of Egypt. *Science*, 1975, *189*: 135–37.

Frankenhaeuser, Marianne. Quoted in Stress on the sexes: how they differ. *Science News*, April 12, 1975, pp. 107, 238.

Frantz, S. C. The web of hunger: rats in the granary. *Natural History*, 1976, *85* (2) : 10–21.

French, J. R. P., & Caplan, R. D. Organizational stress and individual strain. In A. Marrow (Ed.) , *The Failure of Success*. New York: Amacom, 1972, pp. 30–66.

Freud, Anna. *The Ego and the Mechanisms of Defense.* New York: International Universities Press, 1946.

Freud, S. Formulations regarding the two principles in mental functioning (1911). *Collected Papers,* vol. IV. London: Hogarth Press, 1950, pp. 19–21.

————. The dynamics of the transference (1912). In *Collected Papers,* vol. II. London: Hogarth Press, 1950, pp. 313–22.

————. On narcissism: an introduction (1914). In *Collected Papers,* vol. IV. London: Hogarth Press, 1950.

————. *Instincts and Their Vicissitudes* (1915). London: Hogarth Press, 1950, pp. 60–83. (*a*)

————. *Repression* (1915). London: Hogarth Press, 1950, pp. 84–97. (*b*)

————. *The Unconscious* (1915). London: Hogarth Press, 1950, pp. 98–136. (*c*)

————. *Beyond the Pleasure Principle* (1920). New York: Bantam Books, 1959.

————. *The Ego and the Id* (1923). London: Hogarth Press, 1950.

————. The economic problem in masochism (1924). In *Collected Papers,* vol. IV. London: Hogarth Press, 1950, pp. 255–68.

————. *New Introductory Lectures on Psychoanalysis* (1933). New York: Norton, 1965.

————. *The Problem of Anxiety.* New York: Norton, 1936.

Galin, D. Implications for psychiatry of left and right cerebral specialization. *Archives of General Psychiatry,* 1974, *31*: 575–83.

Gardner, R. A., & Gardner, B. T. Early signs of language in child and chimpanzee. *Science,* 1975, *187*: 752–53.

Gilula, M. F., & Daniels, D. N. Violence and man's struggle to adapt. *Science,* 1969, *164*: 396–405.

Glazer, H. I., Weiss, J. M., Pohorecky, L. A., & Miller, N. E. Monamines and mediators of avoidance-escape behavior. *Psychosomatic Medicine,* 1975, *37*: 535–43.

Goldenson, F. M. *Encyclopedia of Human Behavior* (2 Vols.). Garden City, N.Y.: Doubleday, 1972.

Goldman, P. S., Crawford, H. T., Stokes, L. P., Galkin, T. W.,

& Rosvold, H. E. Sex-dependent behavioral effects of cerebral cortical lesion in the developing rhesus monkey. *Science,* 1974, *186*: 540–42.

Gould, S. J. Sizing up human intelligence. *Natural History,* 1974, *83*: 10–14.

———. Human babies as embryos. *Natural History,* 1976, *85* (2) : 22–26.

Greenhaus, J. H., & Badin, J. Self-esteem, performance and satisfaction: some tests of a theory. *Journal of Applied Psychology,* 1974, *59*: 722–26.

Hall, C. S., & Lindzey, G. *Theories of Personality.* New York: Wiley, 1970.

Hall, Elizabeth. Ethology's warning: A conversation with Nobel prize winner Niko Tinbergen. *Psychology Today,* 1974, 7: 65–80.

Hamburg, D. A. An evolutionary perspective on human aggressiveness. In D. Offer & D. X. Freedman (Eds.), *Modern Psychiatry and Clinical Research.* New York: Basic Books, 1972, pp. 30–43.

Hamburg, D. A., Coelho, G. V., & Adams, J. E. Coping and adaptation: steps toward a synthesis of biological and social perspectives. In G. Coelho, D. A. Hamburg, & J. E. Adams (Eds.), *Coping and Adaptation.* New York: Basic Books, 1974, pp. 403–40.

Harris, M. You are what they ate. *Natural History,* 1972, *81* (7) : 24–25.

Hartmann, H. *Ego Psychology and the Problem of Adaptation.* New York: International Universities Press, 1958.

Heckhausen, H. Achievement motive research. In Sebastian, et al. (Eds.), *Nebraska Symposium on Motivation.* Lincoln: University of Nebraska Press, 1968, pp. 1–46.

Herrick, C. J. *The Evolution of Human Nature.* Austin: University of Texas Press, 1956.

Hersen, M. Nightmare behavior: a review. *Psychological Bulletin,* 1972, *78*: 37–48.

Hillman, J. C. G. Jung's contributions to "Feelings and Emotions." In Magda Arnold (Ed.), *Feelings and Emotions*. New York: Academic Press, 1970, pp. 125–34.

Hinrichs, J. R. Psychology of men at work. In P. H. Mussen & M. R. Rosenzweig (Eds.), *Annual Review of Psychology*, vol. 21. Palo Alto, Calif.: Annual Reviews, 1970.

Hogan, R. Moral conduct and moral character: a psychological perspective. *Psychological Bulletin*, 1973, *79*: 217–32.

Holloway, R. L. The casts of fossil hominid brains. *Scientific American*, 1974, *231*: 106–15.

Holmes, D. S. Investigations of repression: differential recall of material experimentally or naturally associated with ego threat. *Psychological Bulletin*, 1974, *80*: 632–53.

Ittelson, W. H., Proshansky, H. M., Rivlin, L. G., & Winkel, G. H. *An Introduction to Environmental Psychology*. New York: Holt, Rinehart & Winston, 1974.

James, W. *Psychology* (1892). New York: Henry Holt, 1907.

Jolly, A. *The Evolution of Primate Behavior*. New York: Macmillan, 1972.

Jung, C. G. *Modern Man in Search of a Soul*. New York: Harcourt, Brace and Co., 1933.

————. *Two Essays on Analytical Psychology* (1943, 1945). Cleveland: World Publishing Co., 1965.

Kaplan, S. The challenge of environmental psychology: a proposal for a new functionalism. *American Psychologist*, 1972, *27*: 140–43.

Kaufman, W. Do you crave a life without choice? *Psychology Today*, 1973, *6*: 79–83.

Kaust, A. Fish are what they eat. *Natural History*, 1974, *83* (1): 78–81.

Keen, S. The cosmic versus the rational. *Psychology Today*, 1974, *8*: 56–59.

King, Mary-Claire, & Wilson, A. C. Evolution at two levels in humans and chimpanzees. *Science*, 1975, *188*: 107–16.

Kinsbourne, M. The ontogeny of cerebral dominance. In D. Aaronson & R. W. Rieber (Eds.), *Developmental Psycholinguistics and Communications Disorders*. New York: Annals of the New York Academy of Sciences, 1975, pp. 244–50.

Klein, D. G. Endogenomorphic depression. *Archives of General Psychiatry*, 1974, *31*: 447–55.

Klein, Melanie. Personification in the play of children (1929). In M. Klein, *Contributions to Psychoanalysis 1921–1945*. London: Hogarth Press, 1973, pp. 215–26.

————. Mourning and its relation to manic-depressive states (1940). In M. Klein, *Contributions to Psychoanalysis 1921–1945*. London: Hogarth Press, 1973, pp. 215–26.

———— The Oedipus complex in the light of early anxieties (1945). In M. Klein, *Contributions to Psychoanalysis 1921–1945*. London: Hogarth Press, 1973, pp. 215–26.

Klein, R. G. Ice-age hunters of the Ukraine. *Scientific American*, June 1974, *230*: 96–105.

Kleinman, D., & John, E. R. Contradiction of auditory and visual information by brain stimulation. *Science*, 1975, *187*: 271–73.

Koizumi, K., & Brooks, C. McC. The autonomic nervous system and its role in controlling visceral activities. In V. Mountcastle, *Medical Physiology* (13th ed.). St. Louis: C. V. Mosby, 1974, pp. 783–812.

Kolata, Gina Bari. Human evolution: life-styles and lineages of early hominids. *Science*, 1975, *187*: 940–42.

Kron, R. E. Studies of sucking behavior in the human newborn: the diagnostic and predictive value of earliest oral behavior. Unpublished manuscript.

Kron, R. E., Kron, V. S., & Phoenix, Marianne D. An analysis of behavioral mechanisms involved in controls over infant feeding behavior: the effect of interfeeding interval on nutritive sucking in the newborn. Unpublished manuscript.

Kron, R. E., Stein, M., & Goddard, Katharine E. Newborn sucking behavior affected by obstetric sedation. *Pediatrics*, 1966, *37*: 1012–16.

————. Effect of nutrient upon the sucking behavior of newborn infants. *Psychosomatic Medicine*, 1967, *29*: 24–32.

Kurtines, W. M. Autonomy: a concept reconsidered. *Journal of Personality Assessment*, 1974, *38*: 243–46.

Lacey, J. I., & Lacey, B. C. The relationship of resting autonomic activity to motor impulsivity. In, *The Brain and Human Behavior*. Baltimore: Williams and Wilkins, 1958.

Lachman, S. J. *Psychosomatic Disorders: A Behavioristic Interpretation*. New York: John Wiley, 1972.

Lamb, W. L., & Turner, D. *Management Behavior*. New York: International Universities Press, 1969.

Leboyer, Frederick, cited by S. England, *N.Y. Times Sunday Magazine*, December 8, 1974; also, Leboyer, F. *Birth Without Violence*. New York: Knopf, 1975.

Leopold, A. C., & Ardrey, R. Toxic substances in plants and the food habits of early man. *Science*, 1972, *176*: 512–14.

Levenson, Hannah. Multidimensional locus of control in psychiatric patients. *Journal of Consulting and Clinical Psychology*, 1973, *41*: 397–404.

Levin, L. *The Holocaust: The Destruction of European Jewry 1933-1945* (1968). New York: Schocken, 1973.

Levine, J. M. Information seeking with conflicting and irrelevant inputs. *Journal of Applied Psychology*, 1973, *57*: 74–80.

Levine, S. Biological approach to stress and behavior. In D. Offer & D. X. Freedman (Eds.), *Modern Psychiatry and Clinical Research*. New York: Basic Books, 1972, pp. 76–93.

Lichtman, C. M., & Hunt, R. G. Personality and organization theory: a review of some conceptual literature. *Psychological Bulletin*, 1971, *76*: 271–94.

Lieblich, I., Kugelmas, S., & Ben-Shakar, G. Psychophysiological baselines as a function of race and ethnic origin. *Psychophysiology*, 1973, *10*: 426–30.

Lifton, W. M. *Groups: Facilitating Individual Growth and Societal Change*. New York: Wiley, 1972.

Lilly, John C. *Programming and Metaprogramming in the Human Biocomputer*. New York: Julian Press, 1972.

Lindzey, G., Loehlin, J., Manosevitz, M., & Thiessen, D. Behavioral genetics. In P. H. Mussen & M. R. Rosenzweig (Eds.), *Annual Review of Psychology*, vol. 22. Palo Alto, Calif.: Annual Reviews, 1971.

Llinas, R. R. The cortex of the cerebellum. *Scientific American,* January 1975, *232*: 56–71.

London, M. Effects of shared information and participation on group process and outcome. *Journal of Applied Psychology,* 1975, *60*: 537–43.

Lorenz, Konrad. *On Aggression.* New York: Harcourt, Brace and World, 1963.

Lott, A. J. Social psychology. In B. B. Wolman (Ed.) , *Handbook of General Psychology.* Englewood Cliffs, N.J.: Prentice-Hall, 1973, pp. 918–32.

Mack, J. E. *Nightmares and Human Conflict.* Boston: Little, Brown, 1970.

Maddi, S. *Personality Theories: A Comparative Analysis.* Georgetown, Ontario: Dorsey Press, 1972.

Maddi, S. R. The search for meaning. In *Nebraska Symposium on Motivation, 1970.* Lincoln: University of Nebraska Press, 1970, pp. 137–86.

Mahl, G. F. Part II: conflict and defense. In J. Janis, G. Mahl, J. Kagan, & R. Holt, *Personality.* New York: Harcourt, Brace and World, 1969.

Malmquist, C. P. Depressive phenomena in children. In B. B. Wolman, *Manual of Child Psychopathology.* New York: McGraw-Hill, 1972, pp. 497–540.

Maslow, A. *The Farther Reaches of Human Nature.* New York: Viking Press, 1971.

————. Deficiency motivation and growth motivation (1962). In A. R. Mahrer & L. Pearson (Eds.) , *Creative Developments in Psychotherapy.* Cleveland: Press of Western Reserve University, 1971, pp. 15–34.

May, R. An interview by Mary Harrington Hall. *Psychology Today,* 1967, *1*: 25–29, 72–73.

————. *Love and Will.* Adapted in *Psychology Today,* 1969, *3*: 17–64.

Mayr, E. *Populations, Species and Evolution.* Cambridge, Mass.: Belknap, 1970.

McHenry, H. M. Fossils and the mosaic nature of human evolution. *Science,* 1975, *190*: 425–31.

Mendels, J. Biological aspects of affective illness. In S. Arieti et al. (Eds.), *American Handbook of Psychiatry*, 2nd ed., vol. 3. New York: Basic Books, 1974, pp. 491–523.

Meyer, H. E. How the boss stays in touch with the troops. *Fortune*, 1975, *91* (6) : 152–57.

Miller, N. E. How psychological factors can affect visceral functions. In N. J. Fina (Ed.), *Proceedings of the First Phillip Morris Science Symposium*, 1973.

Millon, T. *Modern Psychopathology*. Philadelphia: Saunders, 1969.

Milner, B. Interhemispheric differences and psychological processes. *Montreal Neurological Institute Reprint No. 1046*, 1971. (Reprinted from *British Medical Bulletin*, 1971, *27* (3) : 272–77.)

Miner, J. B., & Dachler, H. P. Personnel attitudes and motivation. In P. H. Mussen & M. R. Rosenzweig (Eds.), *Annual Review of Psychology*, vol. 24. Palo Alto, Calif.: Annual Reviews, 1973.

Mok, P. P. I speak your language: test manual. New York: Drake-Beam & Assoc., 1972.

Money, J., & Ehrhardt, A. A. *Man and Woman, Boy and Girl: Differentiation and Dimorphism of Gender Identity*. Baltimore: Johns Hopkins Press, 1972.

Money, J., Hampson, Joan G., & Hampson, L. L. Imprinting and the establishment of gender role. *Archives of Neurology and Psychiatry*, 1957, *77*: 333–37.

Murphy, G. *Historical Introduction to Modern Psychology*. New York: Harcourt, Brace, 1949.

Nager, N. R. Apathetic hearts. *Human Behavior*, 1976, *5* (2) : 40–42.

Niederland, W. G. Clinical observations on the survivor syndrome. In R. S. Parker (Ed.), *Emotional Stress of War, Violence, and Peace*. Pittsburgh: Stanwix House, 1972, pp. 284–88.

Nolan, J. D. Freedom and dignity. A "functional" analysis. *American Psychologist*, 1974, *29*: 157–60.

Norton, R. W. Measurement of ambiguity tolerance. *Journal of Personality Assessment,* 1975, *39*: 607–19.

Olds, E. R., & Milner, P. Positive reinforcement produced by electrical stimulation of septal area and other regions of rat brain. In R. L. Isaacson (Ed.), *Basic Readings in Neuropsychology.* New York: Harper & Row, 1964. Reprinted from *Journal of Comparative and Physiological Psychology,* 1954, *47*: 419–27.

O'Leary, Virginia. Some attitudinal barriers to occupational aspirations in women. *Psychological Bulletin,* 1974, *11*: 809–26.

Parker, R. S. The acceptability and expression of attitudes associated to the Rorschach Human Movement Response. *Journal of Projective Techniques and Personality Assessment,* 1965, *29*: 84–92.

————. The varieties of resistance in group psychotherapy considered from the viewpoint of adaptation. *Psychiatric Quarterly,* 1967, *41*: 525–35.

————. Poetry, a therapeutic art in the resolution of psychotherapeutic resistance. In J. J. Leedy (Ed.), *Poetry Therapy.* Philadelphia: Lippincott, 1969.

————. The patient who cannot express pain. In R. S. Parker (Ed.), *The Emotional Stress of War, Violence, and Peace.* Pittsburgh: Stanwix House, 1972, pp. 71–85. (*a*).

————. Anger, identification, and irrational target selection. In R. S. Parker (Ed.), *The Emotional Stress of War, Violence, and Peace.* Pittsburgh: Stanwix House, 1972, pp. 12–70. (*b*).

————. Some personal qualities enhancing group therapist effectiveness. *Journal of Clinical Issues in Psychology,* 1972, *4*: 26–28. (*c*).

————. Can group therapy be harmful to the individual? *Journal of Clinical Issues in Psychology,* 1972 *3*: 22–24. (*d*).

————. (Ed.). *The Emotional Stress of War, Violence, and Peace.* Pittsburgh: Stanwix House, 1972. (*e*).

————. Psychology, psychotherapy, and the real world. *Journal of Clinical Issues in Psychology,* 1973, *4*: 13–16. (*a*)

_____. *Emotional Common Sense.* New York: Harper & Row, 1973. (*b*).

_____. Ethical and professional considerations concerning high risk groups. *Journal of Clinical Issues in Psychology,* 1976, *1* (7) : 4–19.

Parker, R. S., & Davidson, N. L. A comparison of nursing and hospitalized patients on scores derived from an intelligence test (WAIS). *Psychiatric Quarterly Supplement,* 1963, *37,* Part 2: 298–306.

Parker, R. S., & Piotrowski, Z. A. The significance of varieties of actors of Rorschach Human Movement Responses. *Journal of Projective Techniques and Personality Assessment,* 1968, *32*: 33–44.

Peck, Ellen. *The Baby Trap.* New York: Pinnacle Books, 1971.

Pedersen, D. M., & Shears, L. M. A review of personal space research in the framework of general system theory. *Psychological Bulletin,* 1973, *80*: 367–88.

Penfield, W. *The Mystery of the Mind.* Princeton, N.J.: Princeton University Press, 1975.

Penfield, W., & Roberts, L. *Speech and Brain Mechanisms.* Princeton, N.J.: Princeton University Press, 1959.

Peter, L. J., & Hill, R. *The Peter Principle.* New York: Morrow, 1969.

Phares, E. J., & Lamiell, J. T. Relationship of internal-external control to defensive preferences. *Journal of Consulting and Clinical Psychology,* 1974, *42*: 872–78.

Piaget, J. *On the Development of Memory and Identity.* Barre, Mass.: Clarke University Press, 1968.

Pilbeam, D., & Gould, S. J. Size and scaling in human evolution. *Science,* 1974, *186*: 892–901.

Piotrowski, Z. A. A rational explanation of the irrational: Freud's and Jung's own dreams reinterpreted. *Journal of Projective Techniques and Personality Assessment,* 1971, *35*: 505–18.

Platt, J. Social Traps. *American Psychologist,* 1973, *28*: 641–51.

Provence, Sally, & Lipton, Rose C. *Infants in Institutions.* New York: International Universities Press, 1962.

Prusoff, B., & Klerman, G. L. Differentiating depressed from anxious neurotic outpatients. *Archives of General Psychiatry,* 1974, *30*: 302–11.

Reich, W. *Character Analysis* (1945). New York: Orgone Institute Press, 1949.

Reiser, M. F. Changing theoretical concepts in psychosomatic medicine. In S. Arieti et al. (Eds.), *American Handbook of Psychiatry,* 2nd ed. New York: Basic Books, 1975, pp. 477–500.

Rheingold, Harriet L., & Eckerman, Carl O. The infant separates himself from his mother. *Science,* 1970, *168*: 78–83.

Rickards, T. Group problem solving—a game for brownie points? *Mensa Journal,* International edition, May 1974, pp. 11–12.

Robards, T. The Chase and David Rockefeller. *New York Times,* February 1, 1976, Section 3.

Rotter, J. B. External control and internal control. *Psychology Today,* 1971, *5*: 37–42, 58–59.

Rubin, L. S. Autonomic dysfunction in neurotic behavior. *Archives of General Psychiatry,* 1965, *12*: 572–85.

Sale, P. F. Reef fish lottery. *Natural History,* 1976, *85* (2) : 60–65.

Saul, L. J., & Pulver, S. E. The concept of emotional maturity. *International Journal of Psychiatry,* 1966, *2*: 446–59. (Reprinted from *Comprehensive Psychiatry,* 1965, *6*.)

Schachtel, E. G. *Metamorphosis.* New York: Basic Books, 1959.

Schaffer, R. H. Demand better results—and get them. *Harvard Business Review,* 1974, *52*: 91–98.

Schauffler, R. H. *Beethoven: The Man Who Freed Music.* New York: Tudor Publishing Co., 1944.

Schichor, D. Nonconformity patterns of different types of leaders in small groups. *Comparative Group Studies,* 1970, *1*: 269–74.

Schild, R. The final Paleolithic settlements of the European plain. *Scientific American,* 1976, *234*: 88–100.

Schilder, P. *Contributions to Developmental Neuropsychiatry.* New York: International Universities Press, 1964.

————. *The Image and Appearance of the Human Body*. New York: Wiley, 1950.

Schoner, N., Hoyt, G. C., & Rose, G. L. Quality of decisions: individuals versus real and synthetic groups. *Journal of Applied Psychology* 1974, *59*: 424–32.

Schuckit, M., et al., cited in *Science News,* 1972, *101*: 170 (*American Journal of Psychiatry,* 1972).

Schwartz, G. E., Davidson, R. J., & Maer, F. Right hemisphere lateralization for emotion in the human brain: interactions with cognition. *Science,* 1975, *190*: 286–90.

Seeman, J. On supervising student research. *American Psychologist,* 1973, *28*: 900–906.

Seligman, M. E. P. Submissive death: giving up on life. *Psychology Today,* 1974, 7: 80–85.

Simpson, G. G. Naturalistic ethics and the social sciences. *American Psychologist,* 1966, *21*: 27–36.

Simpson, G. S. The evolutionary concept of man. In B. G. Campbell (Ed.), *Sexual Selection and the Descent of Man.* Chicago: Aldine, 1972, pp. 17–39.

Sims, J. H., & Baumann, D. D. The tornado threat: coping styles of the North and South. *Science,* 1972, *176*: 1392.

Singer, J. L. Navigating the stream of consciousness. *American Psychologist,* 1975, *30*: 727, 738.

Skinner, B. F. *Beyond Freedom and Dignity*. In *Psychology Today,* 1975, *9*: 37–80.

Sternbach, R. A., & Tursky, B. Ethnic differences among housewives in psychophysical and skin potential responses to electrical shock. *Psychophysiology,* 1965, *1*: 241–46.

Stoller, R. J. *Sex and Gender*. New York: Science House, 1968.

Street, W. R. Brainstorming by individuals, coacting and interacting groups. *Journal of Applied Psychology,* 1974, *59*: 433–36.

Strongman, K. T. *The Psychology of Emotion*. New York: John Wiley, 1973.

Sullivan, H. S. *Conceptions of Modern Psychiatry*. New York: Norton, 1940.

————. *Clinical Studies in Psychiatry.* New York: Norton, 1956.

————. *Personal Psychopathology* (1929). New York: Norton, 1972.

Taylor, R. N., & Dunnette, M. D. Influence of dogmatism, risk-taking propensity, and intelligence, on decision-making strategies for a sample of industrial managers. *Journal of Applied Psychology,* 1974, *59*: 420–23.

Theologus, G. C., Wheaton, G. R., & Fleishman, E. A. Effects of intermittent, moderate intensity noise stress of human performance. *Journal of Applied Psychology,* 1974, *59* (5): 539–47.

Thiessen, D. D. Reply to Wilcock on gene action and behavior. *Psychological Bulletin,* 1971, *75*: 103–05.

Thomas, A., Chess, Stella, & Birch, H. G. *Temperament and Behavior Disorders in Children.* New York: New York University Press, 1969.

Thomsen, D. Split brain and free will. *Science News,* 1974, *105*: 256–57.

Toffler, A. *Future Shock.* New York: Bantam Books, 1970.

Tolman, E. C. Cognitive maps in rats and men. *Psychological Review,* 1958, *55*: 189–208.

Topoff, H. The behavioral uniqueness of animal species. *Science,* 1975, *15* (8): 24–28.

Tursky, B., & Sternbach, R. A. Further physiological correlates of ethnic differences in responses to shock. *Psychophysiology,* 1967, *4*:. 67–74.

Vale, J. R. Role of behavior genetics in psychology. *American Psychologist,* 1973, *29*: 871–87.

Valenzi, E., & Andrew, I. R. Individual differences in the decision process of employment interviewers. *Journal of Applied Psychology,* 1973, *58*: 49–53.

Vance, Elizabeth T. Social disability. *American Psychologist,* 1973, *28*: 498–511.

Van Praag, H. M., Korf, J., & Schut, D. Cerebral monoamines and depression. *Archives of General Psychiatry,* 1973, *28*: 827–33.

Vinokur, A. A. Review and theoretical analysis of the effects of group processes upon individual and group decisions involving risk. *Psychological Bulletin,* 1971, *76:* 231–50.

Wahrman, R. Status, deviance, and sanctions: a critical review. *Comparative Group Studies,* 1972, *3:* 203–24.

Walsh, R. N., & Cummins, R. A. Mechanisms mediating the production of environmentally induced brain changes. *Psychological Bulletin,* 1975, *82:* 986–1000.

Washburn, S. L., & Harding, R. S. Evolution and human nature. In S. Arieti, et al. (Eds.), *American Handbook of Psychiatry,* 2nd ed., vol. 6. New York: Basic Books, 1975, pp. 1–13.

Wechsler, D. Intelligence defined and undefined: a relativistic appraisal. *American Psychologist,* 1975, *30:* 135–39.

Weinstein, N. D. Effect of noise on intellectual performance. *Journal of Applied Psychology,* 1974, *59:* 548–54.

Weiss, J. M. Effects of coping behavior in different warning signal conditions on stress pathology in rats. *Journal of Comparative and Physiological Psychology,* 1971, *77:* 1–13. (a)

————. Effects of punishing the coping response (conflict) on stress pathology in rats. *Journal of Comparative and Physiological Psychology,* 1971, *77:* 14–21. (b)

————. Effects of coping behavior with and without a feedback signal on stress pathology in rats. *Journal of Comparative and Physiological Psychology,* 1971, *77:* 22–30. (c)

Weiss, J. M., & Glazer, H. I. Effects of acute exposure to stressors on subsequent avoidance-escape behavior. *Psychosomatic Medicine,* 1975, *37:* 499–521.

Weiss, J. M., Glazer, H. I., & Pohorecky, Larissa A. Neurotransmitters and helplessness: a chemical bridge to depression? *Psychology Today,* 1974, *8:* 58–62.

Weiss, J. M., Glazer, H. I., Pohorecky, L. A., Brick, J., & Miller, N. E. Effects of chronic exposure to stressors on avoidance-escape behavior and on brain norepinephrine. *Psychosomatic Medicine,* 1975, *37:* 522–34.

Wertime, T. A. The beginnings of metallurgy: a new look. *Science,* 1973, *182:* 875–87.

White, R. W. Strategies of adaptation: an attempt at systematic description. In G. V. Coelho, D. A. Hamburg, & J. E. Adams (Eds.), *Coping and Adaptation*. New York: Basic Books, 1974, pp. 47–68.

Wilcock, J. Comparative psychology lives on under an assumed name—psychogenetics. *American Psychologist*, 1972, 27: 531–38.

Wolff, P. H. Ethnic differences in alcohol sensitivity. *Science*, 1972, *175*: 449–50.

Wolman, B. B. Clinical psychology and the philosophy of science. In B. B. Wolman (Ed.), *Handbook of Clinical Psychology*. New York: McGraw-Hill, 1965.

Wood, A. E. Interrelations of humans, dogs, and rodents. *Science*, 1972, *176*: 437.

Wood, M. T. Power relationships and group decision making in organizations. *Psychological Bulletin*, 1973, *79*: 280–93.

*World Almanac*. New York: Newspaper Enterprise Association, 1973.

Wright, P. The harassed decision maker: time pressures, distractions, and the use of evidence. *Journal of Applied Psychology*, 1974, *59*: 555–61.

Yalom, I. D., Green, R., & Fisk, N. Prenatal exposure to female hormones. *Archives of General Psychiatry*, 1973, *28*: 554–61.

Yankelovich, D., & Barrett, W. *Ego and Instinct: The Psychoanalytic View of Human Nature—Revised*. New York: Random House, 1970.

Yellen, J., & Harpending, H. Hunter-gatherer populations and archeological inference. *World Archeology*, 1972, *4* (2): 244–53.

Young, J. Z. *An Introduction to the Study of Man*. New York: Oxford University Press, 1971.

Zander, A. V. Productivity and group success: time spirit vs. the individual achiever. *Psychology Today*, November 1974, *74*: 8, 64–69.

Zohary, D., & Hopf, M. Domestication of pulses in the Old World. *Science*, 1973, *182*: 887–94.

# Index